Baby Shoes

100 Stories by 100 Authors

Edited by Dani J. Caile and Jason Brick

D1614099

Table of Contents

A (Brief) Introduction from Jason Brick

It has been my extreme pleasure to work with the *Baby Shoes* contributors and team, from established masters like Walter Williams, Joe Lansdale and Linda Needham, to up and coming names like Dan Repperger, Eddy Webb and April Aasheim, to incredibly talented folks you'll not have heard of until you read the words down below. It has been a privilege and a pleasure.

I could go on for days, but flash fiction is about brevity. I just hope you enjoy what you find here as much as I did discovering it.

A (Briefer) Introduction from Dani J. Caile

It has been great fun to bring this anthology together. Such a great mix of styles and genres with an intriguing concept. While editing, I myself found many new authors that I will certainly continue to read for years to come.

Valley of the Black Pig
by Scott Crowder

The sniper pulls the synthetic stock of his rifle close to his cheek and sets his crosshairs on the head of the Iraqi man with the little girl on his shoulders. It'll have to be a headshot. A wounding shot may still give the man time to detonate his explosives, and a shot to his torso might set off the bomb anyway. The headshot will kill the little girl too, but there is no more time. He can't hesitate and he can't let the girl pull any harder on his heartstrings than she already has. Not like he did with the little boy.

He breathes in deeply, lets the breath out gently and squeezes the trigger. The Iraqi crumples almost serenely to the ground as the .338 Lapua Magnum round splits his head in two. The little girl is sent flying in a horrible cartwheel, blood spraying in the arc of her tumble. The sniper lost his ear plugs to the concussion of the first bomb, but his ears are still ringing from the gunshot, and he doesn't hear her scream.

. . .

Even before the smoke from the first insurgent's bomb has cleared, even before its thunder has left his head, he straightens the chair from which he'd been blasted and sits back down in it amid the wreckage of the abandoned house. Shame flushes his cheeks scarlet; a moment ago he'd seen, through the Leupold scope on his rifle, the tell-tale signs of a bomb beneath a man's dishdasha, curling wires pushing from beneath the white fabric of the ankle-length garment, the blocky outlines of the explosives themselves. He'd also seen a child sitting on the insurgent's shoulders, though, and he'd hesitated because of it. He'd let the little boy's dirty face give him pause, just time enough for the insurgent to detonate the bomb, and now God alone knew how many people lay dead outside in the courtyard.

The boy, it seemed, had done his job. Subhan'Allah.

Glorious, indeed, is Allah.

9

Once seated in the chair again, he pulls the butt of the M24 sniper rifle close against his shoulder. He peers through the scope out the empty window casing at the people running in panic outside, already beginning to dig through rubble for loved ones. The wailing of the bereaved cuts cleanly through the smoke. Soon he sees the pixilated black and blue uniforms of Iraqi police as they make their way into the courtyard. As the smoke drifts away into the alleys of Baghdad, other people willing to help look for survivors drift in. Now is the time to be most vigilant, the sniper knows. The first bomb was detonated to cause damage, certainly, but also to draw more people to the scene. Another suicide bomber may be lurking nearby, waiting to set off his bomb, as well.

The children are there, of course, to tug at heartstrings. Riding on shoulders, in the backseats of cars rigged with explosives; sacrificed to throw Coalition forces off guard, and at the thought of dead children, the sniper thinks of his own daughter, dead these last two years, sacrificed to satisfy leukemia's hunger.

Why? Carrie had asked in those last few days before her death, sick and drained in her hospital bed, listening at her window to a whip-poor-will cry in the darkness of an Alabama morning. Why does he cry like that, Daddy?

He hadn't answered her then because the answer had eluded him, and his wife Claire had glared at him ferociously, as if his ignorance was a physical blow aimed at her and her daughter both. Claire had left him soon after Carrie's passing, leaving behind everything but some clothes and memories, keeping nothing but her silence. He'd figured it out since then, had come up with the answer his daughter had asked him for.

The whip-poor-will cries, he might tell his little girl if he could go back and do it again, because he can.

By now, of course, the answer doesn't do him a goddamn bit of good.

The sniper peers through the Leupold scope at the people beginning to fill the courtyard, and as he moves the barrel of the gun around slowly he catches a glimpse of another man with a child on his shoulders, a girl this time. The same blocky outlines of a poorly constructed bomb beneath his dishdasha, the same look of zealous determination on his face. The sniper fixes his crosshairs on the bridge of the Iraqi's nose and glances for one instant at the face of the little girl he is almost certainly about to kill.

Allahu akbar, he thinks in her language. Praise be to God. Praise be to God that heartstrings, these days, are a hell of a lot harder to pull than triggers.

10

The Fan
by Cynthia Lang

"The fan! We need the fan!" Burton's wife, sounding even crosser than usual, calls from the front of the house. "Just get a move on, will you?"

Burton knows the attic is going to be hot, hotter than the rest of their cramped, cluttered frame house. Under duress, he makes his way down the hallway. He reaches overhead for the meager rope that hangs from the door in the ceiling. Pulling it down takes more strength than he remembers. But then, as if its hinges have been oiled only the day before, the door gives, and the collapsible stairs unfold in front of him like a ballerina melting into her swan feathers.

No railing, of course, which never bothered him when he was younger. Bending veined hands around the upper steps for balance, he begins the climb. The makeshift stairs shimmy from left to right, enough to remind him he is leaving terra firma. Slowly, step-by-step, he climbs until his head is level with the attic floor and the hot scent of the past reaches out to him. He can see a colony of dust bunnies skittering in the air he's ruffled, overtaking a cluster of stolid, outdated suitcases. There's the Green Giant spinach carton holding his engineering texts from college. There's the wooden milk crate piled with the children's old ice skates. Languid in a corner slump his skis.

The room fan stands where he left it, staking out a footprint on the unfinished floorboards. Its round metal cage catches a ray of late sun from the solitary, dusty attic window.

No easy job, this year, to get the fan down the stairs. At least he should check to see if it still works. Crawling around the edges of the attic, he finds an extension cord snaking its way toward the wall, to some distant source of power. He unwraps the fan's wire from its neat coil and pushes in the plug.

Hands on his knees for leverage, he stands upright, gives two or three half-hearted swipes at the cobwebs veiling the fan's face, and turns on the switch.

Almost at once, the air against his face feels cooler. Set to low some long-forgotten day, the fan oscillates to the left, toward him again, to the right. He remembers a fan like it in college, it stood in the dorm under his maroon-and-white Missouri banner next to bookshelves he'd made himself by propping boards on orange crates. It was the same spring he'd made up his mind to join the dance company, the spring he'd met...

"Burton?" The voice is so distant, he thinks he may have imagined it. "What's the problem now?" He turns the switch to medium.

It is young men's voices he hears now, guys in high school, cheering and slapping their towels against each other's backsides in the locker room, though not him, usually, barely jock enough to make the team. They tolerated him was all; except for one or two who felt like friends, like Timmy. Definitely cooler now, the attic air carries the snap of an early autumn. He remembers sneaking out the window after his father had gone to bed or passed out, whichever came first. Burton would drop from the window sill to the garage roof, from the roof to the sidewalk; he'd make his way to the edge of the river where the guys were gathering to build a bonfire. Even now, he can smell the smoke, see ashy cinders floating into the night sky, taste the burning marshmallow, feel the first few beers of his life buzzing in his throat as he and Timmy passed the brown bottle back and forth.

Curious, Burton turns the switch to high. Chilled, face down on his Flexible Flyer, he hears his mother's voice cheering him on as he braces his small toes against the sled, sees the pristine white hill sliding away. Squinting against crystal puffs blowing like dust in his face, gripping the carved wooden handle, his mittens' damp wool giving off the smell of winter days, he races. Push the handle to the left and he feels the sled curve toward distant trees, push it to the right and he sees through lashes, half covered with snow, the slope banking his way.

Faint as it is, his wife's voice threatens to overtake the clean hiss of metal runners cutting fresh tracks in the snow. Leaving the fan set on high, he creeps backward down the wooden stairs. Groping under the bottom step for the rope and holding the end of it in his teeth so his hands are free, Burton climbs back up to the attic and pulls the door closed after him.

Trapped in a Box
by John James

"Shit!" exclaimed Billy, as he shot up. Startled awake, he banged his head on what he thought was a low-hanging ceiling. He put his hands on his forehead; it was pounding. Nebulous remembrances fulgurated through his mind; the smell of salt in the air, the water, a green Cadillac, Abagail's face, but they left as fast as they had come. All he could think about was the pain. After a few minutes, the pain attenuated, still not pleasant, but tolerable enough. At least he could think. Taking his hands from his forehead he opened his eyes. It was black, pitch black; he could not even see his hand in front of his face. Laid out flat on his back he felt around cautiously with his hands. He was in some kind of box. There was the slight aroma of cedar or was it oak? He couldn't quite place the smell. Billy pushed on the top with all his might. Next he tried the right side, then left, nothing. What the fuck is going on? He attempted to gather his thoughts. Where am I? How did I get here? He could barely piece anything together. Then, like a haymaker from a prize fighter, it hit him. The job.

Billy had been offered a job by the barbarous Riley Tims, which he had accepted with the alacrity of a child accepting a lollipop. Billy had always wanted to work for Riley, he admired the fierce savagery with which he handled his competitors. Most of all though, Billy admired his money. He had always been cupidinous towards money since he was a small child. It's what led him to steal from his mother's slender purse as an adolescent and what landed him his first of many jail stints as a teenager. Recently his avarice led him to work for the capricious and violent Riley Tims. A man who could have a tenth wedding anniversary party for his wife, where he professes his undying love for her, and on the same night have her killed on suspicion of infidelity. Such are the vagaries of madmen and geniuses.

The job was simple. Riley's right-hand man was a stolid guy named Jackson Black. Jackson had an appetency for young girls and a propensity for violence, not a laudable combination of attributes by any standard. If you happened to be a girl of fourteen and were unlucky enough to make his acquaintance, you were in for a bad night. The lucky ones left black-eyed and bruised, the unlucky ones, well…

Jackson was transporting a large sum of money for a purchase of some sort. Billy and two other small-time thugs were hired as escorts to make sure there was no funny business. The job paid 10k, such a large sum for what seemed a little job made Billy wonder what exactly was being purchased, but that wonder quickly dissipated. He had learned long ago not to ask a question you didn't need to know the answer to. Curiosity kills a lot more than cats, especially in Boomtown.

They met at an old dive bar in the center of town called Patty's. Patty's was an atavist, a long-standing reminder of what Boomtown used to be. It was there long before Riley took over the town and filled its streets with blood and bone, and it would be there long after whatever convulsive maelstrom wiped him from its memory. Until then, it, like everything else in this town, belonged to Riley.

They all got into a dark green Cadillac. Billy was at the wheel while Jackson sat, taciturn, in the passenger seat. Jackson was carrying a briefcase in his hand and a .38 special in his waistband. The two other guys were in back. No one talked during the ride save for a few instructions that Jackson gave.

"Keep your mouths shut," and "If anything goes wrong kill them all."

They pulled up to the docks. The sun was setting. The reflection of the fading light off the still visage of the water cast a bluish green pall over the area. It would have been beautiful if it were anywhere else, but this was Boomtown. There was a truck parked close to where they drove in. Four men stood beside it. Their dress was bedraggled and their demeanor was boorish. They were all armed. Jackson told Billy to wait in the car. The three men got out of the car and walked over to the men by the truck. Billy could hear them speaking but could not make out what they were saying. After going back and forth for a while, Jackson handed the men the briefcase. They all walked back to the car. Jackson told Billy to get out. They were taking the truck and giving the car to the four unkempt thugs. The Cadillac drove off into the night. The four of them walked over to the truck. Jackson had a big smile on his face. He unlocked the back and threw the door open.

Billy stood there aghast, his heart in his stomach. He was a seasoned criminal and was not prone to fits of compassion, but this, this was pernicious, this was beyond inhuman. Jackson stood there licking his chops.

"Wanna try out the merchandise?" he said with a laugh. "They're all yours, just don't make a mess." Never has a man looked upon another man with such antipathy as Billy did then at Jackson. Jackson handed him the keys to the truck. "Drive it back to the bar when you are finished, but don't take too long, I have plans for them," he said, then walked off to catch a taxi. Billy was boiling. He could see the look in the other thugs' eyes as they crept closer to the truck. Was he going to let this happen? He thought for a second, he thought about the money, he thought about the consequences, then he thought about his sister Abagail. What if it was her in that truck? Fuck it. He drew his gun. Bang! Bang! Two shots, two men lying dead on the floor, Billy didn't have to think anymore.

"It's pine!" Billy said out loud. He could finally place the aroma. He knew what kind of boxes were made out of pine. He couldn't remember what happened after he shot the two thugs. Did Riley find me? He must've, and now he has me in this damn box and is planning to bury me alive. Billy was feeling very claustrophobic. His mind was racing, panic was setting in. He began banging wildly on the top of the box and screaming "Let me outta here! YOU HEAR ME!" What am I gonna do? Is it possible I am already in the ground? Then Billy heard something faint. It was muffled but to Billy it sounded like the madrigal of angels, it was talking. He could hear it clearer now and it was getting closer. "Help me! Help me!" Billy screamed. They have to hear me. He could hear them speaking right outside. Then in a flash the box was opened. The refulgent light blinded Billy and he shielded his eyes until they could adjust. When his eyes finally did, he looked up. What he saw confused him. He expected to see Riley's cruel eyes staring down at him or maybe even the cops, but it wasn't. There, looking down on him with an amalgam of grief and pity, was his sister Abagail. "Abby, what are you doing here?" he said aloud, but there was no response. A single tear fell from her eyes and landed on his cheek, and then she turned and walked away. Billy sat up quick. He was in shock. There, in a dark, sepulchral room, was his mom, his sister Abagail, a couple of cousins and a priest. "What's going on here!" he shouted but no one looked up. Then he understood. Then he smiled.

His last moments played before his eyes like a vignette. He called the cops and told them everything. He told them who he was, who he was working for, and what was in the truck. He hung up the phone and waited. He knew as long as he was alive Riley would do whatever it took to get back at him. That meant that his mother and sister weren't safe. Billy knew what needed to be done. When the cops arrived, Billy was standing there with his gun in his hand.

15

"Drop your weapon!" Billy didn't like cops and he didn't like to be told what to do. He thought about Abagail again. He closed his eye and pictured her thin, pale face, smiling insouciantly in the lassitude of a warm summer's day, and then he raised his gun. Bang! Bang! Bang!

Anika's Fall
by Jenny Cokeley

When he was awake, she was careful not to stare, but as he slept, her eyes seared every detail of his face into her brain. She memorized everything – his calico beard, the scattering of freckles across his nose and cheeks, the long eyelashes she envied. She couldn't allow herself to forget. Anika untangled herself from his arms, slipped out of bed, and kissed him goodbye. She inhaled the faint smell of cologne on his neck and tasted the brandy that lingered on his lips.

Standing on the threshold between here and forever gone, Anika watched him a second longer than she had to spare. She slowly closed the hotel room door so as to not wake him. A feeling of panic washed over her and she searched her pocket for the train ticket. She knew it was there, she had already checked, but she couldn't take any chances. She ran for the elevator.

The hotel lobby, with its cathedral ceiling and marble floor, played a symphony of idle chatter and ringing front desk bells. On any other day, it would have been background noise. But as she rushed to the front desk, the melody moved her like Mahler's Symphony No. 2.

"Leaving us so soon, Miss James? I hope everything was to your satisfaction," the desk clerk said.

"It was perfect," she replied. "It's hard to say goodbye." It wasn't just hard, it was excruciating. She had almost convinced herself to stay, that he was worth it, that their future together would be worth it. If she didn't leave now, she could never leave.

"I'll take your key then," the clerk said.

Before sliding the iron key across the counter, she felt the weight of it in her hand and traced the amaranthine design with her fingertips again and again, as if rubbing it would reveal how it came to be in her pocket that night on the train. It would spill the secret of how she was transported forward in time when her intention of stepping in front of the train was to stop time

17

altogether. It wasn't depression that led her to the train station that night, although people would recall how withdrawn she had become after the car accident. It was retribution. She was giving a life for the life she took.

She wasn't afraid when she stepped in front of Train 28. She knew it would be over quickly, but instead of oblivion, she watched the world go by from the train's caboose, the iron key in one pocket, a return ticket in the other.

The unmarked key guided her steps to Hôtel S'éveiller and unlocked the door to Room 28 where a stranger she had somehow known forever waited for her.

"Welcome home, my love," he said, and wrapped his arms around her waist. Although she had never seen him before, there was something so familiar in his touch that she welcomed it. She should have been startled and jumped back, but instead she leaned in. The shimmering gold in his hazel eyes sparked a desire in her she couldn't explain. When he kissed her for the first time, the darkness disappeared and when they made love she felt forgiven for every sin. Every day they were together, every vulnerable truth spoken, brought her closer to being whole, but she could never truly be complete. Not until she fixed what she had broken.

The desk clerk cleared his throat and looked around to make sure no one could hear him. "You can stay forever, Miss James. Keep the key."

The agony in Anika's eyes was contrary to the serenity in her smile. She let go of the key and rushed into a waiting cab. "The train station. Please hurry," Anika directed. She looked back as the cab pulled away. The majestic hotel became a luminary and vanished before her eyes. It was too late to change her mind. He was gone and she felt the pain of her decision in every part of her.

Anika's Mary Janes flirted with the platform's edge. The streamliner raced towards the station. It would not stop. The only way on, the only way back home, was a step away – the step that would change everything. It would erase that rainy night after a drink too many; a swerve left instead of right; the twisted metal and shattered glass scattered across Route 28; the shoes of a silenced baby lying in the middle of the road. The train would take her back to the moment she pulled her car keys from her pocket and insisted she was fine to drive.

Anika clutched the train ticket and smiled as she fell forward. The train would rush through her like a spirit and leave her standing at the caboose once again. Instead, she was jerked back and knocked to the platform – the breath leaving her lungs and the train ticket disappearing forever in the night.

"I almost didn't catch you," said the breathless stranger. "Are you all right?" He pulled her to her feet. "Are you hurt?" He had no idea what he had done. His heroism was her loss. Anika fell to her knees, shaking and sobbing into her hands. The baby shoes tied with the red ribbon would never be worn.

A Touch of Christmas
by N.L. Bowley

Milly kicked her legs on the dilapidated porch; a loud and repetitive creaking resounded with each kick. She could hear her parents in the background arguing again; the never-ending subject of money. As their voices grew louder so did the ferocity of Milly's kicks. She didn't notice she was doing this, subconsciously she was trying to drown out the noise.

The noise seemed ever-present in her life and made the negativity stand out like a glowing candle on a Christmas mantle. Christmas, a subject and holiday that never held any happiness for her. Ironically she still looked forward to it every year. It was a hope, a certain hope that came along with the Christmas season that things would change and get better.

Each year she was disappointed. Each year she wasn't given any sort of present. It was not that her parents did not wish they could give her anything she desired, they could not afford new clothes and hardly any food, let alone a Christmas present for their only child.

Milly looked at her surroundings, the drooping aged wood of the porch and house. The cracks between the wood brought in the extremities of each season and the dust of a harsh Oklahoma climate. In summer, she sweated through her bedclothes, her lone sheet dripping disgustingly by the time she had to go to school the next morning, earning her more than one nose wrinkled in disgust by her peers.

In the winters, like now, there weren't enough ragtag clothes to pile on top of her. Cold sleeting rain found its way through the several cracks to pelt her sheltered mound and seep slowly down onto her skin. When it snowed, she shivered and shook, and the east corner of her room had a fair dusting like the first frost of the season.

All of this left her weak, tired, and almost constantly with chills and colds. Another reason for her peers to regard her with disdain. She had no friends and had instead invented an imaginary one instead. Lois was her name, and she was currently sitting by Milly's side whispering in her ear about how much she despised this place. Her clothes were ripped and dirty, her hair greasy and tangled, she stank, and everyone made fun of her.

"Why don't we run away?" she constantly intoned. Milly of course agreed, but she couldn't leave, something held her back. She was only a kid after all and didn't have to imagine that life would be a lot worse than it was now. How would she provide for herself? Answer: she couldn't. So she took Lois' complaining and wishing for a better life with a grain of salt.

She was smarter, she knew that it wouldn't work. Milly got up and walked away from all the noise. What she really wanted more than a new house, clothing without holes, and the friendship of her peers was a real Christmas, a Christmas with a tree, cookies, stockings, and a warm fire to hang those stockings by.

But she would never get any of that, she thought, as she kicked the frost-covered dirt in front of her, fully feeling the biting chill of the wind piercing through her thin layer of clothing. Milly turned and looked back feeling the rage burn in her heart, not the warmth and love that she craved. Why did life have to be like this for her? Why were others allowed to have presents and warmth?

Milly knew that the anger expressed by Lois was her own. That she was the one who wanted to run away and be free of this spiraling hold of despair. Wrapping her arms around herself, feeling that she would go crazy at any moment, she just couldn't take it anymore. She had to run away, but not like her "friend" wanted to.

No, she was going on a mission to find her own Christmas present. She didn't know how she was going to get it or what it would be but she WAS going to find it. Resolved, Milly turned back towards the house, watching her parents through the window.

The light was beginning to fade, the dark bringing more of the cold. She shivered out of fear more than the cold. Would she come back? Once she walked away could she continue? Her mother's shoulders shook as her head went into her hands. Something terrible had just happened, she knew it. Her father, looking grim, tried to control her, not knowing how to console her.

Milly, taking one last glance, tripped into the growing night. Her mind ran with the possibilities of what she might encounter on her journey. She dreamed of sugary candy and sweets that would rot her teeth, of soft clean clothing, lined with fur, like the kind she saw on the rich ladies walking the streets in town.

Thinking of these things muted the cold and warmed her heart. Her stride became faster and within minutes she found the dark rutted dirt road that led out of the poor side of town. The wind whirled and threatened a new layer of snow. Milly's hair whipped, its dirty strands smacking her face like small needles.

She wasn't afraid of being spotted, cars didn't come to this part of town, they were too afraid of its inhabitants. Her mind worked at a rampant pace about how she would finally get the Christmas that she longed for. Milly knew that she so longed for it that she would do anything to obtain it. Even lie, cheat, and steal. She deserved it after all of these years of poverty and cold destitution.

The miles faded away in fast succession until she was staring straight at the iron gate. Milly looked up at the forbidding steel and hesitated. Could she really do this?

Class Clown
by Jim Pahz

To Daniel, the diner was always the place to go. He and Sarah, who he referred to as the girl with the sparkling eyes, went to the diner throughout their high school years. It was their hangout and everybody knew their names. They would sit over coffee in a booth and make plans for their future – elaborate plans. The food was good, the coffee hot, and they had each other.

By the time Daniel and Sarah reached college things had changed. They had grown apart. When they were together they argued over anything and everything. In an effort to repair the damage that time had caused to their relationship, Daniel called Sarah one day and asked her to meet him at the diner. She was reluctant, but finally agreed. Daniel arrived first. Maybe, he thought, it can be like old times.

As soon as Daniel saw Sarah walk into the restaurant he felt it might not have been the best idea to ask her to meet him. It was the body language, and he could tell the sparkle was gone from her eyes. She appeared irritable. She sat down, took a sip of coffee. When she spoke she dispensed with any pleasantries and came straight to the point.

"I came here for the sake of old times. I felt I owed you that much. Daniel, we've had good times in the past. It's been fun, but it's over. We can't see each other any longer."

Stunned, Daniel put down his coffee and asked, "Why?"

"Why?" Sarah repeated, "Because you're a loser. I don't want to be mean to you, Daniel, but you're never going to amount to anything. You don't know what you're doing or where you're going. You're like a child screaming at his parents 'Look at me…look at me.' Well, I've looked, and I don't like what I see. I watch you at the university, when you sit in the cafeteria with your loser friends. What a bunch of misfits – stoners and malcontents. Rich kids with no motivation. Rebels who have no idea what they're even rebelling against. Daniel, you're not the person I once thought you were. Either that or you've changed. Everything is a joke with you. You don't take your studies seriously. All you want to do is play video games and smoke weed. You're a child trapped in a man's body. I don't need a child and I'm too young to be your mother. Quite frankly, Daniel, you embarrass me. I can't afford to waste any more time waiting for you to grow up. I need a man and not a child. Therefore, I'm breaking up with you. My one request is that you forget about me and please don't call me anymore. We're finished."

Finished? Waste of time? Won't amount to anything? What is wrong with her? Daniel thought, can't she see how clever I am? I'm funny, irreverent, a natural comedian. Is the woman blind or just stupid? He couldn't remember being so angry. He thought he would just stand and make a dramatic exit, but then Sarah did it first. She stood and looked at him and said, "Goodbye, Daniel. Have a nice life." Then she walked out of the diner.

Daniel just sat for several moments. He was numb. What a drama queen, he thought. She'll come around. Maybe she's on the rag? When he left the restaurant he got into his car and began to drive. He wasn't going anywhere in particular – just driving. Fuming over the things Sarah had said to him. He felt wounded. He drove fast and recklessly.

Since it was the end of October, the leaves had fallen from the trees. Along the sides of suburban streets, the dead leaves had been raked and piled so the city truck could remove them the following morning. Daniel deliberately hit one of the piles, scattering the leaves in all directions. Smash! It felt good. He knew that someone had worked hard to rake those leaves, but so what? He didn't care. Smash. A second pile went flying. How could she do this to me? Daniel thought. What about the good times we had together? He remembered their high school prom. He remembered three years of dating.

Spotting an especially large and inviting pile, Daniel drove directly at it. And then something extraordinary happened. It was a faint whisper inside his head. "Don't do it. Don't hit those leaves." Daniel remembered a cartoon he had once seen on television. The cartoon character, Pluto, had a tiny devil on one shoulder and an angel on the other. "Do it," the devil on the dog's shoulder said. "No, don't do it," the little angel begged. Now Daniel's was experiencing those same voices. And, he was getting closer to the pile. Fuck

24

it, he thought. That pile of leaves is Sarah. You're going get what you deserve.

At the last possible second, he swerved to avoid hitting the pile of leaves. He didn't know why. He wouldn't have been able to explain it, even if asked. He drove on and glanced in his rear-view mirror. Two heads popped up from the pile, like a two-headed jack-in-the-box. Children!

Daniel could feel his heart pounding. His vision blurred. Trembling, he pulled over to the side of the road. He wiped the tears from his eyes, but he couldn't stop the flow. He sat there for a full ten minutes, just thinking, remembering Sarah, the softness of her skin, the scent of her hair. Maybe I'm smoking too much weed. Otherwise, how can I explain those voices? When he finally regained his composure, he started his car.

Sarah had been wrong he told himself. I know where I'm going. He turned the car around and headed for home.

Lost Sheep
by Crystal Yoner

The air was thick and hazy as Fhaella Arroway passed beneath the forest canopy, her longbow held in one hand. Even here, shaded from the sun, the haze clung to her skin and hair, as insects buzzed around her. She placed each step carefully, not wanting to leave any evidence of her passing. She could hear her mother's voice, advising her how to step and move past foliage, and thought of the countless days they had spent walking through forests just like this one. Her mother had often smiled and praised her ability to walk amongst the trees as though made of the forest herself. She supposed that wasn't entirely untrue; her mother had been as human as they came, while her father was, she'd been told, a wood elf of exceptional talent and beauty.

There were no more of her mother's smiles, not anymore. Twenty years had not dulled the edge of grief as the image of her mother's broken body replaced happier memories. Goblins. She hated the lot.

She hunted a pack of them now, and gave silent thanks that goblins were not among the scourges that hid well. She smelled them long before she could see them – the stench of carrion in full decay. She ignored the insects that gathered more thickly about her face and pulled an arrow from the sheath at her hip. Fitting notch to string, she crept forward, alert for any sound or movement.

She had chosen to come on this quest alone, the need of it burning through her. She had no hope of ever finding the same goblins that had taken her mother; there were simply too many of them and too many hiding places in the mountain pass she'd died in. Fhaella could spend the rest of her natural life searching only one mountain and never find them. She knew this, as core a tenet as the fact that her green eyes and pointed ears would always betray her heritage. At the time, she would have happily paid that price. Now, after years spent amongst the elves, she had made peace with that fact.

Acceptance did not stop her from seeking out work that promised retribution against goblins, however, and sometimes at pay far less than her skills were worth. She held her arrow in place, the string drawn just enough to provide some tension. She was ready.

This company of filth had camped in a tumble of rocks common to this area, rising up out of the forest floor as though by magic. The outcropping was easily defensible, and they had posted something that resembled a guard. Two goblins crouched at the edge, their mottled gray skin blending into the stone. If not for the wicked knives each held, they might have been rocks themselves. Fhaella eased around the camp, wanting to observe it in more detail before she started to lay waste to their number.

As the other side of the outcropping became visible, she saw that this job would be tricky. While there weren't very many goblins, relatively speaking, the prize sheep stock she'd been hired to retrieve was at the center of the camp. She couldn't ignore the small girl-child still clinging to the ewe she'd been riding when the goblins had made off with the flock. It was she that Fhaella was to retrieve above all else.

A few of the animals had been lost on the journey already, but most of them were alive, standing together in a cluster and guarded by more goblins. They were apparently too terrified to run – they were not tethered or restrained in any way. Her plan was beginning to formulate, so she settled in to wait until nightfall.

Night fell. The goblins lit a fire to see by, and then to die by. It illuminated them nicely, and her arrows found their marks with ease. Even the guards were helpful enough to abandon their posts, and now lay next to their brethren. The night was silent, until one of the sheep bleated.

Fhaella eased out of her spot, keeping her bow ready. "Child," she said, her voice just loud enough to set the sheep on edge. A couple more bleated, and they shifted on their feet. "Your parents sent me to rescue you. Are you able to herd these creatures?"

For long moments, there was silence. Then, a small voice. "Yes. Did they really send you?"

"Come by the fire, child. They gave me something to show you." Fhaella moved over to the fire, so she was visible by its light. A small figure crept out of the dark and came closer. Human, female, so small and brave. Her dress was torn and she was smeared with dirt, but her eyes were bright and fierce.

Fhaella pulled the token out of her pouch and held it out. It dangled from the thong it was tied to.

The child crept closer, reaching out to turn the token over in her hands. When she looked up at Fhaella, her eyes were swimming with tears. "I miss my family!" she declared, and crouched down on the forest floor, sobs wracking her tiny body.

Fhaella had no idea how to comfort a child, having been barely more than a child herself when her mother had died, but she tried her best. She patted the girl's shoulder and let her cry. When the tears had passed, she said, "We will leave at first light. Rest, dear one."

They moved away from the fire and the dead. Fhaella settled herself against a rock, bow at hand, and was surprised when the child curled up on the ground next to her. She said nothing, and within minutes, the sound of regular breathing broke the silence of the forest.

Despite herself, she had to smile. Would that she could recover her own sense of trust. Perhaps…perhaps when this job was complete, she would go back to her father's people. They had said that she was welcome with them. Maybe it was possible for lost sheep to return home.

Collared
by S.M. Chandler

She felt they deserved a reward for their hard work providing for the clan all this time, so when she finally tracked and killed the beast, she brought it back to The Home and presented it with a cry of triumph. What a celebration they had, what praise, what songs of glory! Lavish adoration of her efforts came from all quarters, and the rest of the clan looked on her in awe, for she and she alone had defeated the creature. The chieftains honored her in full, singing her praises to the clan and bestowing upon her the greatest of pleasures. When the celebration was over, she devoured her kill to gain its strength, and knew that The Home would sleep peacefully this night.

When she next brought the beast's kin, she made the mistake of only stunning it into unconsciousness, so when she presented it to The Home, the beast-kin awoke and tried to escape, sowing chaos in its wake. The clan was interested and two aspiring hunters tried to make their claim upon the monster, but it was too swift for them. She cornered it again near the cave, but the chieftains knew her failure by then, and were forced to dispose of the creature themselves, refusing to allow any others to taste in the strength of its corpse. There was no praise, no adoration, and the chieftains insulted her to the clan, letting their words pile atop her already obvious shame. She gained no strength from this and she slunk back to the wild to try to resume her duties of protection. She would not let The Home down next time.

Shame did its duty, as her next kill was yet another beast-kin; was there no end to this creature's bloodlines? She brought the kill to The Home and laid it down defiantly, daring those present to deny her strength, her courage, her sacrifice. Gaze upon my power, she dared them with her eyes; dare to call me coward and failure. The chieftains were pleased, and once more she was lavished with praise, adoration, and glory. Once more she feasted upon the flesh of the slain, gaining power, prestige, and awe. The others in the clan once again looked upon her with awe and reverence. She knew they would never match her skill or boast her courage; she could kill beast and beast-kin alike with the greatest of ease, and they could hardly spot one, let alone catch it. Once she had feasted, she looked about The Home territory in satisfaction. It was safe again, thanks to her.

As if to punish her for her hubris, her next bout with the beast's kin went even worse than her previous failure. She had it entrapped, but she could not let it escape, for escape was admitting you could not catch beasts at all, and she, mighty as she was, had caught it even if she had failed to kill it. She rushed to the clan, beast held tight, and presented it regardless, certain that her past triumphs would make this partial hunt worthy.

The chieftains were appalled – how dare she let a beast loose in the sanctity of The Home? The other would-be hunters tried to attack the beast themselves to gain easy status, but the chieftains, mightiest of them all, prevented all attacks, and caged the beast, removing it from sight. She was lectured and would receive no glory for incomplete kills, chastised before the clan! As additional punishment for her failure, and as punishment for all the clan, they sealed the gate leading to the hunting grounds and forbade any to try to leave or face their divine retribution. To see the noble hunting grounds and the easy prey that lay within, but have no ability to get to it, was maddening; nothing anyone in the clan said could change the chieftains' minds. They never saw the stunned beast-kin again.

When the hunting grounds were reopened years later, she was the first to bolt into the green and waiting splendor. She spent long stretches reacquainting herself with the most fertile pastures, the trickiest ambush spots, the choicest places to ensure an easy kill. She knew that her long solitude had only made her skills sharper, for her desire was keener and her will was stronger for the forced detention. She would win back their trust and reward them for their wise decision to reopen the grounds. She was still the best hunter in the clan, and she intended to prove it.

And prove it she did. She brought back larger beasts and presented them with no flourish; talent like hers did not need an introduction. Sometimes, just to prove she was the superior hunter, she brought them back nothing, but devoured her prey in the killing fields. Once, just as a warning to never seal off her freedom again, she found a partially rotted beast and brought half of it back to The Home in the dead of night, leaving it prominently displayed near the chieftains' favorite lounge, just to demonstrate her hunting prowess. As she was not spotted, and she had never before displayed such behavior, the chieftains were unable to pin the slight on her, but her warning was received. She had her status, she had her skill, and she had her killing fields. They would learn to respect her might, and she would accept their occasional gate-closing (but only for the safety of the weak, would-be hunters), but never again would she permit them to keep her from her destiny. She had become stronger than ever before, and she was unstoppable.

...

"Oh damn, what the hell? That's nasty!"

"What?"

"Goddamn cat ate something in here; there's blood and feathers in the carpet!"

"At least she ate it this time. I'm still traumatized from catching that terrified baby bird she didn't bother killing."

"Christ, is that a bird foot?"

"...Fuckin' cat."

Queenkiller
by Adam Thomas Gottfried

Simon Lavaque awoke early, the pitcher of water he had consumed the night before sloshing urgently in his guts. He stood and quickly moved to the window, shoving the shutter aside with one hand while the other plucked unsteadily at his breeches. He relieved himself out the second story window with a soft sigh of release. It was early yet, an hour before the dawn, so no one below was the recipient of his foul-smelling piss, though it would not have stopped him even if there were. In Cheapside, chamber pots were an unnecessary luxury.

After doing his business, he tied his breeches closed and collected himself. The girl in his bed snored and farted in a most unladylike manner, but that more or less described her from top to bottom. She was fourteen, not beautiful, and suffered from the early stages of the great pox. That hardly made a difference. She had been drunk and cheap and willing. Such things were all that mattered, at least to him. He could have stayed at the Tower of course, he had been invited to by the King himself, but the Tower made him uncomfortable. Too many ghosts haunted those bloody halls. He gathered his clothes in silence, not wishing to awaken the slumbering whore. She had been unused to private chambers and had earned her money well the night before: she deserved some peace before she returned to what would undoubtedly be a very short life.

He dressed quickly and simply, in the fashion of his French forebears; tunic and hose, broad belt and tall boots, all of them varying shades of black and gray. He pulled on a midnight blue cloak against the morning chill. The cloak had been a gift from the King and, while Simon thought it hideous, it would do to keep up appearances on this most auspicious occasion. Lastly, he strapped on the broad-bladed sword that had mostly fallen out of fashion in both the English and French courts.

He descended the stairs softly and made his way to the stables. The sore-encrusted stable boy snored loudly in the doorway but Simon simply stepped over him and prepared his huge gray himself. He pulled the double doors open and rode his gray into the pre-dawn morning, not bothering to close the stables again. The boy would catch Hell for it when the stable master arrived but Simon did not give it a second thought.

He rode through Cheapside in the relative quiet. The road was deeply scarred and pitted from the mass of humanity that had trod this way before and would do so again this day, and the next, and the next into perpetuity. However, Simon spared them the same consideration he gave the stable boy. It was early and while he was by no means the only traveler this morning, his huge horse and chivalric bearing – not to mention the broad blade on his belt – set him apart from the common throng. Such were the gifts of his forebears. He hardly noticed.

The soft hoofbeats gave way to a louder clatter as he approached the Tower. The flagstone road was a luxury and had been pointed out specifically by the King to Simon, and Simon had marveled at the extravagance and expense of it. It was his duty as the guest of the King, but he did not much care. He was descended from wealthy sires but he himself was not a wealthy man. He had little use for money, and cared less for extravagance. He did, however, know his duty. The King had wanted him to be impressed, therefore he was impressed. He barely spared the interaction a thought as he guided his steed with skill into the Tower yard. A boy, this one marginally healthier-looking, came out and took the reins of his horse as he dismounted. He spared the child not a glance but handed him a small silver coin, blank of any minting, and met the eyes of the captain of the guard.

The man was slim and pale-looking with deep circles under his eyes. It had been a very long week and he was newly appointed to his role. The captain watched the exchange with mild curiosity. Simon supposed few would have tipped the young page, but then Simon had been raised by common folk and had elevated himself to the attention of royalty through the merits of his skill with the broad blade and the patronage of nobility.

The captain led him into the yard immediately, and Simon mounted the slight knoll with only the faintest twinge of his bad knee. He had a thousand scars crisscrossing his body and the knee was the oldest yet. Atop the knoll, the captain offered him a black hood to mask his features but Simon refused it with a wave of his hand. He had been asked by the King to perform this duty and a black mask would not blind the eyes of God or King.

Kneeling on the ground in the center of the yard was a woman. Simon supposed she was beautiful, if you looked past the grime and bruises and the recently broken nose. He guessed her age to be somewhere on the low end of her thirties but he truly supposed it did not matter. From today, she would get no older. A man stood by, holding a Bible and murmuring words in English. Simon balked only momentarily at this. He recognized the words well enough, but he was used to hearing them in Latin: Last rites. The heathen King had at least given this to her. He waited respectfully until the man finished his catechism and then drew the blade.

She looked up at him tearfully. "Please," she whispered. "Please…make it quick."

He nodded. He moved behind her and pointed the broad-blade at her neck, the flat horizontally in line with her spinal column. With little ceremony, he drove the point into the back of her neck, severing the spinal cord from the head in a swift, precise blow. She died instantly, her final breath whispering out of her in grateful thanksgiving. Before she could fall, Simon withdrew the blade and in a calculated spin, swept her head from her shoulders as was required by the King.

Simon Lavaque drew out a silk cloth and cleaned her blood from his blade, folding it carefully into his tunic when he was finished. It was the blood of a queen, after all. The captain, on seeing her fall to the ground, signaled a man on the tower wall. The soldier nodded, took a torch burning with pitch from a squire and ignited the wick of a large cannon. The blast was deafening but Simon paid it no mind. He turned to the exit, sparing the corpse not a glance. He did not give her another thought. She was dead and his duty was concerned only with the living and ushering them in their passage from one state to the other. That was all, and that, at least to him, was enough.

He silently added her ghost to the grisly host that hovered in his wake, translucent and weeping and as ever, dead, dead, dead.

A Special Child
by Seth Bradley

Joshua was only eight years old. His father was a shepherd. Joshua yearned to be a shepherd, too. Many nights his father stayed out in the fields with the flock, guarding them from thieves who preyed on other people's sheep. Each night, Joshua heard many stories around the fire, as his father and his father's friends told tales of days in the fields. His parents were older when he was born and his mother died during childbirth. From time to time, he would play with the children in his village, but he never really made a friend he could call his own.

There was one story that his father told many times and Joshua felt like he knew the story so well that if he ever got the chance, he could share it with his fellow classmates. He had to wait for the teacher to ask him to tell a story. He couldn't just go up to his teacher and say, "Let me tell you my favorite story." He figured she would laugh at him or the other students would make fun of him, so he kept the story to himself. He hoped one day to get up enough courage to ask his father if the story was really true. As time went by, he started to think that maybe it was just a tale that been passed down from his father's father. Joshua never told the story to anyone or that it was his favorite story. But the tale always made Joshua feel good and feeling good about a story was what made it the best of all other stories told around the fire at night.

The story started out the same way every time. The shepherds were tending their flocks when they all saw a bright star in the Eastern sky. Being shepherds, they had all witnessed the stars shining brightly, because if the moon was not bright, the sheer darkness made all the stars seem brighter. But on this one particular night, one star was so bright it mesmerized them and they decided to follow the star to see where it would take them. They abandoned their sheep, which was unheard of in the annals of sheep herding. The star called to them. Its brightness drew all of them to follow the road to where the star shined the brightest. The way that Joshua's father told the story, nothing could have kept them from leaving the flocks and moving as quickly

35

as they could to the East. Along the way, they ran into three wise men who were traveling on camels. They, too, were following the star. The wise men told the shepherds they knew something wonderful had happened. They were so excited and so amazed they had even brought gifts for whomever they were going to find under this bright star.

The shepherds were grief-stricken because they had no gifts. They were not even sure they would find a person, but they knew that something special was making them follow the bright star.

The shepherds came to a town called Bethlehem and they followed the wise men to an inn. The innkeeper said there was nothing special going on in the town and that as far as he knew there was nothing extraordinary at his inn. But the wise men were demanding and tenacious. They looked all around the inn and found that behind the inn there was a family, a man and a woman, in the stable. In the manger was a little baby boy, wrapped in a dirty cloth and looking as serene as any newborn baby they'd ever seen. They were amazed at the quietness and depth of their feelings. It was like nothing they had ever felt before.

Before them was some kind of deity, perhaps a king or a future ruler. Of this they were sure. The serenity of the moment was heartwarming and sincere and they felt a calmness come over them. The shepherds felt they had to do something for this newborn baby, but what could they do? One of the shepherds went back to the innkeeper and told him about this baby lying in a manger behind the inn and asked why he hadn't given them a room. He told them that there was no room in the inn and the stable was all he could provide for them.

The innkeeper felt bad for the family – a newborn baby with no clothes and no provisions. He left the counter in the inn and went into a back room. When he returned he was carrying a pair of baby shoes. He said, "Take these shoes and give them to the baby to warm his feet. They were once my own child's shoes. He died at birth and never got to wear them." The man fought back tears, dropped the shoes on the counter and retreated to the back room. The shepherd carried the shoes to the stable and gave them to the mother, who put the shoes on tiny little feet to keep them warm. The shepherds felt the warmth in their own hearts as they returned back to their fields.

Crimson Cotton
by Macy Mixdorf

You never know what you'll see on the busy streets of NYC. Whether it be street performers putting on crazy shows, a flash mob pulling off a crazy stunt, sophisticated business workers with their minds in the sky, or just everyday people, kind of like me. It doesn't take much to get lost in New York. It's almost as easy as getting lost in my thoughts.

It was a normal day. Well, at least as normal as my days can get. Nothing seemed to be normal anymore. I got dressed in an old tux that I hadn't worn for five years, splashed on my best, most expensive cologne, and grabbed the black rose that was sitting on the counter. My quaint vintage apartment was on the 22nd floor. The elevator was always crowded, so I headed for the stairs. I quickly stumbled down the musty stairwell and stepped out into the crisp winter air. It sent a chill through my body.

I joined the rest of the hectic crowd and began my walk. Shimmering, pale snowflakes danced slowly down from the sky, blanketing the ground. I stopped in front of a store and stared at my own reflection in the window. The powdery snow speckled my messy brown hair. My cheeks were flushed red from the brisk wind. I looked straight into my eyes. Something about them was different. The warm, bronze shine they always seemed to have had faded away. The bags under them hung low and showed my many sleepless nights. I didn't even recognize my own reflection anymore. It's crazy how the absence of someone will leave you a different person.

I joined back into the moving crowd and continued the walk toward my destination. Everyone in New York always seemed to be in a hurry. I could never understand what they were rushing for. My focus started blurring and the crowd seemed to be one big mass of black and white. Something caught my eye. I immediately turned my attention. It felt like I was stabbed in the chest. I stared, taking it all in. I hadn't seen that color for ages. Not since she left. I zoned out all the honking cars, imprudent people, and chaos of downtown New York. Time seemed to stand still as I was swept away in thought. The crimson cotton scarf that dangled around the stranger's neck was quite intriguing. It reminded me of her. Memories suddenly came flooding back...

. . .

Thinking back to the first day I saw her, I remember nearly falling over. I couldn't believe how stunning she was. The crimson sweater she wore complemented her deep blue eyes, eyes that I would eventually fall helplessly in love with. I worked up the courage and stuttered my first words to her. With some help from fate, I was successful. She had accepted my request for a date.

A few days after our first encounter, I dressed up in my brand new tux. We decided to do a dinner date at a nice restaurant downtown. Neither of us owned a car, so we had to walk a few blocks in the freshly fallen snow. I left my apartment and headed to pick her up. I was so nervous that I nearly passed out when I rang the doorbell. The door slowly cracked open and she flashed a great big smile. I'd never seen anyone more beautiful. The simple cream-colored dress stopped just above her knees. Shining gold curls fell down over her shoulders. The crimson heels added a bit of color to complete her look. Her nails and lips were also painted with the deep, red color. I couldn't stop watching her the whole way to the restaurant. She had sapphire eyes that were hard to resist. The date went perfectly. Things were finally starting to fall into place.

. . .

My mind kept wandering as I thought of more memories tied to the color of the scarf...

. . .

We'd been dating for a year. Everything up to that point had been easy. We were madly in love with each other. I remember taking walks in the fall, admiring the changing autumn leaves. We would sit and stare at the crimson sunset as it faded away into the night.

She had a complex mind, but something about her made me admire the simplicity of our love. One night I showed up at her apartment with her favorite red wine and crimson roses. We took the stairs to the roof of her building and fell asleep under the stars. Sometimes the simplest things are the most magical.

38

. . .

I snapped back to reality and realized that I was getting close to my destination. The crowd had thinned and I was walking much more slowly. But my heart and mind were racing.

. . .

After dating for four years, we had acquired a lot of memories together. There's one that stands out more than the rest. I'll never forget the crimson sheets in which we lay together as I held her in my arms. Little did I know I would never feel her in my arms again. She left me with no explanation, and a feeling of absence. To her, I was just another temporary stop along her journey. The fire in her spirit burned a hole through me. One that I would never be able to fill.

. . .

I had finally made it to my destination, the very restaurant in which we had our first date. I sat down and set the black rose on the table in front of me. Here I am, on our five-year anniversary, at a table for one, not knowing if I'll ever be able to wash away the crimson stain.

Night Delivery
by M.S. Lambert

There's something loose in the back. I can hear it moving – goddamn it, I told the boys to strap that crate down. There's a twelve-foot bed on this truck; it's not right to load just one lousy six-by-eight-foot crate in it. I can run a thirteen hundred pound load from Cheyenne to Laramie and never hear a creak from the back. It's these single item special deliveries that cause problems.

It doesn't sound like the crate is sliding around back there. It's more like a skittering, clicking noise, like a dog trotting over the truck's floor. Not trotting. Scurrying. Damn, there better not be a rat back there.

Sounds too big to be a rat.

Hell, I knew this job was wrong, it was written all over Mac's face like milk starting to curdle. Sick. I never saw a man look as sick as he did when I picked up this load in Cheyenne. He runs the biggest independent shipping company in the Midwest, but he pops antacid tabs like they're his hope of Heaven. Doesn't even dissolve 'em in water first, just puts 'em right on his tongue.

"Just get it to Sioux City," he said, like I couldn't read the order for myself. "Tonight. By sunrise."

"It's a ten-hour drive," I said.

"It's a long night," he said, and gave me a cracked grin. That's when I saw the sweat beading up on his face, running down his bloodless white skin.

"What is it?" I said. The shipping manifold just said canned goods.

"Special delivery," he said. "For a special client. I can count on you, right, Ben?"

"Sure," I said, like the fool I was. "I'll get it there. Don't worry."

Long night. Damn straight it's a long night, the longest of the year. Snow swirls out of the black sky, whirling through the headlight beams and across the empty interstate. I haven't seen another truck in over an hour. No cars, either, but that's to be expected at a little past two in the morning. The CB squats at my elbow, silent, the cord dangling from its mike and swinging a little with the truck's motion.

My bladder's starting to feel a bit of pressure, but it isn't bad yet. I'll give it another forty minutes; see if I can make it to North Platte.

Everything's quiet, except for the rumble of the truck's engine and the skittering of whatever's back there.

Next thing I know, a squeal of metal goes through my brain like a jackhammer. I slam on the brake, startled, and shit, *shit*, I'm skidding across the road. The wheel locks under my hands. I try to turn into the skid, but it's like trying to haul in the Rock of Gibraltar.

I spin a full 360, wheels screaming, headlights bouncing over the empty white fields on either side of the road. I end up facing the wrong way in the westbound lane, the stink of rubber in my nose and the headlights shining out into the falling snow.

I take a shaky breath and release the steering wheel, peeling my fingers off it one at a time. The engine coughs and I switch it off. Now all I hear is the tick of cooling metal and the moan of the wind. There's a draft on my cheek, and I turn my head.

A six-inch gap cuts through the cab's rear wall, like someone slit the metal with a cleaver. As I watch, a claw – hell, it's gotta be eight inches long, but it's a claw, like the world's largest eagle talon – slides up through the gap. It hooks over the edge and pulls the metal down like you'd open a can of sardines.

My seatbelt's locked. It kept me from going through the windshield a minute ago, but now it's like a chain holding me down as I jab uselessly at the release button. *Shit, shit, shit*, the tortured metal screams in my ears as I fight with the unyielding straps locking me in place.

There's a foot-long hole in the rear wall when the claw comes all the way through – five claws, attached to long, weirdly jointed red fingers – a whole fucking hand. One of them hooks on the base of my seatbelt and rips it out of the seat.

I throw the loosened straps off me and yank my door open. The wind blasts my face, hurling snow in my eyes as I stumble down to the frozen road.

When I look back there's a demon crouched in my seat. It studies me with yellow eyes, huge as lanterns in its flat red face. Then it grins, a piranha smile with way too many teeth.

"Which way back to Cheyenne?" it says, and I swear all my ears hear is the shriek of the wind kicking up a notch, but there the words are, burned into my brain.

Not answering is not an option. I point west.

It runs out a long purple tongue, tasting the air. Standing six feet away, I can feel the heat baking off it. Snow swirls down but doesn't land on its tongue. It vanishes before it gets there, leaving little wisps of steam behind. Distantly, I'm aware the pressure in my bladder is gone. I don't want to think about where it went.

"I liked Cheyenne," the demon says. "Things were simpler there. A deal, a crossroads, people respect tradition there. Then I meet your boss, and next thing I know I'm in a box."

It heaves a sigh, its reptilian rib cage lifting and falling like an accordion bellows. "Oh, well. He signed the contract, and payment's due at dawn." Its grin widens. "You'll have to drive fast."

All the Quiet in the World
by Kyle Owens

Crude clouds, light and dark, width a colossal sky. Slides of sound, shaped by fractured voices, prey the mountainside with whispered echoes inside sways of wind. Soft slopes, startled white, paint up against...

"Is it time yet?"

"Not yet. It'll be a few more minutes."

"What's taking so long?"

"It takes a while to travel up the mountain. He'll be here soon."

"I'm freezing."

"I'm not. I'm too excited to freeze."

"You're nuts."

"I'm not nuts. I'm Toby."

"You two hush or I'll take you back home."

"Brenda started it."

"Well, I'm finishing it. Now hush."

Limbs swollen with the dark doves of midnight scanning for sustenance and peering down onto the contrast of dark figures on a white face begin...

"Look at all of them crows up there, Mommy."

"There's a lot of 'em."

"I heard Granny say that a tree full of crows was bad luck. Is that true, Mommy?"

"I don't know..."

43

"Where's Daddy?"

"Never you mind that, Brenda. Just wait quietly like everybody else is."

"But..."

"You heard me."

Faces smudged with melted flakes of snow gazed east as anticipation waterfalled the mind. A quiet mother's thoughts are screaming lost inside the shadows that men play. The mountain ridge edged hard and cold to the touch of the eyes as...

"Did you hear about Tammy?"

"No, what?"

"Bill left her."

"Oh no. They seemed so happy."

"He left her a note and said he was leaving. He said he couldn't handle having a family."

"I can't believe that. How is she going to...?"

Filaments of laughter jewel the ears. Silence and solitude haunt the mind in a backdrop of...

"Look, Toby."

"What?"

"The moon is out and it's daytime."

"That's weird ain't it?"

"Mommy, why's the moon out in the daytime?"

"I don't know, honey."

"I thought the moon only came out at night."

"Maybe it's nighttime and we don't know it."

"It's not nighttime, Toby. It's daytime. Right, Mommy?"

A mother's pale reflection meets her eyes in the window of a Pontiac. Her expression sought escape, but responsibilities swallowed opportunity in the...

"What?"

"It's daytime ain't it, Mommy?"

"Yeah, it's daytime."

Breaking billows of gray smoke sphered the distance as fingers pointed and the crowd paced toward the steel rails that stood pillowed inside a fleece of...

"Be careful now. Don't get too close."

An iron horse crawled the incline charging the senses, tense and sharp, of the small gathering of people fragiled inside wool and cloth. Their eyes stem forward for the engagement to come that is snaking around the...

"There he is! There he is, Mommy!"

A red-jacketed man, trimmed in gentle and white, stood on the deck of the caboose throwing clear cellophane, swallowed tight around colors of effulgent, which were scooped up into tiny hands chased by waves of voices and dreams of plenty into the...

"I got two handfuls, Toby. How much did you get?"

Fists of orange and blue step the air in a...

"I got this much."

"I got more."

"Don't be mean to me. Mommy, she's being mean to me."

"Stop being mean to your brother."

Words shallow out onto the bedded snow as the train's silhouette graves its way into a mountain tunnel leaving only faded drifts of smoke of its ever having been and seemingly leaving behind all the quiet in the world.

"Will Daddy be back tomorrow? Mommy? Mommy? Will Daddy be back tomorrow? Mommy? Mommy?

Mommy?

mommy?

mo my?

mo y?

m   y?

!"

Blue
by Ethan Noone

She looked at him in horror.

He wondered what was coursing through her mind as she stared at him. Her repulsion evident. Her disgust undisguised.

"Why did you show me this?" she screamed.

"Because I love you. You needed to know. Me. For good or bad."

She tried to avoid looking him in the eyes as she began talking. "According to the public records, it has been three generations … eradicated … How?"

He responded quietly to protect himself and avoid an unnecessary escalation. The risk to him was dire. He knew that. "My father protected me. After he murdered my mother for what in his mind had to be infidelity, he ran. I don't know why, but he took me with him."

She was shaking. "But how did he get away with that?"

"He kept me hidden. Bottle fed me. Kept me off the grid completely. No school. No doctors. Travel after dark. Always keeping our heads down."

He paused momentarily, then continued "Perhaps there was guilt that maybe he was to blame."

She looked at him, making eye contact this time. "But the lenses – where did they come from?"

"From the underground market. My kind are not gone completely, despite the official records. Bolivia, New Zealand mostly. Two recessive genes can hide for generations. When they do, solutions are necessary."

"But now I know. We can't go on," she said.

"I feared that. But I need you to know that I love you. I couldn't live a lie if I was going to expect you to live your life with me. Not in good conscience."

He paused, hoping she might back down from her firm position.

She was still shaking, and now she avoided eye contact when she spoke further.

"Only because I love you, the person I thought I knew. I won't call the authorities. But please don't risk putting this curse on anyone else."

"I never planned on having children," he said, knowing the discourse had taken its final turn. "I knew it wouldn't be fair, in case this continued."

She was still looking at him, but still without eye contact. "Please…put the lenses back."

He did as she asked.

She looked at him again. Solemnly, she said, "You have to go now. I'll never be able to see you the same again. Not after you've shown me this."

He stood, knowing she had reacted as generously as anyone could. He walked to the door and looked back to say goodbye for the final time.

Her eyes were tearing as she whispered, "You were so wonderful...how could your eyes have been blue?"

Never Used
by Larry Oldham

I was walking by a decrepit bookstore when a sign in the window hit me like a ton of bricks, as the proverbial saying goes. FOR SALE: BABY SHOES. NEVER USED. I'm the author of various books, so this sign automatically gives me reason to jot down this subject as maybe being the title of a new book. I like the premise and several ideas come to mind. Then the thought hits me, what if the man or woman inside lost a child and was deeply hurt by that tragic event? Suppose I do write a successful book and that title comes back to hurt them even further. The honorable thing would be to go into the store and ask the owner the story behind the sign so I wouldn't cause them any pain in the future. I'm being a tad presumptuous to think that I could write a book with that title that would be a New York Times bestseller, but I do have many thoughts going through my mind about the title. My first inclination is to go in, but I also have the feeling that I should just keep on walking and either forget the idea of writing a book by that title or use the idea, but maybe change the title to something else. What a dichotomy. Torn between writing a warm, tender story about a child who died and how their parents are suffering, or just forgetting the idea and maybe missing out on the opportunity of a lifetime. It's not every day that a good story idea comes to mind or that a title hits you square in the face when you are least expecting it. Ninety-nine percent of me says go in, meet the affected person, get their story, get permission to use some of the facts to make my story stronger and maybe even split some of my commission with them. Maybe they need the money. Maybe they didn't have insurance and that's why they have to sell the shoes. What if they want me to really buy the shoes? I don't have children and my youngest niece is almost thirteen years of age so I couldn't give them to her. What if they want a lot of money for the shoes because of their emotional attachment and I don't have enough money to pay them what they think they're worth? That would be truly embarrassing. No I think my best bet would be just to keep on walking and forget the whole idea of shoe writing. I start to leave the front of the store but my mind keeps saying to me go in, get the facts, write the story, be the author you think you are. Don't be so sensitive

49

about other people. Maybe I'm wrong. Maybe the story isn't a hurting story, maybe the parents just got two pairs of baby shoes as a baby shower gift and they just want to unload the spare pair. If that's the case, that's boring. No one would care that they had an extra pair of shoes or that I was so dumb as to drop in the store, purchase the baby shoes and then find out there's no story. Another way of looking at it is there is no story, there is no trauma, but my creative juices are flowing and I can make up a story about a horrible accident, where a mom lost her life and her baby also died and in the car was a bag with baby shoes that had just been purchased. The father is distraught and he can't stand having the baby shoes in the house so he decides to sell them so another family can enjoy them and the shoes that his baby was going to wear can bring joy and comfort to another family, thus giving his baby at least some extension of living. Yes that would be touching and I could do a masterful job of telling that story. I'm going to do it. I'm going to go into the store and inquire about purchasing those shoes. They will be my inspiration no matter what their story is, I can make up my own story and maybe win an award for story of the year or maybe even story of the century. Either way I will own a pair of baby shoes that has already lifted my spirits and given me hope to write the most famous and the saddest story ever told. As I enter the store I see a young girl behind the counter looking despondent and suddenly I decide I just can't hurt her or remind her of her lost child. I turn and leave the store, saddened by the fact that I have just witnessed and felt a sorrow without knowing any of the facts.

As I was leaving I noticed that an older gentleman came out of a back room and approached the young girl. More than likely her grandfather, or maybe even her father who had become disillusioned by life and the sorrow that had been brought into his life by the loss of his grandchild. I turned back to them and as I reached the counter I ask the young girl, "How much for the baby shoes advertised in the window?"

The girl looked at me and said, "You're an author, aren't you"?

The older gentleman smiled, turned away, and headed for the back room. "Works ever time," he said.

The girl looked at me and said, "I'm sorry, they've already been sold."

I said, "Did you sell them today?"

She said, "No, he sold them twenty-two years ago, but he just can't take down that sign."

An Affair to Forget
by April J. Moore

He walks in and sees her sitting with his imaginary girlfriend.

Damn it! These two were never supposed to meet. How did this happen? Doug slinks into the busy coffee shop and sits at a small table in the corner and watches as his love life disintegrate over lattes and almond biscottis. If Jane finds out Doug dreamed up Marta while they cuddled on the couch watching *Love Actually*, it's all over.

Jane's back is to him, and he struggles to interpret her hand gestures, while Marta responds by nodding and rolling her eyes. Doug chews his lip. What could they be talking about? He instantly thinks of his Lego Star Wars figures meticulously lined up in front of his computer monitor. Jane's always hated dusting around those little piecemeal men, but Marta assured him they were cute. It can't be that, he thinks. He then remembers the cotton candy incident. Laughter erupts from the women and Doug's face reddens.

It wasn't that funny. Besides, shouldn't Jane be furious? Really, what on Earth could they be laughing about?

Oh.

His stomach performs a triple salchow and he wishes he and Jane had decided to meet for a cocktail instead of coffee. A quadruple, venti, half-sweet, non-fat caramel macchiato with an extra pump of remorse isn't going to cut it.

He thinks back to the other night when he had trouble in the sack. Jesus! Come on! He's pretty sure Marta didn't show up that night, but wonders if she sneaked in. Doug rests his elbows on the table and puts his face in his hands. He peeks though his fingers at the diabolical duo toying with his mind and, evidently, enjoying it.

His brain can barely process its racing thoughts as he tries to pinpoint the different occasions Marta hung out with them. Crap. He recalls the day Jane picked out that hideous dress for her boss' wedding. Doug and Marta had a good laugh over that one. Or what about the time he played hooky from Jane's parents' dinner party so he could be with Marta? Hell, it could be anything; Marta's there a lot.

If he could only make out a few words coming from Marta's lips, he might glean something from the conversation. Instead, he gets lost in their glossy red shimmer. He knows he's doomed. Talking to Marta, Jane might as well be looking directly into Doug's brain with his thoughts and emotions being broadcast on a high-def, big-screen TV with full color and surround sound. Not good. Marta knows every inch of his soul; she knows his fears, what he likes, what he wants and doesn't want. Lies he's told. Marta's privy to it all.

As the women converse like old friends, Doug takes a second to marvel – no – fantasize about how well these two very different women are getting along. Jane, with her frilly cardigan sweaters and sensible loafers...Marta, with her exotic and voluptuous features, plus those tall, black leather boots...hmmm.

Marta then taps the toe of her boot on the linoleum and it reverberates like a gong in Doug's head. Her quick and subtle glare extinguishes the burning light bulb over Doug's head.

She can hear me.

He leans forward. Sweat percolates on his forehead and he tries not to move his mouth while his mind asks the questions. Marta, what are you doing? She answers him with a smirk. What are you telling her? She seductively tugs on her ear in response. Frustration sets in deeper as his thoughts – now all in caps and exclamation points – take a turn for the furious. STOP THIS RIGHT NOW!

He's practically on the edge of his chair. To the casual observers in the coffee shop, it would appear that this man, in his khakis and button-down, is experiencing severe muscle spasms in his face. His eyebrows arch, furrow, scrunch and bounce, while his pursed lips dance wildly in every direction. It's over, Marta! His fidgety heels start tapping the floor at a drumroll pace. Struggling to control his hands, he clenches and unclenches them. I know you can hear me.

Marta flips her hair and laughs at something Jane says, ignoring Doug as he nearly combusts.

Just as his hands form a choking motion, Marta pushes her chair out and stands up. Her smug grin feels like steel wool across his face. Then, in a flutter of pheromones and perfume, she walks out of the coffee shop.

With his involuntary muscle movements now at rest, Doug sits frozen, barely breathing and apparently unable to blink. Jane? He wishes he could resolve this telepathically now that they have a caffeinated captive audience. But Jane's still talking, her right arm continuing to gesture, while her left hand is at her ear. She's been on the phone. The whole time.

Doug blanches.

Part of him is relieved, while the other half mourns the loss of Marta. Finally, Jane hangs up and scans the coffee shop, spotting Doug in a solemn trance. Quickly gathering her belongings, she rushes over. "Hon, what's the matter? You look awful."

Doug snaps out of it, but scrambles to explain himself. "Oh, um ..."

Nothing but concern on her face.

"Didn't see you. For a second, I thought you stood me up." He laughs nervously.

She puts her hand on his shoulder. "You have quite the imagination, dear. You know you can't get rid of me that easy!"

He lets out a nervous chuckle.

She smiles. "Let's go home." Like a vice, her firm grasp squeezes his shoulder and it terrifies him. "I feel like watching *Love Actually*."

Penumbra
by C.M. Crockford

He walked along the dirt road with nothing but darkness before him. The sun that had burned liquid heat earlier in the day seemed to have vanished into thin air, wiped from existence itself. Only the stars lit a path for him now, and even they glowed far from reality, distant, oblivious. The route back to his house was familiar to him, but all memory of the daytime journey was gone along with the sun. Perhaps it was the alcohol clouding his thoughts, a remnant from the daytime barbecue that had faded as dusk drew near, but he couldn't be sure. Vacant blackness loomed over all, silent in dominion.

He had lived in the countryside all his life. He was familiar with the quiet of the earth, the wind that spoke through the rustle of the trees, the white winter that buried the light and the green. He loved it, hated it, understood its patterns and mutations. He took comfort in its permanence and its eternity. But the dark here was a different animal entirely. The dark was hidden and deep and kept its terrors protected from sight. It was not like the night of the city, where the street lights provided a shield of some kind and there were apartment buildings filled with stinking humanity, with technology and plastic and burning screens. At least that was a barrier against the catacombs and secrets of the natural world, the secrets of the dark. The dark of the country, of the endless, treacherous forest, whose sounds and cries would enter your skin and never leave you, had no such protection. Thus, in the fevered rush of his mind and the fear that was quickening his heartbeat, shadows crept behind him in every direction.

His pace quickened. He was a young man, but childhood fears seemed to have overtaken him. He now remembered when he was a little boy walking down the stairs into the basement, staring down at the void between each step. He pulled the metal string turning on the light, but the sickly glow made little difference. As he stepped down to grab the laundry his mother had asked him for, he could hear the eerie thrashing and thrummmm, hummmm of the machines, the water churning. He gazed into the dark abyss looming before

54

him, struck with thoughts of the unimaginable. It was as if one could hear other sounds alongside the thrummmmmmm, hummmmm, the whispers of another world that he did not know and could not comprehend. He finally bolted up the stairs, his shoes clomping on wooden finishing, and slammed the door; then he breathed deeply and feel the relief of being back in the real world, one of light and color and things known and seen, a world that felt sharply, nauseatingly familiar. The unknown was forgotten.

Returning to the present, he flinched at a sound somewhere in the distance. He tried to look for the source, but could only see great oaks and birch trees; most were devoid of any greenery, naked and empty. Their frail branches were as harsh as claws, one arm pointing upward as if in accusation. Others were brambles and ferns that would soar in color in the daytime; in the shroud of darkness they became great shades, monsters in waiting. The trees and plants had altered into beasts of nature of their own slumbering power.

He stumbled on hard gravel and his leg teetered, getting caught on a bramble patch on the edge of the path. He could feel the thorns scratching at his skin. Pain seared upward and he cried out in surprise. A little blood oozed from a cut in his thigh as he pulled it away. He stared at the landscape, uneasy and tired, and he wondered then if his wound could attract...something. Something that liked the taste of blood, that could smell it leaking from his body and would lick its lips in anticipation, lurking, readying itself for movement. It could hide in the dark, inching forward little by little, stalking him, and then...

You're being ridiculous, he thought. Why the hell was he sweating, why did he keep making darting glances back and forth? There were no monsters, no ghosts or ghouls out to get him. It had been hundreds of years since vampires or witches were seen as more than old stories...it was the 21st century after all. Logic and reason were what mattered, not blood and old stories and fears of the dark. There was nothing unnatural out there that could hurt him, only bears and owls and deer and wild raspberry patches and the leviathan trees, beautiful and humming all the days. It was a gorgeous night after all. The world was silent and still, his footsteps crunching and alive on the gravel. And he could see the mountainside up here, the living painting that he and the residents of his small town had grown so used to. His house was close now and he'd arrive home shortly. There was nothing out here, nothing.

"Nothing to be afraid of," he said to himself.

"I agree," something behind him replied, something ancient and large and knowing and sharp and dark and breathing and not of the known world, something talked about in the old stories, something with teeth and claws that had been following him all this time. "Nothing at all." Suddenly he could feel hot breath on the back of his neck and a heavy weight on his shoulders. And he looked back and began to scream.

And then it was upon him.

Beneath London's Streets
by Carrie Uffindell

Ninety-two feet below London's war-torn streets on a balmy September night in 1940, Harry Bell sat on his old, ratty bedroll on the Strand Underground Station's west platform.

It was hot and musty, the air stagnant and rank from hundreds of men, women and children seeking shelter from Hitler's bombs. The platforms, corridors and stairwells stank of urine, sweat, blood and sticky flies.

Harry squinted, reading a novel under the faint yellow lights. With his one uninjured hand, he carefully flipped to another page but stopped reading when he heard a low moan. A filthy woolen blanket undulated in an unmistakable rhythm nearby.

Bloody hell. Harry cleared his throat loudly. The couple under the blanket slowed a moment before redoubling their sensual pace.

Harry sighed. Time to find a new spot. He glanced around, frowning. Trouble was that most underground dwellers claimed the same space each night during the air raids.

"Oh my gosh," whispered a young woman seated next to Harry. She leaned toward him. "Are they doing what I think they're doing?"

The woman's accent was smooth and measured, her "Rs" pronounced, like an American. Harry glanced over at her. "It appears so."

The woman looked to be ten years his junior, which would place her in her mid-twenties. Her lively hazel eyes peered at him from beneath arched brows, her red mouth curved in a puckish grin. She wore navy blue trousers and a bright blue coat with a silver knot work brooch pinned to her lapel, a battered leather satchel beside her.

"Pleased to meet you," she said. "I'm Eleanora Hart."

"Harry Bell."

"And what do you do, Mr. Bell?"

"Do?"

"Your profession, your job, your calling. Your mode of employment."

Suppressing a smile, Harry closed his book and accidently banged it against his bandaged hand. Pain shot up his arm and he sucked in a deep breath.

"Are you all right, Mr. Bell?"

"I burned my hand last night whilst fighting an inferno caused by a bomb blast. I volunteer for the Auxiliary Fire Service several nights a week, you see."

"Oh dear, I hope it wasn't too serious."

Seeing her bright eyes dim, Harry said the first thing that came to mind. "A bookbinder."

"Excuse me?"

Harry winced. "My profession, I mean. I restore and bind antique books."

She smiled, a dimple forming on her right cheek. "How interesting. Do you enjoy your work?"

His heart pounding, Harry nodded again, uncertain how best to respond to this strangely compelling young woman. Miss Hart wasn't what he'd call a conventional English beauty with her dark hair, freckled nose and wide mouth.

But then Harry also knew he'd never been a conventional Englishman.

"I can tell by the way you're staring at me that you'd like to ask me something."

Harry cleared his throat. "Yes. Are you an American, Miss Hart?"

She nodded. "Please call me Nora."

"Then you must call me Harry. Why are you in London these days, Nora?"

"I'm a journalist from New York City. I'm covering the war effort."

58

"Which newspaper?" Harry said. "*The New York Times*? The *Herald*?"

"You're familiar with New York newspapers?"

"I read – or studied, as you Americans would say – history at Barnard College."

"Really? I attended journalism school at Columbia University." Nora paused. "Ah, sounds like our neighbors have finished their business under the blanket."

A snore drifted from the now-still blanket. "Hopefully now they'll sleep through the night," he said softly.

Nora's brows arched and she chuckled, covering her mouth. "Lucky them."

Before Harry could form a response, Nora tapped the cover of his book. "What are you reading?"

"A novel." He inched the volume under his bedroll. "You never told me who you work for."

"I'm working on articles for *The New Yorker* magazine. Now, what book are you reading?"

Harry shifted. "*The Thin Man*."

Nora's soft laugh warmed him. "Oh my goodness," she replied. "An antique bookbinder reading American pulp fiction. What would your customers think?"

"Uh, well, I may have a fascination with American crime fiction," Harry said.

"I swear I won't tell." Nora traced an X across her chest. "Cross my heart and hope to die." She extracted a thin paperback book from her satchel. "I'm rereading my favorite pulp story, *The Big Sleep* by Raymond Chandler. Have you read it?"

He nodded just as a sharp whistle sounded. A rush of air shot through the platform as the nightly refreshment car slid to a halt.

Harry stood. "I'll fetch us some tea." He returned with two battered tin mugs.

"Thanks, that's very kind of you," Nora said.

"What do you miss most about New York?" he asked.

"Hmm. Horseback riding in Central Park. And you?"

"The New York Public Library."

They continued to talk about New York, detective novels and Nora's recent magazine articles until she yawned and lay down, drawing a thin blanket over her. "I hope you don't mind, I'm so tired and the dim lights and awful smells down here have given me a headache."

"Eh, Nora?" Harry wondered if he dare ask her before she dropped off. "There's a café that serves breakfast a few blocks from the station. I sometimes go there after a long night. Would you be interested...?" He coughed and started again. "I'd like to continue our conversation..."

"Me too," she replied.

"We can walk over as soon as the all-clear sounds in the morning," Harry suggested.

"I'd like that very much."

Harry tucked *The Thin Man* into his rucksack and closed his own very tired eyes, careful to not lie on his bandaged hand. It had been a long time since he had talked to anyone, man or woman, with such ease.

Since his wife had died, in fact.

Rubble
by Tiaan Lubbe

A thin string of smoke rises in the air on the mountain. Then another and another and another. People are settling in for the long night ahead as the sun says its red goodbyes over the peak. They're stupid. Letting them know exactly where they are. Making it easy for them.

Like killing an ant.

Around me, smarter people hide under the trees and next to the rocks as the long grass of the field keeps guard. A small river breaks the field into two. It runs with a steady stream of water only interrupted by the occasional floating, rotting island. A year ago people would have cared. They would have tried to get them out, but now it just seems like a task that would waste energy and make too much noise. Rubble and remnants of structures that were once houses line both sides of the street that was once home. Up closer to the mountain, I know, stands another, collapsed and empty. A creative mailbox would have proudly displayed its number as 831. 831 Alexandria Road, Pretoria. I can still remember my address. Useless, I guess. But it's like a memento of yesterday. Just a piece of it that can't be stolen or taken away.

"Why are you standing in the middle of the street," I hear a voice from behind me say. "Aren't we going in there?"

I look around to find her standing behind me, a frown settled on her brow and a look pointing past me to a bare, concrete structure.

"Maybe it would be better to sleep in the field," I say. "Safer."

She doesn't even take time to think about it. Her brow frowns deeper and her lips pull tight.

"Bubba!" she says, the word still as innocent in her mouth as ever. "You promised we wouldn't be sleeping in a field again. You know I hate the…"

"The rats and the spiders and the snakes," I finish for her. "And the crickets and the grass sticking to everything." I look to her with a grin.

"Well I do," she says and walk closer to me. "Please can we just sleep in there?"

I know we shouldn't. The field will hide us from troublemakers and FF troops. The structure won't. I listen for a familiar crackling sound, but none meets my ears and I let a sighing breath escape from my lungs. She still stares at me with those big blue eyes. The same ones my mother used against me to do the dishes.

"Fine," I finally give in, "but just because it's your birthday, Anne. Tomorrow we're sleeping in the field and you're cuddling the rats. Okay?"

She laughs and pushes past me. "Race you there!"

The structure is cold. A breeze runs around its corners and whistles at the next. No one else occupies the destroyed space and we walk toward a section that still has some of its roof intact. I set our bag down and point Anne towards the floor under the roof. A few tiles still managed to survive their cracked siblings. She does as I instruct and I decide to take a look around before settling in myself. Here and there something different peeks through the normal piles of rubble. A television, its screen broken, lies next to a shopping cart with only two of its wheels still attached. The television once would have shown his face declaring war against anyone that opposed him or he simply didn't like. It would have shown those first few months drenched in red and it would have shown the week that the bombs started destroying everything. I walk back to Anne where she sits rummaging through the bag. She looks up as I come closer.

"Where's the juice box I found?" she asks.

"I gave it to that kid remember," I say knowing she wouldn't. I didn't tell her.

"Not again," she moans. "You always give our stuff away."

"We have enough. Bread and water. Those kids don't even have brothers or sisters like we have. Right?"

Her lips tighten again, but I don't let the frown climb back up her forehead. I tickle her and she falls onto her back laughing.

"Shhh," I say lowering my voice. "We're making too much noise." I laugh at her and then help her upright. Then I reach into the bag and pull out two slices of bread and a bottle of water. We sit there, eating in silence as the moon takes over the shift from the sun.

"Bubba," she says after a few bites. "Do you think Mommy and Daddy would have been here if I didn't cry?"

I sigh. She always asks this and I always give her the same answer.

"Mom and Dad died protecting us. They wouldn't have wanted it any other way."

"I still remember her smell, you know?"

"I know. Me too." I breathe in the night air and she mimics me. "It's getting late. You better sleep. We're heading past the mountain tomorrow."

She takes the last bite of bread into her mouth and lays her head down on the bag as she chews for as long as she can.

"Happy birthday, Anne."

That night as the moon kept rising and the air became colder my eyes shot open at the sound of a familiar crackling.

A Wanted Man
by Shelley Widhalm

I crafted my personal ad as if some fairy godmother could wave her magic wand and usher in a tall, handsome man with blue eyes. This, I wrote trying not to think about Derek.

He managed the front of the sushi restaurant and I, the back. Sans ring, he rode the rollercoaster of those going through a divorce. His smile blew heat to my toes, causing my eggrolls to crisp.

A response to my ad took me on a date. We decided on Italian. He ordered water and for dessert, we split a tiny cup of spumoni.

To his inquiry for a walk, I said I had to check my email.

"I might have a freelancing job. I'm a writer, you see…"

He leaned over to kiss me, mouthing the air as I stepped back. Anger painted his doughy cheeks.

"Gotta run," I said.

I had made the mistake of letting him drive us, so I alternated jogging in heels with jagged walking from newly formed blisters. My punishment for being stupid.

Really, I wanted a fortune cookie romance.

One slow night, Derek and I were in the kitchen after the dimming of the restaurant lights. Studying the paler skin on his third finger, I raised my eyebrows. No, his head shake said. I gave him a diamond dust smile as opulent desire shimmered across my chest, flashing up to my throat.

"Your food is delectable," he said.

My throat was unfavorable to sound.

"And so are…"

"Don't…" My voice came out rusty, as if unused.

"What's this thing between…?"

"Is your divorce…?"

"Pretty much."

Derek slammed me against the steel table with the force of his kiss. My brain sparked. I fell into him, losing my recipes and commonsense as bright lights exploded. What did my fortune say, the one I read to add to my purse collection of good advice, lucky numbers, and future of blessings?

"Better things are to come." But did it have to be so literal?

A telegram of love. Stop.

"You are so delicious." Microwave hot breath on my face.

The divorce papers from the wife arrived. I let my breath go.

Derek broke down, asked me to take over both sides of the house.

"Are we…"

"That," he said, "was a…"

I didn't hear the last word as his foot smashed a misfortunate cookie.

Running in wonton soup-stained shoes, I slid on the floor, tackled the employee's entrance, and chased after fairy dust. Derek's fancy BMW wheels spewed bits of pebble, clouding my wave.

A rub at my eyes informed me that, yes, I would have to get over another man, but was he worth it? He was cheap in a different way than my personal-ad-cheapskate date.

The Apocalypse According to Dogs
by Marquita West

The dogs have always been happy. But they miss people now.

Loki scratches himself and whines a little. It's harder to wake up. He had his routine. Tail thumping on the floor, wet nose prodding a sleeping face. Dr. Phillips, his human, mumbling, groaning a little, heaving himself out of the warm bed, taking a piss, long stream, good noise, shuffling down to the kitchen. Kibble plinking into Loki's dish.

Then, out Loki goes, banging his pet door behind him, running to meet his pack. Giselle, little and sweet-smelling, how he loves to stick his nose up her heinie. Bart, huge but friendly, unless Loki spends too long with Giselle. His little pack runs and runs and runs, leaves rising up to fly in their wake. All day long they guard and patrol the neighborhood, barking at interlopers, chasing cats and sticking their muzzles into dead things, trotting home, paws clicking on pavement, turning off into their own yards, nosing around their food dish, slurping water, tossing squeaky toys in the air, greeting their humans.

It's different now. Something's happened. Something that smells bad. Mr. Parson's horse Dudley died right away. Grandmother Stone's chickens went too, same day – don't eat them, the Irish Setter across the way barked. They're bad. Soon, rotten smells fill all the houses. But some of the meat is okay. Loki misses his kibble, must eat what he can find. It feels strange to shove his nose into Dr. Phillips's face now. Cold. Dr. Phillips is gone, Loki realizes. He is Meat now. Giselle whines about Baby. She liked Baby best, so nice smelling, like a well-tended puppy. But Baby is gone and Mother, too. Giselle feels sad but the meat is okay. She doesn't get sick. Nickels down the street gets very sick. He dies. Did he eat something bad, they wonder. The things he ate were too dead, they decide. Poor Nickels.

It's more fun running around now, though. Safer, too. No cars to dodge. Little hurdles everywhere, bikes, skates with their wheels spinning on their own, toy wagons on their sides to jump over, lawnmowers.

The bad thing that happened – it's not so bad for dogs. Maybe it's a good thing.

Reclaiming Childhood Memories
by Sharon Rezac Andersen

Growing up on a farm during the 1950s in a family that embraced the "Dick and Jane" ideal innocent childhood world culture, I had little to fear except for an episode each day that scared the Hades out of me. My most scary ghost-like fear involved an incident each morning when my grandpa would drive his newly purchased black Kaiser into our farm yard. He kept one foot pushed down hard on the gas pedal and the other on the brake, and the roaring car sounded like a loud thunderstorm. When we heard him coming down the road, my brother and I would sprint quickly to the top porch step for fear of getting run over. Our parents constantly reminded us that we had to stay out of Grandpa's path and pardon his poor driving ability because he had just received his driver's license from the Montgomery Wards catalog. We knew Grandpa was "learning to drive" while turning into our driveway and circling around our farmyard, before stopping in for his homemade breakfast caramel roll and coffee. We dearly loved our jokester grandpa who lived next door and enjoyed the stories he would tell us children.

On a magnificent summer sunshiny day he and I went walking through the woods and I asked him why some trees were white and all the others green, and he exclaimed, "One day when I had nothing else to do, I painted the trees white so there would be diversity in the woods." As a four-year-old, I was impressed with my grandfather's painting ability and believed his story until I started school and my classmates laughed heartily at me when I bragged about my creative tree painter grandfather.

My brother and I knew he was a better storyteller than a driver; we loved him most for his storytelling ability, but hated his hazardous driving. I recall this particular episode as if it happened yesterday, for it was the day Grandpa left my brother and me burning red with anger. Grandpa as usual came driving into our yard, sounding like a rumbling tornado. My brother and I barely leaped to the top step when his Kaiser came to an abrupt halt right in front of our porch. Holding hands, we felt safe until we saw our cat, Lusabizza under the front car tire. We started crying with anger and together screamed, "Grandpa why did you run over our cat?" He said he was sorry and assured us that he would find us a little kitten, but we both knew no cat could replace our beloved Lusabizza.

Grandpa left our yard, and after wiping tears and snot on our shirtsleeves, we got a posthole digger, dug a hole, decorated our cat coffin with red ribbon and buried our cat. We placed a marker on the site that read: "In Loving Memory of Lusabizza." However, neither of us had forgiven Grandpa for our cat's death. On the same day, following Lusabizza's funeral, Grandpa and Grandma's chickens wandered over into our yard. We hadn't put the posthole digger back in the garage, so in frustrated anger, and with coaching from me, my brother threw the posthole digger at the closest hen, cutting off one of her legs. We were both astounded by the sight of a chicken hopping around on one leg, and together recited the phrase, "She's running around like a chicken with her head cut off."

We were not sure what to do next but trembled with fear when we thought that our parents, grandparents and older sister would discover the chicken's amputation. We decided to kill the chicken as revenge for Lusabizza's death. We ended the chicken's misery by cutting off its head with the bloody posthole digger and then buried the hen some distance from Lusabizza's memorial site so it could not contaminate our beloved cat's grave.

To our surprise, the next day when Grandpa stopped in during his "driving lesson" he announced that they were missing one chicken and we should all be aware that there must be either foxes or wild cats in both farmyards: ours and theirs. My brother asked if he should set a trap, and when I heard his remark, I could hardly hold the laughter that was exploding inside me.

Our secret remained between the two of us for about three years. But like all siblings, we often got into arguments as we grew older so I coined the phrase "Grandpa and Grandma chicken killer" as a threat to my brother. Two years younger than I, he feared I would tell our parents. He knew the punishment for a period of time would be taking away Lady, his horse he loved to ride. Therefore he ended up playing dolls each day with me, whether he wanted to or not, so I would not reveal our secret.

We never told our parents or grandparents before their deaths the truth of all that happened the day Grandpa ran over Lusabizza. However, my brother often reminded me and my children about the childhood threats to him that mandated he would do all I asked him to during our younger years growing up on the farm.

Psychologists suggest that our personalities are influenced significantly during our first five years of life. Within this story resides the questions, "What is the result of living with life threats in our childhood? Does one reclaim the influence of a grandparent on her or his grandchildren, or recall that a pet was killed as a result of a grandfather's driving accident?"

Stories like the ones grandfather told us have a way of resurrecting themselves throughout time, including a variety of embellishing episodes, don't they? My brother's sudden death does not provide us with the opportunity to tell this story together. However today I am heartened by the quote from Ralph Waldo Emerson: "It is one of the most beautiful compensations of this life that no one can sincerely try to help another without helping him or herself." Today, I delight in Emerson's quote while reclaiming these fond childhood memories.

Second Chances
by C.A. Verstraete

The strange flu came from nowhere. The news blared the rising death tolls hour by hour. Then came the panic and looting, especially once the real disaster became clear – the dead didn't stay dead.

Lucky for me, being the "crazy hoarder" in the rundown house on the hill had some advantages: The zombies had easy pickings of the panicked citizens below, and I had a house full of goods. With everything I could possibly need on hand, from ointments and paper goods, to baby items, to all kinds of food, along with my rain barrels and homemade solar panels, I almost never had to leave home.

As I stood on my roof, rifle in hand, and watched people fleeing and trying to fight off the ghoulish hordes, something hit me. The fate of the adults didn't matter. Heartless as it might sound, I knew it was them or me. But what about the truly helpless and defenseless? I didn't want to go out, but I couldn't stop thinking about the day care center in town. I had to find out what had happened there.

I headed inside and threw some supplies into my backpack, my eyes drawn to the old box of baby clothes on the shelf. This time, instead of making me mourn my own loss, it filled me with purpose.

The back roads remained empty, most of the action centered along the main streets where people frantically tried to escape the encroaching undead. My ancient but reliable van putted up and around the hills, my luck holding as I encountered only a few ghouls wandering here and there. They turned and moaned at the sight of my vehicle, then shambled after it at a snail's pace. I let them be, not wanting to draw others with the sound of gunfire.

To my relief, downtown appeared pretty deserted as well, because most people had been at work or home sick with the flu. The worst part was that many died at home, alone and forgotten, until they emerged undead.

I edged the van next to the day care, in my mind the only place around here worth visiting. I enjoyed seeing the little ones and bringing them the toys and baby clothing I'd kept after my own infant son's death all those years ago.

Seeing no one about, I hurried out and tried the side door. That it opened eased my mind somewhat. It told me the staff had time to escape, at least I hoped so. To my relief, nothing moved. It remained quiet.

Once my eyes adjusted to the dimness inside, I noticed the chaos – the discarded toys and overturned chairs, and the signs of struggle. I bit back a sob when I spotted the box with a new, unused pair of baby shoes lying discarded on the floor. I prayed someone had taken their owner home.

Both playrooms stood empty. I moved toward the last room when an odd sound stopped me cold. Not even my pounding heartbeat drowned out the unusual noises on the other side of the door.

I steeled myself and slowly pushed the door open, relieved when nothing jumped out at me. The sounds I'd heard, little growls actually, grew louder as I neared the toddler still seated in his high chair. Dark blond locks stuck out like porcupine quills all over the little boy's head. A lone, dirty curl hung limp on his grayish-blue forehead. He reached for me with dark, chubby hands and chomped his mouth, his few little teeth clicking against each other.

A shiver crawled up my neck as the boy turned and watched my every movement from faded blue eyes clouded over with an opaque white film. Seeing a playpen, I inched closer and stared at the infant lying there. She kicked and gurgled, her gray skin and odd, sightless eyes telling me all I needed to know. Somehow these two had become infected, yet they had survived.

Knowing I'd better hurry, I tucked the infant into a carrier. She wrapped her mouth harmlessly around my hand and nuzzled me with toothless gums. The toddler snapped at me as I struggled to get the uncooked beef bone up to his mouth. Finally, he held the bone in his fat little fingers and sucked in contentment.

The loud groans of the approaching zombies told me I didn't have much time. I strapped the boy into a car seat, secured the baby carrier, and took off. Somehow I managed to dodge most of the ghouls, but had to run over a few as a precaution before pulling into my driveway without being followed.

Once inside and the house secured, I set up the infant's playpen and gated off a play area for the little boy. The two ate heartily, the boy chewing on bits of raw beef, the infant sucking on the bottle of meat juices. They appeared as happy and healthy as any other living children would be before all this happened.

I listened to the soulless keening of the undead drifting in on the breeze, and the sounds of fighting in the distance, and whispered a prayer of thanks that I'd been so well prepared.

The irony of it all didn't escape me. The house that others called a neighborhood nuisance and a disgrace had become a safe haven for me and my new family. I smiled, relishing my second chance at being a mother and caring for young ones who truly needed me.

Burned
by Jeb Brack

The fire swept through the city, fanned by the winds of February 1904. The fire brigades did their best, hampered by the cold that froze hydrants and split hoses. Companies from other towns responded, only to find that their hoses would not fit the Baltimore hydrants. Sparks and cinders lofted into the gray skies and descended on new sections of the city. Men in tall hats and women with parasols went about their business, unaware that the fabric above them smoldered and withered, leaving only the stovepipe or the skeletal brolly frame. For two days and nights the glow of the fire lit the sky around the port, and Sims watched from his flophouse in Cheapside, cursing.

On the second day the clamor of fire and alarms died away. Sims joined the ranks of citizens drawn to the edge of the burned area, some wealthy men whose businesses now lay in ruins but most simply onlookers, hoping to see what remained of the city and perhaps acquire some abandoned valuables. They halted outside the ring of devastation, held at bay by police and soldiers with rifles warning of the dangers of smoldering rubble and unstable structures still standing. The crowd craned their necks toward the piles of brick and ice that clogged the streets, but showed no sign of more until Sims yelled that it was vital to get to his office, how dare they hold him back? Others took up similar cries and moved forward against the cordon; Sims circled around the press and ducked down an alley as more police rushed up to aid their fellows.

Skulking through the streets, Sims tried to get his bearings, but none of the familiar landmarks remained standing. He thought he passed the John Hurst & Co building where he had set the fire two days before; not even the façade survived. Sims clambered over uneven mountains of debris and jumbled furnishings, badly balanced by his heavy satchel. His inclination to rush he resisted, knowing that undue noise would attract the National Guardsmen. He would never get another chance at this.

When he spied the National Exchange Bank ahead, he almost failed to recognize it. The shell of the once-imposing structure still stood, but sheets of ice coated it, evidence of the sheer volume of water spent on the blaze. Through the now-empty windows Sims looked up at the sky; the floors and roof lay on the bottom floor as a pile of frozen, murky ash. Sims scrambled through a first-floor window. He cast about in the fading afternoon light, sure that his prize huddled under tons of wreckage, unreachable.

No, there! In the corner, canted over at a rakish angle, sheathed in ripples of ice, stood an enormous oblong: the massive safe that once adorned the office of the bank president on the fourth floor. When the floors weakened, the fireproof monstrosity had plunged through the blazing building, remaining whole as the rest of the bank went up in flames, hidden beneath the torrents sprayed by the firemen.

Sims breathed a silent prayer of thanks. Since lighting a small fire in the cellar of the Hurst building two days ago, nothing had gone according to his plan. First the fire flared out of control, drawn by the breeze that swirled up the elevator shaft. In fifteen minutes, instead of creating a Sunday morning distraction, the entire place burned like a torch and set other buildings afire as well. Then the quiet district exploded in panic as businessmen flocked to their establishments with every manner of wagon, cart, and buggy to evacuate valuable goods and materials. Instead of quietly entering the bank while passers-by watched a small fire, Sims found himself helping load furniture and filing cabinets onto milk wagons until he retreated along with everyone else, fleeing the advance of the flames.

Alone now, he set about breaching the safe. A few taps with a hammer and the ice sheathing fell away; the scorched metal of the safe still radiated warmth. From his satchel Sims drew a pry bar and wedges. He preferred quieter methods of cracking a box; forcing sand into the lock mechanism, say, or searching the office for the combination that the banker could never remember. Those options were destroyed as utterly as Baltimore itself. But inside the safe lay a bundle of bonds, their presence revealed to Sims by an embittered clerk who had lost his position. The bonds, worth half a million dollars to anyone who possessed them, made the risk of noise acceptable.

Sims applied the pry bar to the seam between the safe door and the frame, just over the hasp of the lock. Fire had melted the combination dial and likely fused the works as well, so finesse had no place here; this was a job for brute force. Sims leaned on the pry bar, then drove a wedge into the minuscule gap. He repeated the process below the lock, wedging it deeper. Then back to the first, the second, the first, each time spreading the frame away from the door a little more. Every so often he paused to listen but heard nothing outside. The light had nearly drained away when the frame, creased beyond endurance, made a slight pop as the hasp came free. Sims drew a deep breath of gratification, then swung the safe door wide.

He caught sight of the stack of bonds, still safe inside their treasure chest, as the raw heat inside smote him in the face. The cold air rushed past him and struck the superheated interior. The fire, deprived of air until now, erupted inside the safe. Sims cried out and lunged for the bonds, searing his hands and face and drawing back only fragments of burning paper that crisped into ash as he held them.

The fire burned merrily for a short time, but Sims remained where he was long after the warmth faded and the cold returned, turning the tears to ice upon his cheeks.

Blow
by Gerri Leen

It's an easy ritual. Duck into the bathroom. If the place is in use, pretend to be checking the stock of paper towels and toilet paper. Sign off on the sheet on the back of the door – a good way to get extra snaps from Rick. Just be careful that some dickweed doesn't crash through the door and slam it into your nose as you're writing. That happened to Jimmy over at the Glass Pheasant, and he's looked like shit ever since.

The place is empty, so no towel-checking for you. You head for the last stall, pull out the little vial that hangs on the cord around your neck, unscrew the lid, and dip in with the spoon attached to the lid. You hold it for a second just at the lip of the vial, inside where it's safe from spillage, willing your hand to hold still.

The door slams open, and you're glad you're not standing behind it, trying to write on the list under Ramon's illegible handwriting – he takes up three lines despite Rick's lectures on only taking one. You wait for footsteps, either to the urinals or to one of the stalls, but there's no sound.

You eye the spoon, just barely in the bottle, ready for you to lift it to your face. It's too damn quiet; the sniff as you take in the white powder will be too loud. And if it's Rick standing there, he'll can you. Rick's a reformed cokehead from the eighties, and he's pretty smug about that.

You wish the guy would hurry up so you could finish the ritual. Snorting coke is different from smoking out or letting Valium melt under your tongue. You hoover the powder up into your nostrils, and then you're not sure what happens 'cause you never paid attention in science. But you know somehow it gets to your bloodstream, and that's when the drug kicks in, and you can forget your life is going nowhere and your home's about to be sold because your stupid parents can't get along anymore.

77

The guy goes into a stall. You can hear the door swing shut, hear the lock being turned. Once, when you were still bussing at the Glass Pheasant, you went into the first stall, locked it, dental flossed the lock into place, then crawled into the next stall and repeated the process. You don't know why you did it, but it was funny. It was even funnier when Vinnie the manager realized it was cinnamon-flavored dental floss, the kind that straight-A prick Melvin used on his breaks.

Vinnie had a real nasty temper. He and Melvin had words, which meant Vinnie talked with his fists and Melvin listened with his face. And then Melvin was on bathroom duty for weeks even though he kept saying he hadn't flossed the doors. You helped him with the bathrooms, not because you felt bad, but because you always help out when people are watching. Makes it easier to do weird things later.

You wait for the guy in the next stall to do something so you can have your coke and get the hell out of here. Then you hear him start to sob, and it's the perfect white noise to cover up the sound of you snorting the spoon you've been waiting on. You jam the vial back under your shirt, flush the toilet, walk out of the stall, and the sobbing stops suddenly.

The door opens, and Rick steps out, his eyes all red. "Shit, Jeff. I didn't know you were in here."

"Had to pee."

"Ruth's out there."

Ruth is Rick's wife. Ruth isn't all that hot-looking, but she has this way of looking at you that says she's interested in people – that she cares about what you have to say.

"Why are you in here, then?" You don't always get Rick. He's nice and all. And he's pretty lax on how you do things as long as the customers are happy and the health inspectors don't bitch. But he doesn't say much. And you're not sure how that works with Ruth, who seems to want to listen.

Rick holds up a big wad of paper.

"Looks official."

"Is. Divorce." And he starts to cry again, and you remember he's from the eighties and wonder if you're going to have to hug him. And he does reach for you, but it's not to hold you. He's grabbing the cord to your vial, and he's pulling it out. And it's clear he wants some.

78

You drag the cord over your head – no way you're letting him handle the operation the state he's in – and you unscrew and load up and hold the spoon out, and then he's helping himself to your blow.

And you let him. Because maybe now he won't be so damn self-righteous about having given it up back in the "We Are the World" eighties.

And because, somewhere in the part of you that didn't feel bad for Melvin, you do feel sorry for Rick. So when he looks like he could go for another dip, you screw the lid back on and say, "This shit's bad for you, man."

"So's divorce, Jeff."

You're putting away the vial, and Rick's looking pretty nostalgic in that way you get over Laura Johnson every now and then. You aren't sure what to say, so you just nod and go check the paper towels. And Rick does the toilet paper, and when he goes to the door, he starts swearing, and you know Ramon's taken up too many lines again.

Rick takes the pen from the list and signs the sheet, then he signs the divorce papers without even reading them. He pushes past you, and you look on the door to see what he's signed on the list, and he's written, "The kind of guy you leave."

What a frickin' downer. Maybe you should have given him that second snort?

Ready to Face Home
by Derek Knutsen

The rocky terrain Private Pottersman walks has become more familiar over the past several months. Dust coats the ground and there is no vegetation for miles. Palegain's land has suffered greatly under the global war. He stoops down to put a leather-clad hand flat on the ground. The tingling of magic courses through his palm, up his arm, and manifests as a blue glow behind the eye patch covering his right eye. As soon as his palm lifts off the ground, the blue glow disappears.

Looking over the crest of the hill, Pottersman sees smoke from a campfire. He drops to his stomach, pulling his blowgun and a needle from the stash he keeps on his left upper arm as he low crawls to the edge. On the dusty plain below, a solitary figure sits by a campfire despite the lack of wood in the area.

The man has a large cooking pot sitting next to him. Unlike a normal pot, this one has gears surrounding it, a conical cover, and a long hose attached to the side of the pot. A pair of straps allows the pot to be worn as a backpack. The man, who Pottersman knows as Specialist Spoon, wears a patched infantry uniform. Across Spoon's lap is his trusty ladle. Spoon looks blankly into the fire.

Pottersman drops the blowgun and pulls a pan pipe from one of his pockets. He starts a haunting melody that carries through the bleak landscape. Spoon quickly looks up, searching for the source of the melody. After a few seconds, he gets lost in the melody, closing his eyes. A bass guitar appears in Spoon's hands. He joins in the song.

The empty space behind Spoon becomes active with eddies of dust. Each eddy gradually becomes a recognizable form. Fifteen double bunks form in the middle of the empty plain. Other humanoid forms resolve themselves out of the dust. Two of these new forms become younger versions of Pottersman and Spoon. Young Pottersman helps young Spoon make his bed. Silently, they talk to each other. Young Pottersman laughs at something young Spoon says. When they finish the bed, they sit next to each other on the bed frame continuing to talk.

The scene abruptly changes to young Pottersman and young Spoon graduating, becoming soldiers. Once the formation breaks, a human-looking woman happily runs to Pottersman, giving him a hug. She is lithe with red hair and pale skin. As she runs, her hair bounces, showing pointed ears. Young Spoon laughs. Young Pottersman introduces his fiancé to young Spoon.

The dust drifts off, but quickly re-forms into a beautiful outdoor wedding scene. A priest of Chuula, the Palegain god of nature, stands in front of the Pottersmans, uniting them. Spoon stands beside them, as the best man. Both Spoon and Pottersman are dressed in formal uniforms. Pottersman kisses his new wife and the scene shifts again.

Inside a large tan tent, a hardened soldier points a rifle at Pottersman. Spoon sneaks up behind the soldier and uses a ladle to strangle the soldier, forcing the soldier to point the muzzle of his rifle to the ground. As much as the soldier struggles, Spoon will not let go of his ladle. Eventually the soldier passes out. Pottersman takes his rifle and shoots the downed man. Spoon looks questioningly at Pottersman, who calmly lifts the edge of the tent and looks out at the night.

Dust blows and re-forms into a burning farm house. Muzzle flashes inside the house staccato the dancing flames. One wall blows outward. Through the smoke, Spoon runs outside carrying Pottersman in a fireman's carry. In the building three figures hang from rafters. Their bodies are covered with symbols. The bodies of priests of Nested, the mad evil god, lie in a heap. Bullet holes riddle their bodies.

Spoon lays Pottersman, who is crying, down on the ground. Dropping to the ground, out of breath, Spoon holds Pottersman. A young human man carries Spoon's normal-looking pot to the pair. Out of it, he pulls a couple of rags. Spoon wipes the dirt from Pottersman and himself.

The dust dances and then forms Spoon, who angrily kicks down a door. Inside the newly formed room, Pottersman, now with an eye patch covering his right eye, holds a lemon over shallow cuts on a bound man's arm. Pottersman's hard eye looks at Spoon, who is surprised to see the scene before him. Spoon shakes his head no. Pottersman levels his rifle at Spoon and gestures for him to leave. Disgusted, Spoon quickly leaves the room. Pottersman sighs and slowly closes the door.

Outside the room, Spoon packs a small bag. Then he puts his pot that has been modified with gears on his back. The young human man who was at the burning house confronts Spoon. There is a silent argument between the two men. Spoon stands with his gear and walks away. Quickly the man packs his gear and runs after Spoon.

The song the current Pottersman and Spoon play comes to a close. The dust slowly stops dancing and falls to the ground. Spoon sends the bass guitar back to the pocket dimension where he stores it. He looks to the cliff above him with a sad look on his face. Pottersman puts his pan pipe back into his pocket. He slowly low crawls away from the edge.

At a safe distance, Pottersman stands up, puts his large pack on his back. With his blowgun in safe reach, he takes a deep breath. A little magic sends to Spoon, Pottersman's deep sad whispered words, "I'm afraid of what my wife will see in me. But I got to face home at some point. Best to do it with you. Come get me when you're ready."

Never Used
by Christina Dudley

It was the year 2014 and I sat quietly in my room. My life was far from boring. I was adopted into a very loving family when I was around two years old. I will never regret who raised me or the morals they instilled. My parents were a special kind of "Heros." They helped me through changes within myself that would have scared off the normal person.

I was told by my parents at an early age about being adopted. When I asked why they felt the time was right, I received the response, "Sweetheart, you've always been a mature soul. Your father and I have talked a lot about this, since the moment we realized you were special." They told me the truth when I was just ten. I knew I was special from the first memory I have. My mind worked in amazing ways.

I think the only thing my parents were ever really scared of was how unique I really am and what people would do if they found out.

My parents had referred to me as "special" on many occasions. I knew they were talking about my abilities, which were not public knowledge. I was raised to protect myself against people that would try to use me.

See, my parents had been through fertility doctors and treatments and tried to adopt for a very long time, but seemed to be getting the runaround because they weren't made of money. My parents lived comfortably but that was because they used their money wisely and didn't try to live above their means.

My father, believing in fate and faith, went to church like clockwork, where he met Father Keith. My mother told me that Father Keith was their savior. I grew up, looking up to him like an uncle. He came to all our get-togethers and holidays, he was a welcome part of our family.

My mother is a natural, my father has always told me. Nicolette is a strong woman with a brilliant smile and a soft heart. When Father Keith came to them with a young child that needed a home, they stepped up immediately.

My parents got out in the yard with me and played soccer games that were filled with laughter. My dad would be trying to get the ball away as my mom would cover my eyes with her hand and trip me. They helped with every science fair project and every essay, my family really interacted. Life with my parents was a good one.

My parents were never scared of me when my abilities started to present themselves, they always embraced me with loving arms. My abilities included beyond-perfect vision, amazing hearing, above-average strength, a wicked sense of smell, a perfect immune system and a mind filled with possibilities.

My dreams were filled with vivid color and surreal accuracy, they were as real as historical events. My dreams were amazing. My parents were fascinated with the stories of them every morning at breakfast, it was our morning ritual and a treasured one.

My mom, Nicolette, used to tell me all the time, "God didn't want us to conceive children because he needed us free to bring you into our loving arms. He needed us free so we could help you grow into a beautiful, smart young lady that might one day change the world."

I remember my bio-mom, she was a fighter. When I say fighter, I really mean it. My mom was something close to a superhero. She brought me to Father Keith in order to keep me safe and give me a chance. A chance at a real family and a normal life, well, as normal as my life could be. I had my bio-mom's see-through amber eyes and her high cheekbones, along with dark autumn-colored hair and freckles.

She explained the truth to me as she held me in her arms for the last time. She left me in Father Keith's care, wrapped in a hand-stitched, warm blanket, along with handmade slippers and a note within a note.

Note #1

I trust Father Keith with my secret along with my life. I am entrusting my daughter to him, so he can find her a good and loving home. Somewhere she can grow and feel welcome. You must know, Shyanne is special in a way few will understand and even fewer will be able to accept. Father Keith can answer any questions you may have. Thank you and God bless you.

To my angel, you know why I cannot be there to see you grow into a beautiful young lady, but you will always be in my thoughts and my heart. When I thought my life would be brave but all-consuming, you surprised me. God blessed my presence with you, my miracle. Your father was a brave fighter and gave his life to protect us before you were born. His name was Joseph. You have the shape of his sweet face.

If there comes a time when you need me, I will be there. I promise that you will be, forever, what drives me to rid the world of these unholy creatures. Just place a classified ad in a national newspaper with a simple statement "For Sale: Baby Shoes. Never Used." and a phone number. I will be there no matter what. I love you, my dear Shyanne.

Protect yourself and hold your loved ones close. I pray that you get to experience the life you were always meant for. Until we meet again my darling daughter.

I have had a great life with my mom and dad, they put me in every sport and school activity I ever thought of. I've had best friends and boyfriends, I've been the captain of my debate team and class president. They've always been very proud of me and wanted the best for me, so when I said I wanted to look for my bio-mom, I knew they'd be okay with it.

We talked more about it over the next week, and together, all four of us put the ad in the classifieds "For Sale: Baby Shoes. Never Used." I think Father Keith was really excited to see my mom again after all these years, almost as excited as me. I knew my family loved me but there was still a piece missing.

A couple of days after I placed the ad, my phone rang; it was my mom. I assured her that I was fine and asked for a meet. She agreed, I would only have to wait two more days. I wondered if she still looked the same, smelled the same or sounded the same. I missed her so much.

When the doorbell rang, I almost jumped off my seat on the couch. As the door swung open, our eyes connected and I threw myself into her arms. It was amazing and my family was finally fully complete.

3:27 AM
by Dan Repperger

For Steven Michael Brodeen

I used to look through this bedroom's keyhole all the time. I would bound
out of bed when the sun had barely crossed the horizon, wide awake and ready
to conquer the day. I had to remain quiet until my mother was awake, so I'd
creep down the hallway again and again, trying to dodge every squeaking
board. When I got to her bedroom, I would peer through the antique keyhole,
trying to see if the curtains were open and she was up.

Now, decades later, I knelt on the other side of that door in the middle of
the night.

When my mother died, a kind man that rented one of the rooms raised me
like his own son. Then he, too, died and the house became mine. I lived in my
old room for years before accepting that the biggest bedroom was meant for
the home's master. Then I gave up keeping it as a museum and moved in my
belongings.

I don't remember waking up or getting out of bed this particular night. I
just remember being at the keyhole again. I remember it being dark, the room
barely lit by the glow of a streetlight. My alarm clock read 3:27. It was early
in the morning – and I lived alone – yet a bit of golden light was shining
through the keyhole. I remember leaning in, pressing my face to the door,
strangely afraid to just open it and look.

Every light in the house was on. I might have forgotten one, but surely
not this many. I never even used most of the rooms in this old, yawning place.
Stranger still, the decorations were all wrong. I'd never bothered to hang up

much of anything, yet now pictures of relatives and paintings of landscapes were everywhere. A boxy TV was flickering in the den, its screen never resolving into a meaningful image. And there in front of it I saw a child in red pajamas, sitting at the feet of his mother, opening a present wrapped in white paper. They seemed completely comfortable, as if unaware they were in my house.

I realized what I was seeing, perhaps dreaming: the pair looked at home because they were at home. I remembered those pajamas. I loved them. My mother could hardly get me to wear anything else. And there she sat in her easy chair, just a few feet from this child, dressed in a brown skirt and lighter top.

"Mom?" I whispered. I reached for the door knob, but the moment I touched it, the whole room went cold. My skin crawled, and my muscles froze solid. Dream or dark spirit, it would brook nothing outside of its script.

I saw the child—I saw me—pull a toy from the box. Bright. Yellow. Soft. I knew it well. I'd wanted a pet bird for years, but she couldn't afford one, so this plush animal was the closest she could get. It was just like the one the renter had, and I suppose that's where she got the idea. He was buried with his, but mine still sat atop my dresser.

Why this present? Why this memory? What am I supposed to see?

Then I remembered. I tried to move but couldn't. I tried to scream but had no breath. I wanted to pound the door, rush out, do something to stop what came next, but I couldn't. As the child clutched his toy to his chest, his mother arose, tears on her face, careful not to let him see. She mouthed something to a picture of my father and then opened the door to the basement, closing it softly behind her.

I heard her footsteps on the stairs, but something was wrong. As a child, the moment I first noticed she had left was when I heard the bang of her falling. She got hurt and died. But tucked behind the keyhole, I heard every step, all the way to the bottom. There was a long silence. My heart stopped. Then I heard the bang. To a child, it could have been anything, but as an adult I understood. That wasn't the sound of her slipping – it was the sharp crack of a gun.

"Mom?" the child called out, rushing toward the stairs. He wouldn't see her again. He would find the door jammed shut.

I slumped against the bedroom door, tears hot on my face. It wasn't just my mother that I never saw again. My father's gun went missing as well. And a section of the wall got replaced. My mother's death was no accident; she had abandoned me. Did some part of me know all these years? Is that what I needed to see?

I tried to remember what came next. Who opened that door? Did I call someone? Maybe Uncle Greg? No, he didn't arrive until later. It was the renter. I don't think he heard the bang, but he heard me struggling with the door and came to help. He was the one that called Uncle Greg. They talked for a long time, and then agreed that, even though not family, he would stay here and raise me.

I turned back to the door, watching the other bedroom doors along the hall, watching the panicked child yelling for his mother. But nobody came. I struggled to think. Which bedroom did he come from? I couldn't remember seeing him emerge, just him being there. He knew exactly what to say, exactly what I was thinking. He knew me better than I knew myself. And he had a bird on his dresser that was just like mine.

A Sealed Letter
by Owen Palmiotti

I was raised in a culture where anyone who did not look like me, speak like me, or pray like me was an enemy. My elders often said that it was simply The Way. I was trained to fight, to kill, to preserve our beliefs. I grew into a hardened soldier who was feared on and off the battlefield.

When The War began, a part of me was excited for what was to come. There would be countless stories and adventures that would be remembered forever, whether I was alive to hear the tale being told, or not. I took a boat across the sea, wearing the colors of my tribe, waving the banners high above my head as my colleagues and brethren lusted for battle.

I had my warbag with me: spare clothing, provisions, ammunition, and many other weapons of my choice. I liked options. The more, the better. If I could not kill you with my rifle, I had my pistol; if that didn't work, I had my bayonet. And somewhere in between, I could either throw a grenade, slash you with a knife, or set a remote explosive. There were so many ways for you to meet your end and I was excited to bring you to your maker.

I also carried a picture of my family inside The Good Book, a gift that had been passed down from father to son over the last few generations. I had taken that leather-bound book everywhere I had ever been since my father gave it to me when I became a man, or at least when society deemed me worthy of becoming a man.

We stormed their beaches, killing just as many as we lost. We pushed forward, moving further inland. Half my unit was injured or killed before we surrounded their capital, but that did not stop us. I saw a muzzle blast from a sniper high up in a tower. If I didn't make my move, I knew more lives would be lost. I signaled a few of my men and under protective cover fire made my way to the base of the tower. I kicked open the door and killed several of my enemies that poured out. There was no hesitation, no delay: my movements were well-rehearsed from many years of training.

I finally made my way to the top floor.

I changed the magazine of my pistol, chambered a new round, and then whispered one of my favorite passages out of The Good Book. I crouched at the top of the staircase and exhaled deeply. It was time to move: I kicked the door off its hinges, sending splinters everywhere.

He heard the commotion from behind and quickly grabbed his handgun. Just as we both aimed for the other, a loud explosion rang out from above. A mortar hit the roof of the building, sending a concussion that knocked both of us to the ground. Smoke and flames filled the air.

Without realizing it, I was lying beside my enemy, mere inches away. I could have easily reached over and plunged my dagger into his heart, and I'm sure he could have done the same to me if it were not for the rubble that buried us alive. We both knew escape was no longer a possibility. We were to die there that day.

We made eye contact once more. There was something in that momentary exchange that connected me more to him than anyone I had ever known. It was as if we were the only two people left alive in this shitty world. We let out moans as our bodies were being crushed.

I managed to reach into my pocket and pull out The Good Book. I slid it over a piece of roofing, angling my hand away from the encroaching flames into the reach of my enemy.

"If you survive, take this to my family," I said to him with struggling breath.

I didn't expect him to reply, but to my surprise he pulled a sealed letter from his breast pocket. There was not even the slightest hesitation with his hand reaching out to mine.

"And if you survive, take this to mine."

All I saw next was darkness.

I awoke some time later in a hospital bed, several miles away from the skirmish. I was not sure how much time had passed, but I knew that I was badly injured. Over the long weeks and months that followed, I slowly healed. I began to borrow maps and catalogues from the volunteers at our little makeshift hospital, attempting to find the place I would soon visit.

As I write this now, I stand at the outskirts of the village that was written upon the letter. I hold it in my hand and wonder if he is possibly in my hometown, about to bring news to my family that I am dead. I am a stranger in their eyes. I do not belong here. I am different from them, just as they are different from me, but that will not stop me from delivering this sealed letter.

I move slowly forward and with each step, notice more eyes on me. People come out of their dwellings. Word passes around quickly. I soon have an audience. They are not blocking my passage, but rather lining the way to where I need to go. I feel hands prodding, touching my clothing and face. I continue forward because that is the only direction that I know. After having been to Hell and back, I will no longer dwell on the past. The hatred and violence that I have known for so long is now behind me, a mere memory.

I couldn't believe my eyes as I saw him standing there beside his mother and father, a smile large on his face as he saw the sealed letter in my outstretched hands.

The Crash
by Charles Loomis

No doubt about it, I was slowly losing altitude; I was going down. The engine was misfiring and wouldn't respond when I eased the throttle on. I gently coaxed the throttle and tried not to force it for fear of choking the engine and having it quit on me altogether. It coughed a bit and spewed some dirty smoke as I gently pulled back on the yoke, trying to avoid a stall and hoping to gain some altitude from my present height of about a thousand feet. A little higher and I could circle back to the airport, land, and hopefully save my butt. However, when Mother Earth calls one of her children and his machine back into her arms, it's sometimes ugly and there's very little that a child of the earth can do except try to make the return trip as safe and gentle as possible.

I radioed in a Mayday and the control tower tersely confirmed that they would have equipment waiting for my possible return or rescue, whatever the case might be.

The cockpit alarm systems were sounding off and jangling my nerves. I was busy piloting, but I still had time to wonder what went wrong. She never skipped a beat during takeoff. What the hell was bothering her now – dirty fuel, electrical problem? Who knows? I tried to think of everything, but now had my hands full and no time for idle thoughts about mechanics.

I was losing altitude fast now. I was definitely going down. The scrub brush and a tree here and there reached out to me, wanting me. "Not yet, dammit," I declared out loud. I'd try to pick my earthly spot and settle in as easily as I could. I deftly applied a little rudder now and then, looking for a clearing. Too much of any control surface would send me spinning or stalling into a nose down dive to earth. I put the nose down a little to gain some glide speed and to gain a little steerage. There was no clearing, but I saw a spot that didn't have trees, just scrub brush, and decided to go for it. All I had to do was

92

make it over one tree that stood high in my path and then maybe the scrub brush would slow me down to a survivable stop.

It was the only choice I had as all the other landing sites were dotted with trees – no clear path anywhere. Besides, now I was committed. I had no choice unless the engine suddenly roared to life – fat chance!

I had misjudged my approach and was a little too low. I was losing airspeed rapidly. That damn tree seemed to be reaching for me. "Never make it," I said. "Got to make it," I declared back to myself.

I carefully eased back on the yoke, again risking a stall. "Dammit; at least I'll pancake into that damn tree instead of diving in head first."

I quickly killed the engine and shut off the ignition and fuel pump. At least I'm going to cut my chances of burning to death if I survive, I thought.

I was sweating now and I struggled against the fear that was trying to surface. Stay cool, stay cool, was the mantra repeating over and over in my brain. I thought of my college days and all my flight training. Here I am, experiencing a lesson I hope I learned well. I thought of that corporate logo "No Fear." I'll bet those fools have never been in an airplane crash, I thought.

It seemed like the upper branches of that accursed tree were alive and reaching for me. The branches whipped by my windscreen and I braced myself. I heard a loud banging and screeching noise as the tree enveloped me. It seemed like my heart was beating a thousand times a minute and was thudding against my rib cage. I was thrust roughly forward and I felt the harsh but welcome bite of my safety harness. The plane shuddered and lurched but suddenly sunshine streamed in on me. Hallelujah, I had made it through that spawn of the devil, that beckoning goddess of death.

The plane quickly pitched down but still had enough speed to glide and soon the short scrub brush tried to grind me down too fast. The banging and scraping started again as the little brush people grabbed at me. I gripped the yoke as long as I could, but realized there was nothing more I could do. The machine was out of my hands and control. I threw my arms up in front of my face and uttered an audible yelp. Finally, I came to an almost gentle stop as the plane pitched forward nose down in the dirt.

I realized I had stopped breathing and drew in a huge gulp of air. I dropped my arms to my lap and my body slowly relaxed. I was aware that I was alive and well and I had made it.

With sweaty and shaking hands, I climbed out of the simulator to the derisive hoots of my laughing classmates.

The Shadow Figure and the Old Woman
by Monroe Truss

May sat on her old weathered front porch nestled on handmade cushions in a wooden rocking chair, slowly extending her left ankle to rock. Her eyes were frozen on the path through the forest that emptied into her yard. She anticipated company and she full well expected someone even though it was just a sense. She puffed on her corn cob pipe and exhaled a small stream of swirling smoke from her pursed lips.

The colors of sunset were being painted against a dark blue western sky. The chickens that roamed the yard chasing grasshoppers and bugs had all gone to roost. Her old faithful flop-eared hound lay beside her rocking chair, his droopy eyes keenly aware of every movement.

May finished her pipe, leaned forward and placed it on the railing. She grabbed her cane and held it firmly with both hands while leaning forward in her chair. Her aged eyes revealed a strong spark of life and a knowing smile crossed her face. She laid the cane against her left leg, lifted a Bible with worn pages from her la, thumbed to the 23rd chapter of Psalms and read out loud as if someone was listening.

The wind began as a small breeze and built little by little till the trees bowed like servants. Everything not fastened down was tossed about and blown violently until it lodged against a solid surface. Leaves were lifted and danced dizzily, swirling round and round. May held the pages open, pinched between the index fingers and thumbs of both hands, and continued to read, ignoring the wind.

May placed her left index finger on the page to hold her place, closed the Bible and held it tightly in her left hand. She leaned back in her chair and again looked down the path. She could see the shadow figure of a man walking down the path toward her. She began to hum an old Gospel tune, and rocked slowly. She laughed a little to herself, and let her emotions rejoice. She knew her guest would soon arrive, and was prepared to greet him.

The figured walked to the opening of May's yard and stopped. Her old flop-eared hound stood, walked to the steps, and moaned a low-pitched growl. May laid her Bible on a small round wooden table beside her and pulled her cane across her lap. The wind ceased and everything became still.

"Well don't just stand there staring, come on up and visit with me," May said very loud and clear.

The shadow figure didn't budge, and stood like a dark statue at the edge of her yard. He wore a large-brimmed black fedora and a long black trench coat. His features looked chiseled, with deep defining lines.

May laughed a short laugh, and cleared her throat. "You can't stand there all night because I'm not going to sit here all night waiting," May hollered very clearly.

The last rays of sunlight lit up the horizon. May arose from her rocker, lit an old kerosene lantern, and hung it at the edge of the porch. She walked to the steps, stood beside her old flop-eared hound, and leaned on her cane.

"No need to be afraid of this old hound, he ain't gonna bite you," May yelled out. "If you think you're going to just stand there all night, you are mistaken. This old woman is tired, and I'm going inside soon. You can leave or come up here and talk with me," she continued.

The shadow figure didn't stir or make a sound. He stood ominously staring at the old woman.

May reached for her corn cob pipe, pulled a tobacco pouch from a pocket, loaded her pipe, and lit it with a kitchen match. She puffed on it till it was fully lit and took a long drag. She blew the smoke toward the shadow figure, and smiled broadly.

The smoke lingered in the air just past the steps and floated gently to the ground. The small stream of smoke rose like a serpent and danced slowly toward the shadow figure.

"I thought you might like a smoke," May said.

May raised her cane and waved it in circles, and the smoke spun as it danced closer and closer to the figure. The faster she waved her cane the faster the smoke spun. Then with a quick jerk she whipped her cane forward and the shadow figure was consumed in the smoke.

May lowered her cane and pounded it on the floor of the porch. A large boar hog rounded the house and ran into the smoke. May swept her cane across and the smoke blew into the forest. The boar squealed and ran down the path from which the shadow had come. A small pile of black cloth lay on the ground where the shadow once stood.

May patted her old hound on the head and chuckled to herself. She lifted the lantern from the hook, picked up her Bible, and looked one more time down the path.

"Come on old boy, time for us to turn in," she said to her old hound. "I was hoping tonight would be more entertaining," she said with a chuckle as she opened the screen door and went inside.

Confessions
by Zephyra Burt

Her lap was full of red paper hearts. She looked up at him, back down at the card, pink and marked with swirling black letters.

"It's beautiful," she said finally, and he knew something was wrong. Her long silence was a sword of Damocles hanging over his head, and he could feel the thread fraying like his nerves. His implant showed no elevation in her heart rate, no heightened conductivity of skin…she wasn't excited, in any way. If anything, she was anxious.

She frowned, then glanced up at him, quick, too quick to read.

"I probably should have told you," she said, chewing her bottom lip. "I'm on inhibitors. I'm sorry."

"Ah," he murmured, putting his hands in his pockets to hide the shaking. He glanced out the window, feigning nonchalance, swallowed the lump in his throat and waited for his symbiote to kick in. The sun was going down and the city was lit in neon colors, the arcing electric rails of the skyway trains forming a net over it all. Cars hung from the rails on thin wires, transparent stabilizing wings quivering in the wind. They always reminded him of dragonflies, or puppets. Giant silver puppets of dragonflies. Tears welled up and turned the mechanical vista into a bright impressionist smear.

A few seconds later the symbiote sensed the chemical imbalance and he felt it pulse beneath his skin, a little above his heart. His cheeks cooled, the stab of betrayal receding with the anger and sadness.

"I'm sorry. You're great, you know, but I can't. I'm just not biologically capable." She shut the card and put it in her letter box. The letter box was only the barest courtesy. He knew where the things in that letter box went. If the recycling chute was Hell, that was Charon's ferry.

"No, I understand now." It was not a lie. "Why didn't you tell me before?" He was still watching the city, and he felt very calm. It was all in perspective now, and somehow that was emptier than raw rejection. His eyes had filled with tears a moment ago, but they meant nothing now. His implant helpfully noted their relatively high salinity and suggested he drink more water.

"It's just a part of my life at this point, I guess," she said, sweeping the paper hearts into a heap and putting them on the desk. They were translucent, the size of rose petals, different shades of pink, orange, and red. "You understand? I mean, you're not a naturalist." She smiled with half of her mouth and he did the same. Automatic. It meant nothing.

"No," he agreed.

A Cobbler's Curse
by Bam Leslie

The bells on the door jingled and clattered behind Sarah as she walked into the musty store. There was nearly half an hour before her prescription at the pharmacy would be ready, so she had decided to walk down the street to the shady pawn shop on the corner. She had been to enough of these stores that she knew exactly what to expect before she walked in. It was the typical assortment of hand-me-down junk that people in desperation had probably sold for loose change, just to try to get by. Sarah cringed a bit at the thought: A pawn shop was not a respectable business in most aspects. However, she took solace in knowing it was simply a matter of having time to kill, and that she likely wouldn't buy anything.

Behind the glass counter (a smudged, poorly lit display of old jewelry and watches) was the shop's proprietor. He was a tall, dark man, slightly hunched over, with long black hair and a thin beard that outlined his long, bony face. He projected a creepy vibe that Sarah could not quite ignore, and his eyes seemed to be following her around the room as she idly viewed the various items on display.

She was almost ready to walk out of the store when a particular display, different from all the others, managed to catch her eye.

It was a small, open shoe box, faded from a once-vibrant pink, with two tiny infant shoes. The hand-scrawled display, also faded with time, read:

"For sale: Baby shoes, only worn once."

The shoes were obviously old, fashioned from the finest materials, with craftsmanship both unique and fantastic. Sarah looked at the shopkeeper, who was focused very intently on her by now, and almost worked up the courage to ask about those shoes. The shopkeeper's very pale face and deeply set, dark eyes made her hesitate. Thankfully, he saved her the fuss.

"They're cheap for what they are," he said, in a tired, shrill voice, one that belied his size.

Sarah forced a polite smile. "They seem lovely, but I have no need for them. Not yet, anyways."

"I'll offer you a deal on them, they could be a gift or something. For someone you know, perhaps?"

Sarah approached the counter, moving boldly now that the silence had been broken. "What's the deal with those shoes, if I may ask? You don't really sell clothes or shoes here."

The tall man shifted on his feet, looking deeply into Sarah's eyes. The intense scrutiny caused her to quickly look away. "I acquired them when I acquired this store from a desperate woman. This is the story as she told it to me. Of course, I didn't believe it then, but it's true."

"A cobbler made these shoes, a special order for a very strange customer. The customer was a dark woman, who was rumored by the townspeople to be a witch. The cobbler assumed this to be balderdash, so he crafted the order as best he could for the woman. The woman's child died and, as she was indeed a witch, she became angry and placed a curse on the poor cobbler. As if it could have been his fault somehow! The curse has been passed on to me, and in order to break the spell, I must sell these shoes."

Sarah stood silent for a moment, trying her best to digest the tall tale that this strange man had divulged to her. "So what is it? What's the curse?"

"I'm bound to this place. I can't leave here. This is the same store that the poor unfortunate cobbler used to fashion his wares. I bought the store and many of these items with it, including the shoes. If I could sell the shoes, I would, at last, be free."

The handwritten sticker on the side of the shoe box read $1.50. It was dirt cheap for the handmade footwear, even if the style was a bit dated. Sarah chuckled a bit as she carried the box from the display table to the counter. The old, dark man watched her every step. It would be well worth it, she thought, just for the story alone. It would also make a great conversation piece for guests when she hosted parties, as she often did.

"You know what?" she said, smiling. "I'll buy them!"

The store owner did his very best to hide his elation as he counted out her change. He placed the lid on the box and handed it to Sarah, returning her broad grin. He then held up a long, bony finger as if signaling her to wait for a moment. He walked past Sarah without another word and exited the front door of the pawn shop. Much to her surprise, he then turned and disappeared down the sidewalk to his right. Sarah started to follow but found as she approached the door that some unseen force kept her hand from the door-handle. She was unable to progress any further, despite her best efforts. She screamed, crying for help, but it was of no use. People walked by the store without a passing glance, as if she could not be heard...

. . .

A young couple entered the quiet old pawn shop on the corner one lazy summer afternoon. The husband smiled as he held his wife's hand and she glowed as she rubbed her swollen belly; it wouldn't be much longer before the patter of little feet would hit the floor at their home. The only other person in the shop was its owner, who looked up and smiled hopefully as she saw the young couple enter...

On Spilling on the Train
by Robert Eversmann

You're on the light rail. Everyone's spilling.

Spilling orange juice. Spilling milk. Milwaukee's Best and bodily fluids.

-liquids sloshing-

Nothing is sacred. Nowhere is safe. The floor, the chairs, their bodies.

-sticky feet-

Your legs are still wet from moments ago. The wet Cheerios, your shirt is globbed with raspberry yogurt. A whole cup clings to your sweater like little white rats in amniotic fluid.

They've spilled on you all morning. But you're persistent. A long way to go.

You: I'll see this thing through.

The train comes to a stop, some of the spill rushes out. Two men with a shipping crate full of milk, shoddily made and leaking…

An unfamiliar man, long coat, wide eyes, sits beside you. Nothing spillable though.

He sniffles. He stretches and scratches under his pits, brings a finger below his nose.

You: Oh.

-violent sneeze-

Politely, he takes out his hanky and wipes off your knee.

Sneeze-man: Hee-hee, I'm sorry.

A man nearby immediately coughs—

-retching-

—ten-pack-a-day smoker.

Hint of a new smell, subtle, growing—

-bursting, gushing-

Little old man: Oh…

Such a little old man, his colostomy bag. Pops like a watermelon and runs down.

Green, green, green from his bag full of bile.

A smell like no other—

-mass disgust-

—and the passengers relocate, revile, spit. Another stop, a dozen more pile on. One clumsy man catches his toe and out comes his fruit cocktail. He stands up and smiles.

Clumsy man: People are really crowding that upper level.

You offer a jam-soaked old woman your seat, unfortunately full of gummy bears and fondue.

Woman: Eww…

You shrug.

A seat's a seat you think. But okay, you sit down.

You see across the lake of milk and wave to a little boy. Waving back, he spills his orange juice into the milk. He cries.

A woman complains of pain in her stomach.

You're not a doctor.

You: Ma'am, what's the matter?

Her body spills.

Woman: I think my water broke!

Oh.

Looks like you're here to deliver a baby in the river of milk.

104

-hee-hee-hoo-

-screaming-

You're a natural, Doctor.

-baby crying-

And so she names her baby after you.

In all the excitement you miss your stop.

But word has spread. The next stop, they're prepared—one big group steps onto the train ready: snorkels, shorts and flippers.

A pack of runners get on in a flash flood of sweat. Stop after stop, it's too crowded to ever get off.

You cry, the baby cries and everybody else cries too.

Ballerina
by Jess Kapp

Her dream was to be a ballerina.

It was a cliché, but ever since she was little, twirling in a yellow sateen recital costume, gold sequins flashing, feathers fluttering, she had imagined a life on the stage in New York City. She started dancing in the seventies, at age three, when the uniform was pink tights, tutus, and those tiny leather ballet slippers with the elastic band across the top. The best ones were always a perfect baby pink, unlike the faux leather version, which came in black or white. She always begged her mother for pink, the most expensive of the colors, but had to settle for white, the color that dirtied easily and showed all the flaws. Even at age three she registered the difference between her scuffed up white knockoffs and the other girls' pale pink leather slippers. By age seven she was taking jazz lessons, again coveting the soft, flexible leather shoes worn by the other girls in her class. Their jazz shoes had supple, soundless soles while she clunked around in noisy fakes that blistered her feet. By the time she was twelve her goal was to own silky, baby pink toe shoes, the slip-ons abandoned for the footwear of a real dancer.

When she was sixteen, her father was dying. Her biggest fan, he came to all of her recitals, bouquets of carnations at the ready. Now he lay confined to a hospital bed he would never escape. "To the prettiest Cinderella ever," read his last card to her. It had been nestled in among a tangle of pink roses he had splurged on for her first starring role that spring. Now it was summer, the season when, under normal circumstances, she would have spent her days helping him out at his store, running the cash register, maybe ducking out early for an evening with friends. Her dad would have taken her fishing ridiculously early on a Sunday morning, because, "That's when they're biting," he said. But this summer, she worked every day at a job she hated, saving up to buy her baby pink toe shoes, and spent every evening next to the hospital bed that held the withered shell of her once vital father. What passed between them in those days was mostly non-verbal – an understanding that he

106

didn't want to leave her, but that it was inevitable and life would go on. The cancer affected his voice, reducing it to a whisper, but somehow when he did speak he managed to exude his humor and his wit as fiercely as ever. The slipper-footed ballerina inside her was afraid of that hospital bed, and so she lay dormant somewhere deep down, below her guts.

Her dancing had gone dormant, too, in the past year. With high school came friends, boys, and new interests. She started running. She never knew she could run like that. Her father, struggling to walk the distance from the parking area to the racecourses of her cross-country meets, appeared, rain, snow, or shine, to cheer her on. Instead of a pretty ballerina in a white dress she was a sweaty, pimple-faced teen in blue and gold running shorts. He still brought her flowers. He managed to show up somewhere midway through the racecourse, when she was at her worst, and lift her up out of misery. He had a bum hip, and limped in a way that appeared painful and cumbersome. He would get himself to the finish line before she crossed it, inspiring her to kick it into high gear for the last hundred meters of the race. Her feet were more often in racing shoes now, metal spikes poking out of the soles, than the ballet slippers she had grown so accustomed to. But that was all before the hospital bed, the cancer, and the whispers lodged in her ears.

Her toe shoe fund still sat untouched in a jar in the back of a drawer full of leotards. One Saturday morning while rummaging through that drawer her fingers grazed the cold glass of that jar. She grabbed it, shoved it into her oversized duffle. She wasn't sure why she was taking it.

At the hospital, he patted the mattress next to him. For the first time in her life she was uncomfortable around this man who had taught her how to bear hug. She tentatively sat by his left hip, the bum hip, and turned to look at his face. He smiled, revealing the face of the man she had trusted above anyone. He told her to get an education. It was a heavy whisper. She knew it was his dying wish for her. Did he know the jar was in her bag? Had he sensed that his only child was considering the rough road of a starving artist? He had traveled it himself, guitar in hand, and worried for what his daughter might face. He was trying to whisper it out of her mind.

Later that day she bought those baby pink toe shoes. At home, she hung them on the post at the foot of her white canopy bed. She never put them on her feet. They were never used. Never danced in. They hung on her bed until she was twenty-six. Her mom called her at graduate school to claim anything she wanted from the bedroom of her youth before the house was sold. Sitting cross-legged on her old peach carpet she ogled those shoes, then put one on her foot, running her thumb over the silk. She delicately wrapped the ribbon around her ankle. She was tempted to stand in that toe shoe, just to see what it felt like. But she wasn't a dancer anymore. She was about to be a PhD in some subject or other, she couldn't quite remember at the moment. Educated. Dumbfounded.

The next day she placed an ad in the local classifieds. For Sale: Baby Pink Toe Shoes, never been used. The pink part seemed important.

Sexual Liberation for Married Ladies
by April Aasheim

An angry orange box bleeped across my computer screen.

WARNING: *We have detected spyware! Your boss, family, and even God will see all of the terrible things you have been looking at. Install our **Spy-Be-Gone** software and we can keep this to ourselves. Operators are standing by.*

Alarmed, I quickly scanned my browsing history. There were no porn sites, sex manuals, or Craigslist's Casual Encounters ads, but just to be safe I installed **Spy-Be-Gone**. After a quick scan it shrugged apologetically, then offered me my money back.

When my husband returned home he found me huddled in a Snuggie, watching Lifetime Television. "Uh-Oh. What's happened now?"

"The computer thinks I'm boring."

"A computer can't think, and even if it could, why would it think you're boring?"

"It said it was going to reveal my most disturbing secrets to the world, but all it came up with was my obsession about Toddlers and Tiaras."

"Well, that is disturbing," he said.

I nestled my head into the sleeves of my Snuggie. My own mother had once called me a prude, and now my software was confirming it.

"I blame our generation." I sniffled. "Just listen to the music. The Boomers had a song called Love the One You're With, and the Millennials sing about kissing girls and liking it. All we Gen Xers had was a song about learning to relax if we wanted to enjoy ourselves. It made us not only repressed, but neurotic!"

My husband sat down and patted my knee. "I'll help you unleash your inner deviant."

"You will?"

"Gladly."

Our first stop was an adult toy store. I had driven past the neon-pink sign many times but had never been inside. I slunk in behind my husband, astonished to see that it wasn't even noon but the place was swelling with customers.

"What do you think?" My husband gestured toward a case with an assortment of what appeared to be large, animal-inspired Pez dispensers. One of the rabbits flicked its ears at me.

I took a step back. "I think I'm going to check out the rest of the store."

I left as my husband asked the clerk to see something called The Grape Ape and headed for a room labeled Arcade. I might be sexually repressed, but I could play the hell out of Miss Pac Man. Two minutes later I left the room, knowing I would never look at Donkey Kong the same way again. I grabbed my husband's arm and rushed him to the door. "Let's go," I whispered. "I don't think this place is the answer."

"Let's try a bar," he suggested. "I'll take you to one of my old stomping grounds."

If there was a place to find sexual liberation, it had to be at one of the bars my husband frequented when he was single. I could probably find other things there too; things that required an insurance card to cure.

The bar was so dark I could hardly make out the shapes of others. "You used to meet girls here? How could you tell what they looked like?"

He took a swill of his beer. "It didn't matter. That's the beauty of liberation."

"But what if she had warts, or a hairy back? You wouldn't know."

"Nope."

"God, I hate men."

"Now that's an idea," he said, his eyes gleaming in the dark. "You want to broaden your sexual horizons? Maybe you should try a woman."

"Maybe I will, just to serve you right."

"Okay, then."

"Maybe I'll like it so much I won't come back to you."

My husband pointed to a shapeless figure at the far end of the bar. "That woman has been eyeing you since you walked in."

I took a shot of whiskey. "Fine. I'm going over."

"You do that."

As I marched towards the shape, I realized I had never hit on a man before, let alone a woman. I lifted my chin. This was progress, of sorts.

"Excuse me," I said as she turned her stool to face me. "I've never kissed a woman and I wondered if I could kiss you? Just to see what it's like."

She nodded and stood up, dwarfing me by six inches. I felt my husband watching as I craned my neck upwards to meet her lips. The moment her mouth touched mine, I freaked out.

"Sorry," I said, knocking over a stool as I ran away. "It's not you, it's me."

She slumped back onto her stool and mumbled something about *experimentalists*.

"There's no hope for me," I said, returning to my husband. "I *am* repressed."

"No, my dear, you are straight and this is a lesbian bar. But I thought I'd try."

...

When we arrived home I settled into a deep funk. Why was everyone else so confident in their sexuality, while I blushed when someone caught me buying underwear in Target? I was a prude, just like my mother said.

My husband brought me my Snuggie and a bowl of ice cream. "I don't think you're repressed at all."

"You don't?" I took a spoonful, remembering the fake handcuffs he had once brought home. I was so alarmed I hid them in the sock drawer. When he asked about them later I said they had been burgled.

"You're just you," he said. "And that's marvelous and amazing and sexy."

"And boring?"

"You, my dear, are never boring." He pulled me from the couch, wiping ice cream from my chin. "Let me prove to you how unboring you are."

"Okay," I said, following him into the bedroom. "But can we turn off the lights? The ice cream is settling on my thighs."

"Of course."

I gave my husband a sly smile. "I think the burglar may have returned those handcuffs."

"That's great. Maybe he'll return my Babes in Bikinis video next."

"Doubtful," I said shutting the door behind us. "But you never know."

Weeds
by Ian Christy

There's whispers in the weeds.

Turtling after a mother's desperate shove triggers an avalanche of clothing, camouflage in a closet covering up a child with cauliflower hair. Finger pressed to whitened lips as her Mama backs out of the bedroom.

Drowning in the smell of stale laundry, peeking through gaps between fingers, sound muffled by cotton and polyester.

Straining to comprehend with every sense, to understand.

Cringing at the roar of a monster's opera sung over a symphony of shattering glass and bursting furniture. Wincing for Mama's voice, shrill and hoarse, details lost in the whirlwind. Thunderous cracks when there hadn't been rain in weeks. She scuttles backwards away from the sound and the pain it represents, clutching her injured arm to her chest. More garments pour down upon her head.

Eventually couldn't hear much of anything at all, just the hot evening breeze sifting through the dry weeds outside, brushing against the skin of the doublewide.

Papa used to keep the field groomed. Take pride in who you are no matter what your station or circumstances, he'd say.

Until one day. Something changed that none talked louder than a mumble about.

Papa stopped mowing the field. Stopped trimming back the weeds from around the trailer's flat tires, checkerboard apron, and cement block porch. The weeds began to grow, became ragged and restless, full of hostile opinions scratched from raspy throats.

Papa stopped talking much. He stopped celebrating refrigerator drawings and telling bedtime stories and leading expeditions to the creek for crawdads.

Left room for the voice of the weeds.

After a couple of weeks, Papa just disappeared. His husk still stood around. Shadow he cast more alive than what came from inside. After a little while, Papa disappeared altogether. An empty sack shoved into the back of a county sheriff's car.

The weeds grew tall and strong, a ragtop mane that set the mobile home adrift atop gilded waves, insects flitting and forming orchestras.

She strained to hear anything more than the scratch of weeds and crawled close to threshold of the closet door. Swelling her chest with all her courage, she pulled the protective barrier away and crawled to clutch the bedroom doorframe. She listened with all her might and could only hear herself, feel her breath hot on her forearm where she pillowed her head against the doorframe, her other arm clutched to her chest, hand tucked up into her armpit.

Out of the bedroom, she scuttled across the disemboweled living room into the tiny kitchenette, to her cupboard. A cubby accessible without a stepstool. Afternoon snacks and self-serve breakfasts. Cereal with marshmallows, the kind in the bag pretending to be that kind in the box. Plastic bags, yellow labels, white boxes, black stars.

Thoughts raced through her head. Need to pack up and go. The monster could come back. Need to run away. Need to brave the weeds.

She began to select supplies and tried not consider where her Mama might be.

Mama would bring home snacks from her work. Tiny white donuts. Packet of 8 plus a little shape and the powdery ghost of the one that went missing. Pack the donuts. Pack the raisins too. Slow to do with only one hand holding things right, other still folded up close.

Scour the living room for keepsakes and prized possessions.

Bag of pirate coins to purchase train tickets or a pony. A bracelet made at the country fair. A book she liked to hear her Mama read aloud.

Stuff everything into a burlap bag. Struggling to stuff precious things in with only one arm, trying not to jostle that broken wing.

Rest for a moment. Feeling sleepy, cold, and alone. Swooning as a baby bird might when the nest has been flung away. Hearing waves.

Slapped awake by angry sounds and seeing a terrifying parade of shadows dancing across the walls. Red and blue lights causing her to blink and scurry back into the cupboard, hermit crab finding refuge.

The sunshine has gone out and left seething oil behind.

Yelling outside. Something crashing through the weeds. Pops and explosions, something slams heavily against the side of the doublewide. Everything rattles. Her tiny teeth feel loose against her tongue.

A howl that causes an ache deep inside her is cut off by a final gunshot.

Even the weeds go still.

Creak of someone stepping into the trailer, footsteps shuffling across the floor. Shuffle and crunch, getting closer. Dazzling light etching the edges of the cupboard door.

The door opens and stabbing light blinds her. A gentle voice speaks and she feels shame for the tears spilling down her cheeks, juts her chin.

The voice tells her help has come.

She lets the sheriff attached to the voice lead her out of her cupboard. She clutches her grandpa's bag with her one able hand. She refuses the woman's attempts to pick her up as she shuffles to the door and stands on the stoop feeling the cooling evening air.

A loud rustling sound catches her attention, she turns and sees a tarp settling over something the size and shape of her papa on the ground outside her home. She feels a touch on her shoulder and jerks away, her vision beginning to swim.

"Someone go get the mother," the sheriff says, sounding far away, scooping the child up mid-swoon. "We have the child. And get me some blankets over here, this kid's freezing. Where are the paramedics? Her arm looks a mess."

A whisper of wind passes through the weeds. She feels soothed by the sound.

A fresh, cool breeze sweeps up an ovation as a mother's arms fold around her child, pull her away from the sheriff's chest. "I'm here, baby. I'm here. We're safe now."

Gentle rain begins to fall, the first in months.

The weeds bow beneath the falling drops.

I Know Doe
by Cody May

When you look at him and he doesn't know it, when he's staring at the air, he's got the look of a sociopath. I forget about it for a while and then – whoops! – by accident, I face him when he's not facing me, and I catch that vacancy, that apathy in his popping blue eyes. And then next time I see Doe and he laughs and smiles and says, "Hey, man, how's it going? It's nice to see you," I feel a bit of distrust.

Is it nice to see me? Do you really care how I'm doing?

I don't think he's a sociopath. Not really. But I do feel his distance from me – from everyone, I guess.

It's like he's a well-drawn apparition. He's got the thick, meaty appearance of a human being, but then you talk to him, you spend some time with him, you poke a hole, just a tiny little hole in his skin and all you hear is hisssssss. There's nothing in there. Air, that's all. That's how it feels.

Everyone else: We're all twisted and mysterious and proud of the fact that we're worth more than six words. You think you know me? No. You think I know you? No. But I know Doe. I know him like a drumbeat; I tap my foot to everything he says, no matter what he says. He never surprises me.

I gotta watch out for everyone else, but he's a puddle that'd barely get my shoe wet if I stepped in it. What kind of person is that shallow?

He's a nice guy, a relaxed guy. He doesn't make me tense with a façade, because I don't think he cares who I am and especially not who I pretend to be. He enjoys good music and "isn't a big fan" of his parents. Other than that, he doesn't seem to ever have an opinion. And even though there's nothing really to him, even though I have a hard time telling you how simple he is because of how simple he really is, you know what? He's refreshing — just a little sip — which is nice, considering the salty, depthless, literally shitty sea of people around me.

You ever heard of Occam's razor? You know, "the simplest answer is often the correct one"? Well, he's the simplest answer to a best friend I've found, and he just might be a sociopath. It's as simple as that.

Sweat Man (The Worst Superhero Ever)
by Dan Marshall

"So you're telling me you woke up yesterday with a new superhuman ability, and your power is that you...get sweaty?" my friend Keith asked, eyebrow raised.

"Yeah, but there's more to it than that," I said, taking a swig from my beer and placing it back on the bar. "I can do it regardless of my physical state: lounging in bed, riding in the elevator, standing in line at the grocer. I can do it during the most mundane tasks you can imagine, even ones requiring no physical effort. I can sit in a walk-in freezer and sweat like I was in a triathlon. I know because I went into my sister's restaurant last night and did it until she yelled at me for sweating all over the food, then kicked me out."

"That is so dumb," Keith replied, shaking his head and rolling his eyes. "What's the point?"

"The point? Watch this," I said, closing my eyes and feeling the perspiration spring from my forehead almost immediately. This gets easier each time, I thought. I swiped my hand across the expanse of skin below my hairline, gathering a handful of my salty excretion, and slapped Keith in the face.

"OW!" Keith exclaimed. He wiped his face with the sleeve of his button-up shirt. "Dude, what the hell?"

I smirked. "That's right. Don't dis the Sweat Nap."

I was surprised by how loudly Keith laughed. After he caught his breath he said, "Sweat Nap? Is that your superhero name? Wow, man."

"Yeah, it's a play on wet nap, but with swea–"

"No, I get it," he interrupted. "I definitely get it. Still stupid."

"Hey, it's a work in progress. Think you can come up with something better?" I demanded.

Keith looked up at the ceiling and rubbed his chin with his hand. "Hmm," he said. "Sweat is salty, right? You know, sodium chloride? How about 'The Psycho Sochlo' . . . maybe 'Lean Mean Saline'? Oh, I know, 'The Saline Solution'!"

"Jesus, Keith," I said, pounding the top of the bar with my fist. "I want to sound like a badass, not have people call me when they need their contacts cleaned. Come on."

Keith opened his mouth to reply, but before he could there was a slam behind us from the direction of the bar's front door. We turned to see the door resting open against the wall. In the entryway stood two men dressed entirely in black, wearing balaclavas and long jackets with an uppercase "A" surrounded by a circle on the breast. One was tall and skinny, the other short and fat. "Shit," Keith whispered. "Anarchists."

"We're the black blocheads," the taller of the two said. He swung his arm out from under his coat, showing the sawed off shotgun he held in his hand. "And we're here to free you from the bonds of capitalist oppression." The shorter man standing next to him grinned and brandished a knife, flicking it open and stabbing the air menacingly.

"Uh," I said, unsure of how to respond. "We're both unemployed, so we've pretty much already been freed from our fat cat overlords."

Keith snorted. "Yeah, what he said. Plus, we spent most of our money at the bar." He motioned across the wood platform separating us from the rows of bottles. We all looked, but the bartender who'd been standing there only moments ago was nowhere to be seen.

The taller man stomped over to Keith and smacked the barrel of the shotgun against the side of my friend's head. "Shut the fuck up and give us your wallets!" he yelled, lowering the gun's barrel to point directly at my best friend's chest. Keith rubbed his head and looked over at me pleadingly. I could see blood smeared on his fingers when he pulled his hand away.

It was then I knew I had to try saving us by using my new power. I closed my eyes and began to summon my sweat. I could feel it gathering on my forehead, on my upper lip, even under my eyes. It began to run down my face, but I knew I'd have to do something more drastic if Keith and I were to make it through this night alive. Focusing all my concentration on the liquid that was sliding toward my chin, I began to imagine it as a stream – no, a mighty river! – springing from my forehead.

I opened my eyes and my head forcefully jerked back as a blast of sweat the size of my forearm burst from the top of my head. It struck the two anarchists like a hose, instantly drenching them. Thinking quickly, I aimed the stream at the eyes of the smaller man, then those of his large companion. They started gasping and rubbing at their faces.

"It burns!" the fat man squealed. He dropped his knife with a clatter and began hopping around, rubbing his eyes with both hands.

The taller anarchist grunted and shook his head wildly. "I got some in my mouth," he whined, spitting. I stepped over and smacked the shotgun from his hands, then reached down and grabbed it. The two men rubbed at their faces for another few seconds, and when they opened their eyes they were staring at the business end of the weapon, coughing and sputtering as tears streamed down their cheeks.

"You blocheads are all washed up," I said.

"You're so bad at this," Keith groaned from behind me. "But, you know, thanks for saving me."

I turned to him and replied, "Of course...don't sweat it."

The Centenarian
by Maya Silver

I knew the pink lipstick mark was appearing on my cheek again because the chick I was helping cocked her head sideways and looked at me funny.

"How'd you do that?' she asked. She thinks it's a trick, just like everyone else.

"If you want to know the truth," I said, hoping to impress her and earn a bigger tip on the Italian grinder I was making her, "it's a natural response to pretty girls like yourself, sort of like a blush, if you know what I mean."

Since maybe two, three weeks ago, pink lips started appearing randomly in various locations on my face. Typically, the cheeks. Occasionally, the neck. It all began around the same time some old lady died after eating Korean barbecue at the food court.

I'd been staying away from those delicious, saucy Korean meatballs ever since but I woke up yesterday with an I-can-conquer-those-meatballs mentality. So I went to town on half a dozen with steamed rice during my dinner break.

The rest of my shift? Hazy with a 40% chance of projectile vomit. Those meatballs got to me. I lunge-walked my way back to Steve's Sandwiches, tried to keep it together and avoid knives. Put on sunglasses so customers couldn't see my eyes. Finally, we closed. Just a little cleaning between me and some quality time with the toilet.

I stopped in the bathroom on my way out of the mall and, boom, slumped back against the wall, hit my head on the floor. Out. Woke up in the dark way later and saw my blood, thick like Sriracha, on the gray bathroom tiles. I propped myself up and took a look in the mirror. Nothing too crazy: an epic cut on my head, definitely a concussion, two lipstick marks, one above the other, on my right cheek. And, as I wiped the blood off – surprise, surprise – another pink lipstick mark materialized on my left cheek.

I stumbled out into the hallway, where it was dark as shit. Dark and quiet – no more soulless workers, zero tweens, 86 the gossiping moms beelining to Macy's.

Of course, the doors were locked – I checked every one. My best chance was the possibility that the security guards weren't sleeping on the job and would notice me on their cameras.

I started down the hallway in search of an armchair to curl up in and noticed a little pink circle hovering at about eye level in the distance. After a few steps, I could see better. It was a pair of pink lips. Pursed, a little dry, with a healthy application of lipstick.

I called "Hello" in a prepubescent voice and just northeast of the lips, an eye appeared. Then, another eye. Then, a bony little nose. And finally, a whole freaking lady, hovering about ten feet away, wearing a magenta velour jumpsuit and those shoes with built-in cushions to make walking extra challenging. Her old-school yellow Walkman blared "Hard Headed Woman" by Wanda Jackson and I straight-up stopped breathing.

Finally, grandma looked up at me. Her eyes had no pupils. They were like windows – you could see through them to the other side.

"It's about time," she said.

"About time what?" I mumbled.

"I was doing my exercises," she replied, "I take my powerwalks here."

"What are you?" I asked, because how could I not.

"I'm Edna and I have an escalating suspicion that you're the young man who served me the meatballs that ultimately led to my death. It was my steadfast goal to live to 100. My sister is 102 now. My friend George-Ann is 106. I was 99 when I ate those bad meatballs."

"Do I look Korean to you?" I asked.

The old lady started to shake like a washer on its final spin mode. She began busting out jumping jacks, which were extra bouncy due to her crazy plyometric shoes.

"Look, lady," I reasoned with her, "I'm sorry about the meatball incident and everything but it wasn't me. I work at Steve's Sandwiches. In fact, I got sick off those balls today, myself."

Edna's pink lips opened up and got wider and wider until her mouth was the size of a cantaloupe. She reached into her pocket and pulled out the largest, fiercest dentures I'd ever seen, snapped them into her mouth and hissed.

"I had one month left until my 100th birthday, son," she continued, violently convulsing toward me, backing me up against the locked gate of the Sharper Image store.

If you think you've been harassed by a close talker, you got nothing on me. Edna's lips were half an inch from my face and her breath smelled like the toxic, powerful stench of a wastewater treatment plant.

"100 years, son!" she wailed into my face.

Out of the corner of my eye, I noticed that the Sharper Image guys had left their model Roomba, the floor-navigating, circular vacuum cleaner, outside the store. I ducked down to grab it, flicked it on and pointed it at Edna, trying to rip Bill Murray's technique. And, boom, the suckage commenced.

It caught the sleeve of her jumpsuit, swallowed up her arm, flipped her horizontal. Her body waved back and forth like a flag as it surrendered to the insane suction power of the Roomba. Her lips were the last to go so you might say she went out with a kiss. I set the Roomba down, wondering if it needed to be quarantined or destroyed.

Needless to say, I was on the cranky side the next day at work after barely sleeping in the fetal position on a dirty carpet. I headed straight to work to layer shit on bread again and nurse a haunted, meatball-induced hangover.

"Anything else with your Rambunctious Rueben, ma'am?" I ask the lady across the counter.

She tilts her blonde head back with a sassy half smirk.

"What?" I ask, kind of scruffily.

"Nice lipstick."

Nightly Sin. Morning Penance.
by Maria Clark

Time was running out. The commotion downstairs beckoned her, but she wasn't ready. These feelings, these monstrous thoughts that visited her at night. The way her body reacted; no matter how hard she tried they kept coming. Each night she saw him standing there. And she went, despite crying out against it. She fought herself with every step taken. She tried to stop it. But she went, like she went every night. And every night they ended up naked on a large bed, his beautiful, powerful body at her side. She tried to keep away. She knew she shouldn't want him – it was wrong. This was all sick and vile, but she went to him when he reached for her with his long muscular arms.

His crushing weight on her, their dark cravings came alive and through her pleasure she wept. The tears came to her eyes and when she opened her mouth to shriek, only a moan escaped. She tried again and again but the moans only got louder and more passionate. When she reached to fight him off she only clawed at his back in sexual ecstasy; this was wrong. This was evil but she couldn't stop the pleasure it was bringing her; her desperation was overridden by their sick, shared passion.

At the peak of their odious desires she awoke, like she did every morning, with a convulsive shudder, feeling satisfied and flushed. Her chest heaved and her eyes were not wet with tears, but her face was pink with satisfaction. She changed, the dirty panty falling in the hamper. She needed to do laundry again.

Exhausted and defeated, she lay on her bed in her underwear, looking up at the blank ceiling as if it held the answer to her nightmare. "Why? Please. Can someone help? Why can no one help me? I can't do it alone. I can't stop loving him. I can't stop longing for him. L – lusting – that *disgusting* word. I'm so sorry. I can't stop this." She curled on her bed, folding in shame and self-loathing. How could she have allowed herself to entertain such abominable hungers? "I'm sorry," she whispered miserably into her comforter and she sobbed. The tears softly came and she sniffled in silence, trying to be as invisible as possible to the people downstairs.

The miserable cur wanted to pull out her hair – single hair by single hair – maybe that would help her. Maybe she could bleed this stain out of her soul. Maybe she could wash this sin from her wretched body. She was foul, gross, revolting – her soul putrid and crippled. Her womanhood yearned for the filth that lurked into her mind every night. She groaned in frustration at the lust she could not stop; lust for someone never destined to be hers. But God had decided to trifle with her and He laughed at her misery. She knew He did.

There were steps coming up the stairs and a vice grip strangled her heart in panic. He was coming. She knew those footsteps. She knew the weight of his walk and the rhythm of his gait. She knew him anywhere. His fist pounded on her door, and she gasped as if he'd landed the blow directly on her pounding, asphyxiated chest. "Rebecca? You ready?"

"What? It's still early!" She feigned sleep and willed the dirty feelings and misery away.

"You know how Mom gets about church."

"I know, I know." Rebecca breathed deeply to finish collecting herself and walked to the restroom. Her face did not betray she had been crying, but just as a precaution she put on light make up.

"Rebecca. Rebecca. Rebecca. Rebecca."

"I heard you the first time Marshall!"

"Oh. So that's how it's going to be, huh? Well I'm not stopping until you're out."

He resumed his chant and Rebecca couldn't help but smile at his deep baritone voice. "Alright! Alright!"

She threw on a sun dress and slipped on her wedges; very appropriate and very lovely. As Rebecca looked in the mirror, she took a deep breath because despite herself, somewhere deep in her soul, she was hoping he thought she looked a little more than lovely too.

"Rebecca. Rebecca. Rebecca."

She threw open the door, a wide smile on her face.

"Okay, okay! I'm ready, Dad!"

126

(Not) For Sale
by Barry Koplen

Just before I began my morning walk, I glanced at a letter from Dad. He'd written it to me while he was stationed at Lake Charles Army Air Field in Lake Charles, Louisiana when I was a little less than a month old.

Prior to receiving it, I had known the joy my Dad experienced whenever he was with my two daughters. With them, he was inventive and creative, loving and giving. As far as they were concerned, sadness was remote.

But I knew better. He never mentioned a loss so profound to him that he guarded his feelings about it with decades of silence. It concerned my sister, Nancy. When I was five, she died of a congenital illness. She never walked. Before she was one, she passed away.

Much of her life had been spent in Baltimore hospitals. Although my parents had prayed for a cure, they had known, since shortly after she was born, that only a miracle could save her. That miracle never came.

I knew that story more than fifty years before I was given Dad's letter. Mom had kept it with mementos from my childhood, items she had saved and put away when Nancy was born. By the time she gave it to me, Dad had died. Framed now, it hangs on the wall beside my door.

Daily, I glance at these paragraphs on my way out:

Tonight I am a very lonely man. I am away from you and your darling mother. I hope that soon I will be with you again forever.

As I sit here, I envisage wonderful things for you. I see in you the beginnings of a man who your mother and I will be proud of. I see in you a man capable of the wonderful kindness, courage, ability and love inherited from your wonderful mother. I see in you the love for your mother that will equal or surpass the love of any other man for his mother. I say this as she is the finest in the world and I want to say this for you to remember always.

Because it had been stored away for so long when it was given to me, I regarded it then as I still do, as a monumental gift. If it had been given to me too soon, I might have undervalued it. In retrospect, I can see how his words reverberated in the love that he shared throughout his life.

His statement "I want to say this for you to remember always" has had the ring of a clarifying mantra, a most significant lesson in the sense that I have come to realize that fathers are supposed to instill beliefs "to remember always."

Knowing that has stirred considerations that, on occasion, have shaken me. At times, I have pondered the enormity of that responsibility.

That's why I'll never forget being with my daughter and soon-to-be son-in-law at their wedding in Jerusalem. Just before they marched to the chupa where they would be joined in marriage, it hit me.

For the last time, I would hug my daughter, my child, and entrust her life to a man I knew she adored. I burst into tears. Questions that hadn't tormented me until that very moment shaped themselves into words.

"Have I taught you enough?" I wanted to ask. "What have I overlooked?" I asked myself. "What if I've missed something important?" I shuddered and I wept.

Had I suitably prepared my wonderful daughter for this, her life's most important venture? Wasn't there so much more for me to do?

I didn't know. My tears fell onto her stunning wedding gown as I held her. I'm not sure she understood why.

Her attendants led her away; she was radiant. She probably thought I was just being the Dad she had come to know as the sometimes teary-eyed guy who wasn't very good at reining in his emotions.

Maybe she was right. Maybe I had taught her those few basic elements about life and love and their roles in attaining a harmonious and joyful relationship. Perhaps those loving relatives and friends who had been so important to her had imparted much more than me. Somehow, I consoled myself, somehow she may have gathered from them all that I had missed.

128

Accepting that took a few minutes as well as many deep breaths. By the time vows were being made, I felt more like a proud father ready to cheer for the newlyweds I loved absolutely.

Unobserved, I looked up, as if to speak to Dad, as if to tell him I had remembered the mantra he had instilled in me. Hoping he could hear me, I felt my tears return.

Those tears weren't unlike the ones I'd cried when I attempted to read that same letter he'd written to me at his funeral. On either side of me were my daughters.

At the wedding, they were there too, close by.

That was not the time to ask which one might want the letter my Dad had written when I could no longer read it. Trying not to think about that during the wedding, I consoled myself with the thought that one of them might want instead the shoes I'd also treasured, the ones Nancy had never been able to wear.

Suddenly, those thoughts were swept away. A crowd of men had come to get me. It was time for the father to dance with the bride.

Consummation
by Danika Dinsmore

Fire is contagious. She knows this from the way her hands burn when he approaches. Fire is what happens when we collect oxygen, fuel, and heat. Anyone can oxidize over time. Anyone can burn slowly. She bears the heat because it is slow. She can, on a daily basis, write down one word of him, and it is enough. She can write down wrist or chin or thigh or shoulder. Feeding the flame. But sooner or later, she will combust. She is combustible.

She begins to collect small things, slips them into her pockets. Flame-resistant things. Paper clips he has put in his mouth while on the phone. A dry pen tossed into the trash. A spoon used in the office kitchen before he fed it to the dishwasher. Days later, she can still feel his heat in the objects, fading campfire embers. She warms her hands over her little dish of trinkets on the altar she constructed for them. Spends an evening melting them into each other until she can't distinguish their separate parts. Her heat and his heat, coalesced, liquid metal hearts.

Reading in bed, she pulls herself from a daydream on the page. She must be careful how long she stares at one place in her book. If she gets lost in thoughts of him, the page in front of her inevitably catches fire.

She grows tired of not knowing endings.

She reaches thermal apogee on a Thursday just after lunch, blue sky crisp with promise. As the door to her elevator car is about to close, he slips inside. Presses her backward, smelling of sushi and soap and radiating from the bright day. He is full. Fuel. Her sharp intake of breath startles them both, and he drops his take-out bag as it ignites. He blinks into her face. Eyelashes, she thinks. Consumed.

130

Harried Hal
by Wes Choc

Hal struggled to be right, unhappy when not.

Born Virgo, Hal was oft reminded of strengths and weaknesses of his nascent earth sign after tasting mud pies or walking barefoot, by flaming Sagittarianistic retorts from a fire-sign mother. Her opinions had singeing impacts amid motherly hugs. Dad's Piscean pacificisms caved in regularly with "yes, dear" as if she knew what she was doing. She did. Family expectations persisted: piano, chess, grades, enough church to assure the right crowds. Hal's role model dad taught him chess...his mom, everything else.

"You'll be first in the family graduating from college," mom reminded Hal after dinner twice a week, whereupon he dutifully itemized school tasks, commentaries, and grades. Smiling through horn-rimmed glasses, "yes, mom" responses reflected his adaptation to an almost-adult role.

. . .

On campus, Martha, Hal's special cafeteria mate and love focus, always had presents: chewing gum, ballpoint pens, bananas she said were too much for her to eat. She insisted he call her Marty. In return, he said "sure" to all suggestions. Marty never asked for much; she knew what he could deliver and liked it when his potentials were exceeded. They chatted mornings and evenings over coffee and donuts. After messy chocolate, Hal always washed his hands. Marty always declared washing was a worthy habit.

Hal's weakest grades got Marty's attention; improvements received smiles. Hal earned solid Bs and a few As thanks to her. Pleasing her pleased him. In a semester, they'd both get diplomas. Marty considered graduate school. Hal figured a tech company would let him develop, create.

Geek-head Hal was preoccupied by Marty's impending birthday, disconcerting for him guessing what to buy. What did she really want? Ready and willing, he must get this right. She received gifts from home plus silly

131

over-the-hill cards from girlfriends. But they were going to dinner right after that 4 o'clock midterm. He disguised exam shudder; she displayed mental prowess.

Deliberating whether they were ripe for yet deeper feelings, he considered a ring, but changed his mind, unsure whether oh-so-beautiful Marty might become disappointed about pledges she couldn't have predicted. Seeking to feel right but feeling doomed for not trying hard enough, instead he bought one red rose like that book said to do. In a long red-bowed box her 21st birthday card scripted the message:

Twenty-One! Only once, only you, someone with such class,

Only one special touch for this one-of-a-kind lass.

They ate a nice dinner with legal glasses of wine to toast the future. They held hands. They kissed good night at her dorm door after she looked up and down the corridor. Graciously accepting the flower, her eyes were moist. Conversations were always more comfortable than intimate; Hal thought that's what she wanted. She smiled, "You shoulda studied more for that exam, Hal. An A is achievable." After warm embraces, she kissed him gently, her hand caressing his cowlick.

. . .

Hal read books about proactive male behaviors.—.opening doors, eye gazing, then other books about courtesy, respect. So many shoulds…so much information.

One day with endearing smiles, oh so judiciously, Marty asked if she might be his best friend, pressing his hand over her heart.

"Sure, Marty" Hal smiled back. But things changed. Twice-daily visits evolved into one or two times a week until Marty had too many events with girlfriends. Watching laughter at a distance at least made him feel she was happy even if it wasn't with him.

. . .

Hal and his friend Lennie met for a beer. Hal didn't like beer, but at 21 he did like being seen as adult. Lennie talked about how his girlfriend, Suzie, wasn't very smart though she was cute. She made him feel good all over; that's what counted. Amid mutual commiseration about school and women, Lennie finally frowned and asked, "Would you rather be judged by risks you took, or for never making any mistakes at all?"

132

"I'm trying. I still like her."

"So what? Besides the ante, what've you got in this poker game?"

"I just wanted to be right." Studying his fingerprints, Hal rubbed them to see if they might disappear.

. . .

Hal took a long walk. No dinner with Marty tonight! Hal used to walk long distances regularly. It cleared his mind, cleansed his spirit; but, Marty changed all that. Now he was aboard the Titanic. He walked into a bar for a beer; happy hour over, the place was almost empty. After carding him, a wrinkle-faced bartender asked, "How's school?" recognizing him as a student.

Hal was glum. "Gotta another B+ day."

"B+? That's pretty good!"

"Coulda been an A."

"Think of those getting Cs. Is perfection the goal?

"Nah. Just the best..."

"You sound down."

Staring into his glass, "Girlfriend's looking for better material."

"Ah...different story...a little B-plus-iosis?"

Looking with pursed lips, "Yup, got that disease eatin' my insides out."

"Y'know, sometimes it's all how you see things. If you want it to be right, there's always someone righter. Being right isn't always the right thing to be."

"'Course you're right." Hal muffled a chuckle.

Nodding, "Most people would rather be right than happy, don't you think?"

Moving his glass in circles, "You're right; does that make you happy?"

"I'm seldom right! I'm just pretty at good creating an atmosphere where folks can think, relax, and be happy. Being happy is merely a byproduct of accepting things we cannot change, changing things we can. Being right creates another list of things we can never change."

133

Hal thanked him and dropped a five, giving him a gracious nod. Walking home was different. A survivor, the Titanic wasn't sinking.

. . .

"Hey Marty, let's grab dinner. Yeah, it's late; I know you're busy, but I wanna talk about exams. What? I don't care. I need your opinion. Yeah, now!" Hal rambled about choices, discoveries, even enjoying the process with someone like Marty. He had her attention for maybe the first time, and she listened.

Heart stirred, Hal was finally discovering what Marty wanted. He was delivering. Tomorrow he'd go ring shopping.

Dead Sexy
by Jason Brick

for Larry Oldham

"Dead hookers," Luie crooned to the tune of a song I remembered from my very brief actual childhood.

"Dude, shut up."

"Dead hookers," Luie continued as if I hadn't even spoken.

"Dude. Shut. Up."

"Dead hookers aren't much fun."

"I'm begging you here."

"They don't come when you call, they don't turn tricks at all. Dead hookers aren't much fun."

"What the fuck is wrong with you?"

"Nothing, man. What's wrong with you is you don't know how to respect a man's process."

"The fuck you mean by that?"

He gestured in front of us, at the four prostitutes in nineteen or twenty pieces, jumbled all together on the concrete floor of the city's third-shittiest self-storage operation.

"You see some fucked up shit like this, and you get all mad and quiet, start thinking on how you're gonna put accounts straight when we find out who did it."

"Are you saying we're not going to do that?"

"Oh, we're gonna do that all right. We're gonna bring down some biblical shit on the heads of everybody who even thought about being a part of this. This shit would be heinous even if it happened to girls we didn't know. But where you get all mad and quiet, I get hilarious. It's just part of my psychological process."

"Well, it's a fucked up process."

"Racist."

We stood there a while, saying a quiet goodbye. They'd been nice girls, or so we heard. Two weren't exactly friends but they'd been nicer than they had to be when we'd done business: Sindee, who I'd first seen barefoot and pregnant scrubbing out pans at the Silver Lemon, and Kismet, who I swear had a crush on Luie even though she claimed to prefer girls. Outside, Bobbey was waiting with a van and an address.

Luie nodded slowly, and said "Ready to do the thing?"

"Yeah," I said. We turned our backs on what was left of our friends and ducked out through the half-closed rolling door.

Whistler's Dilemma
by Lawrence W. Paz

Mark Whistler sat in his cubicle, as he had every day for the past eight years, sipping a latte and wondering what this day would bring. He was troubled by yesterday's assignment. Mark was a very thoughtful person with high ethical standards. His wife of over 15 years, Julie, had suggested he might be a bit too ethical at times.

"Mark, if you want to get ahead in this world, you need to go with the flow," she'd say. "Just because you believe something is unethical doesn't make it so."

Mark considered this many times, but he always came to the conclusion that "What is right is right and what is wrong is wrong."

He attacked each assignment with enthusiasm and the intention of contributing to the welfare of others as well as his own. This current task was different. He was having difficulty getting his head around this one. Something was not quite right. In assigning Mark this particular job, Amanda, the general manager, had skipped over two levels of management.

"Mark, this assignment is highly confidential," she had said with quiet determination. "I know I can trust you to approach this task with discretion."

Amanda was a bottom-line manager. Paying attention to the almighty dollar had gotten her promoted to top management in record time. Amanda trusted Mark to research the various business options without leaking it to others in the organization. Amanda also knew if she didn't make the decision Mark recommended, there was the risk she might lose a valuable employee.

Mark pondered Amanda's motive for giving him this assignment directly. Was he the best person for this task? Mark was more people-focused than monetarily motivated. He considered product safety a paramount objective. Customers trusted his company to create products that would not cause harm.

Mark deliberated on how to gather the necessary information to make a principled recommendation. He knew that at least 23 cases of misfortune had been reported. Were some misfortunes, or even deaths, not reported? So where should he begin? What outcome did he want to achieve? How could this negative situation result in a positive solution? Whom did he need to speak with, and how could he maintain confidentiality? Did he need a cover story? If so, what might it be?

He wanted a win/win outcome for company and customers alike. It was difficult for him to treat this issue in a positive way. However, he was determined to give it a try. He made a list of eight people within and outside the organization he felt could be trusted to contribute significant information on the issue. The cover story had to be consistent with his position as a researcher analyst. He would "invent" a representative product for his investigation.

Mark's first interview was with his direct boss. Mark posed the hypothetical new product.

"George, what steps are taken to warrant that company products are fully tested before being offered to the public?" George assured Mark the company extensively tested a product internally before bringing it to market. No independent tests were made. George felt left out and asked why Amanda had given Mark this assignment directly rather than through him. Mark hesitantly suggested he direct his inquiry to Amanda.

Jeff, director of customer relations, was his next interview. Jeff assured Mark that his staff was well-versed in the features and uses of each product and that they did their very best not to disseminate any data that might put the company in legal jeopardy.

John, director of media, didn't have much time for Mark. John said he worked closely with a legal consulting firm to make certain any advertising in print and electronic media include disclaimers, even if only in small print.

Mark concluded that insufficient testing had been done to ensure that a safe product would be released to the public. "Rush to market" seemed to be the underlying goal of the company, rather than fully disclosing information to the public.

It was time to go outside the company for advice on how to proceed with this deceptive information. Clarence had been Mark's family lawyer for years. He was a bit conservative, and not averse to taking a calculated risk.

His advice: "Whatever you decide, I can help protect you legally."

Cynthia was a new financial advisor to the Whistlers. "You have the financial resources to stay afloat for six to eight months," she told Mark. "Whatever your decision, protect yourself financially. I'm here to help."

Charles was an excellent spiritual advisor. He listened intently as Mark explained his dilemma. Mark was convinced that products were not fully tested and that any difficulties were being covered up with legal mumbo jumbo and customer disservice. Charles shared his concern for the product users.

Mark deliberated over his findings and brought them to Amanda. He suggested a reevaluation of the testing methodology, a major product recall, and full disclosure to the public. Amanda listened to Mark's arguments but only committed to reevaluate the company's testing process. Mark concluded that Amanda's profit obsession was overriding the public's common good.

Although this assignment was confidential, he did not keep secrets from Julie. She always had a thoughtful and unbiased viewpoint. That evening, after the girls were asleep, Julie and Mark sat at the kitchen table where they often discussed significant issues. Mark briefly gave Julie the background of the task at hand and shared the results of his research, as well as his suspicions.

Mark had always tried to live his life with integrity and empathy. When faced with a similar dilemma in a previous job, he had left the company rather than confront the issue directly. This time Mark needed the income to support his growing family of two preteen daughters and a son due in three months.

What was the honorable next step? With his hand poised over the cell phone, and his eyes on the Whistle Blower Hot Line number, he contemplated his next move.

Rescue 911: The UFO!
by Peter Boadry

At a farm in Southwick, there was a mystery brewing, for something was dumping trash by the barn and chicken coop outside, but what?

"It's the weekend, we should set up a watch by the barrels and catch this thing!" Peter said.

"Like what kind of shifts?" Charlie asked.

"Like maybe 4-hour shifts to catch this thing, we're all tired of picking up this trash, right?" Peter asked.

"I can park the station wagon by the barn and you can watch from there," Charlotte stated.

"So there will be one inside, one outside every shift hooked up by walkie-talkies!" Peter stated.

"Okay, that's what we will do!" Charlie replied.

They finished picking up all the trash and headed in for supper.

At the dinner table their father stated "It could be a bear or even a raccoon!"

Any number of things can be dumping the trash!

So the boys made up a schedule; 8 pm to 12 am would be Ronnie, with Theresa inside the house. Then 12 am to 4 am would be Peter with Denise inside the house. And last would be Charlie with his mom Charlotte inside the house, 4 am to 8 am.

They even set up a cage trap cage near the barrels in case it was a small enough creature to catch.

So first was Ronnie armed with flashlight, walkie-talkie, and some comic books to read out in the station wagon.

It was a peaceful night. Then about 2 or 3 hours in, this God-awful racket and commotion started.

Strange noises, howling and such.

Theresa ran into the rooms and woke everyone up, saying something is outside making a racket and "I can't get Ronnie on the walkie-talkie!"

We all looked outside and tried to get Ronnie on the walkie-talkie, there was no answer!

"Did he get eaten?" Theresa asked.

We saw a shadow of something down by the car with its head in a cage. At one point it stood on its hind legs but since this was a dark area we couldn't tell what it is.

Their father suggested his bear theory again.

We started clanging pots and pans from the porch because we couldn't check on Ronnie until this thing was gone!

When the thing got the cage off its head and left, we went to see where Ronnie was.

Ronnie was fast asleep in the back of the station wagon!

He wanted to know what it was we caught, it made enough noise to wake the dead, and we're surprised it didn't wake you up!

So now we knew it came during the first shift, so we could do away with 12 am to 8 am shifts.

We needed to revamp the schedule!

Double up on the guards and surveillance.

So the next day that's just what we did.

Ronnie and Peter were in the station wagon armed with flashlight, walkie-talkie, comics and snacks, ready for another interesting night!

Theresa was in the kitchen manning her station.

Ronnie fell asleep again, and Peter was starting to.

He tried to stay awake.

Peter was struggling to stay awake then it happened!

A flying saucer appeared, hovering outside Ronnie's window of the wagon.

It spun around and looked like it had church windows, it was above the wagon and off to the side.

"Theresa, there's a flying saucer outside get everyone up!"

"Ronnie, wake up! Do you see what I see?" Peter asked.

"Ah, yes I do!"

"I'm not waking everyone up, you guys are playing!" Theresa replied.

"We're not joking, there's a flying saucer out here!" Peter stated.

"I'm not falling for it, sorry!" Theresa said.

Just then, just like in the comic books, it zapped a ray and made a direct hit on the cage we had there.

The ground shook, the cage rattled and a skunk appeared.

"No one will believe us." Peter stated.

"Maybe they were collecting animals for testing and the skunk sprayed them!"

So they dropped it, and it just so happened it landed in the cage.

The next day at breakfast no one would believe the flying saucer story!

"Well for all you non-believers there's a skunk in the cage for someone else to get rid of then, we're not!" Peter stated.

They all kidded and joked all through breakfast.

We were kids, why would they believe us?

But when the morning paper arrived, we had the last laugh, for it seems two police officers had also sighted this UFO and reported it and gotten their pictures in the paper!

A dog was the real trash dumper; the owner from down the block wasn't feeding his dog.

He must have been scared to come out that day 'cause of being caught in the cage.

Based on a true story.

The Swell
by Laura Scott

I run to the Howth Road, unable to answer one more question, field one more comment about travertine or enamel or whether or not I'll ever want to open up that wall between the kitchen and living room because I'd better figure out where the grotesquely tall radiator is going to go. I run until I reach the edge of the bay, and I'm standing on the footpath, looking out across to Bull Island, and beyond that, to the Irish Sea. I stand there for several moments. A couple with a small dog passes me. The wind gathers under my hair and I can feel the surge of the tide coming in, the salt in the air. My breathing slows. I am transfixed by the cloud formation over the shallow layer of water that is now gaining on itself. These are low and large, grey-bottomed and impressionist-quality. I have never seen a scene like this up close that is impossibly simple but beautifully perfect all at the same time, something that so clearly belongs in a gallery. The sky speaks to the water, the water reflects the conversation back up – dove grey and quietly sparkling. I am calmer now.

I walk along the path, raised up above the bay on the one side and along the traffic on the other side. I decide to walk all the way up to the Marine Hotel. It's easily 30 minutes each way, but I'm in no hurry. The path gradually curves around, slightly to the right, and I am able to look over my shoulder toward the two stacks and south Dublin City. The bay's horseshoe shape clearly reveals itself and I feel somehow less anxious, less harried, as I watch these clouds and this bay gently close in and envelope me.

I arrive at the entrance to the parking lot and half expect to see Martin, my husband, there waiting for me in the car, but he is not. I walk up slowly, past the cypress trees, toward the butter-colored two-story hotel with its dark grey eaves and gold lettering. Inside, there are several men at one end of the bar, the end next to the flat screen, and they are always here at this time, we've noticed. They have three or four pints, discuss the most recent matches, settle outside for several smokes, and eventually move off in their own directions for the rest of the evening. I take our usual spot, now on my own, in the snug almost directly across from them, and well within earshot. I place my

144

order for a house white and an order of chips, because who am I kidding? The small bottle of wine will actually fill my glass almost twice and the chips are hot and good and dripping in malted vinegar, and I'm in no mood for messing around.

And so what if he did come and join me, slide into the seat next to me and order a pint? What would I say? Sorry. I'm a lunatic. It's not the travertine, or the enamel. It's the everything else. I can't make one more call, give one more answer. On anything. You know that shrink you told me not to see? He says I'm overwhelmed. He says a death in the family like that is just overwhelming. And then we moved here.

He keeps asking me where home is. "Where is home?" And with a different intonation, "Where is home?" I never have an answer. I don't know anymore. My father's briefcase is still sitting on a shelf in the garage behind a power tools. I think I should be able to find something in it, but I can't bring myself to look inside since the funeral. I found my letter to him the last time I peeked, with a feeble attempt to invite him up north to our place, that I hoped he'd feel better soon, that he should try to keep busy. It clearly hadn't worked. But it must have meant something then for him to carry my words around with his passport and his will. There was that at least. But I couldn't look in it again. I think my father may have had it all wrong. He was always first to leave the table, never had dessert or coffee, on to the next thing. He left his own life in much the same way.

I down the rest of the wine. I am overwhelmed. I think, that's why I can't look at the news, and why I fear something is going to go horribly wrong whenever I leave the house, and why I can't talk about the showerhead we chose. If Martin were here, he would give me that look that says, "It's the psychiatrist's bill that's overwhelming, Love."

I pay the bill and head back out onto the path. It's dark now. I'm still anxious, without any reason to be. I walk back, warm from the chips and rosy from the drink. The wind whips up and the lights across the bay in Sandymount twinkle as I walk. My heart slows. I think about my husband and our child together. I think about the ways in which we, he and I, will carry our family on: about acorn walks, laundry folding, zucchini planting, and table wiping. There are thousands of little things we do every day that I am so grateful for, that are not chores, but that are ways in which we show our appreciation for one another.

I have to settle for this moment. It's a swell or a surge. It will, almost certainly, pass by me. And him. And I – we – will let it past. And we will

145

finish this house. If I can make a decision, and if we can make a home. And we will have to be content in those moments, those impossibly simple but beautifully perfect moments, in between.

Captain Lewis Meets His Demon
by Mark R. O'Neill

The men of the Corps of Discovery knew the fauna of the forest, for most of them grew up on the Kentucky frontier. But the animals became bigger and stronger as the mountains of the west part of the Louisiana Purchase grew taller. The Corps of Discovery did not always know where to go or which direction to head, but they knew that generally they headed west, and that direction was easy to figure out because that was the way the sun headed. Their leader, Captain Meriwether Lewis, had taken point duty as he led them away from the river they had just named for the sitting president, Jefferson. They were leaving what was left of the Missouri river and making their way across land. Captain Lewis walked ahead, carrying his musket loaded with black powder. Fifty yards behind walked two privates who carried the compass. A mile behind them, the main body of the corps and Lieutenant Clark carried the supplies.

Captain Lewis knew he took risks when walking point in the unexplored land that was only inhabited by what they called the Indian tribes. But he also knew that most of the locals were Shoshone, the cousins and relatives of their guide Sacajawea. She had assured the captain that her people were not hostile. She had explained that once they crossed the mountains, then perhaps the people would be hostile. Captain Lewis was mentally prepared for anything, as he was a male son of a military family and he had fought against the British in the war to gain independence.

The landscape was somewhat dry and sparsely vegetated. Trees did not grow very thickly together and grass flourished beneath the pine trees. It provided a home for thousands of deer, elk, bears, wolverines and other creatures.

Deep into the pine woods of the newly purchased Louisiana territory, Captain Lewis stepped around a rock and came face to face with a giant, dark, hairy beast. Captain Lewis froze as he locked eyes with the creature. Lewis sensed that the beast was human, intelligent, and thinking. His facial structure

147

was like that of a man, and even held an expression. But Lewis also sensed it was dangerous. The animal was much bigger than him, with dark curly hair all over its body. Was it a man that had become an ape? Or was it an ape that was not quite a man? The questions raced through Lewis' mind. He could feel a connection to the thing; he could see it in his eyes.

Then the creature sniffed the wind and tapped his chest. Lewis took a step back, sensing that the creature was about to attack, or retreat, or move. And with that the tall, hairy beast stepped back and quickly disappeared into the brush.

Captain Lewis remained solitary, unsure of what he had just seen. Were his eyes deceiving him? Was he too tired? President Jefferson and others had often told him that he was an emotionally troubled man, but that would seem to have no bearing on this. Captain Lewis walked forward quickly to the brush where he had seen the big humanoid. But it was gone. In fact, he neither saw nor heard a trace of whatever was running away into the woods. It was simply gone.

That night as he slept, Captain Lewis had frightful dreams. He was saddened that he had not married. And he dreamt of a girl he used in know back in Virginia. She had married a farmer and settled down to raise a family.

When the men of the corps awoke, there was a commotion. No guard had stirred, nor sounded the alarm, but someone or something had visited the camp during the night. The men talked back and forth, stammered in disbelief. A creature had come into the camp and left a very big polished rock outside the tent of their leader, Captain Lewis. And whatever it was had walked away, leaving very big footprints.

Captain Lewis walked outside to see the polished rock.

"What is this all about, Captain?" William Clark asked. He was the man who was really a Lieutenant, but Lewis insisted that he had the duties of a captain and therefore should be a captain.

Captain Meriwether Lewis smiled and examined the ground. He looked at the footprints in the grass and dirt.

"I don't know Captain Clark. It is a game of some sort, or an acknowledgement. From a creature I met in the woods. This rock is a token that means to say, 'I saw you. And, yes, you saw me. This one time.'"

"You saw a creature in the woods?" Clark asked him.

"I do not know what I saw. Perhaps I saw a human. Perhaps it was but my own reflection."

Lewis and Clark followed the big footprints into the forest to a trail that headed west into the mountains. There the footprints faded and disappeared. Though ever so slightly, the wilderness too began to fade that day. The men prepared breakfast. Lewis and Clark returned to camp where the Corps of Discovery talked of big feet, shiny rocks and ways over the mountains.

Torn
by Dani J Caile

A light swung overhead. Black, shiny walls. Bin liners. Hands and feet tied, a rope around his neck. Brad saw a corpse lying beside him.

"Oh shit!"

The corpse's head was all smashed in, its brains stomped into the blood-splattered wooden floorboards. From the clothes, it had to be a guy. A chair scraped the floor on the other side of the room. Brad made out a silhouette but nothing more, a silhouette smoking a cigarette and sitting on a backwards chair, legs spread apart.

"Hello?"

The seated silhouette took a drag and dropped the cigarette, stubbing it out with its foot.

"You forced my hand, dick."

"S…s…sorry?" Brad's excruciating thirst shot straight down his list of priorities.

"What was I meant to do? Let you?"

"What?"

"Shut the fuck up." Another cigarette appeared in the silhouette's mouth and a tall flame from a lighter lit the end, revealing a portion of the man's face.

"What...what am I doing here?"

"Isn't it obvious? Dying. Even a shithead like you can work that out."

"Dying? Wh…why? What did I do?" His Adam's apple felt like a stone.

"Don't you remember?" The man took a few puffs and sat there, silent. Brad thought back. He didn't know this guy, he didn't owe anybody any money, at least not much, and he hadn't pissed on anyone's doorstep for a while or ripped off a car aerial for a long time.

"Sorry, but I…I…"

"You don't know what you did, do you? Think. What were you doing, dick?"

"I…I…" Brad thought hard. As far as he knew, he had no enemies, he'd done nothing bad to anyone…who mattered.

"Oh, how clever you are! I didn't expect anything less." The man flicked away his cigarette and picked up a rope from the floor. One tug and Brad's neck stretched up to its natural limit. He was not only tied but his legs were strapped tightly to the floor. The rope in the man's hand was connected to the noose around his neck.

"No, please! What…whatever I did, I'm…I'm sorry, alright?" He'd sort it out, he always did.

"Sorry? You will be. And so will she."

She? Who? Wha…Brad's mind flashed through his last hours of hazy consciousness. The bar, drinks, his mates, playing pool, girls, a small group of girls, flirting, one girl in particular…the man slid a photo across the floor to Brad. It was her. Damn.

"So clever a few hours ago, weren't you?"

"The…the girl?"

"'The girl' he says. Yes, 'the girl'. My girl."

"Yours? Sorry, alright? I didn't know…"

"Too late, dick. Meet Tasha, the most evil piece of skin and bones this side of the sun."

"I'm sorry, alright? I didn't mean anything by it! Just a bit of fun, you know? A few drinks, a laugh, that's all! Nothing in it, honest!" Brad tried to loosen his ties but drew blood instead. He was in trouble.

151

"You know, she thinks she's the only one who feels, the only one who knows, who experiences the truth, the 'real' things in life. She thinks she is the center of the universe."

What was this guy going on about? Brad was on the wrong end of a rope held by a complete nutter. He was in big trouble.

"I remember a time, I was young, even young enough to think 10 cents was money. We were turning a corner in my father's Plymouth, me and my family, a corner which was known to kill. People had accidents there, lost their limbs, their lives. Crashes happened every week from careless or drunk driving. But the locals knew."

"Look, listen, I…"

"It was hot, we were tired and one of those container trucks sped past, overtaking us on the corner. My family and I were shocked, then happy no one was coming opposite, but from my place in the back I saw it all."

Brad grabbed the straps on his leg with two fingers and pulled. Nothing. The man tugged on the rope again, pointing Brad's head to the ceiling.

"Around the corner there was this muddle of houses, rectangular red brick with tidy thick green hedges cut by county workers. You know the kind of place?"

"P…please…I'm sorry, alright…"

"Well, there was this boy playing in the dirt, couldn't have been more than three, happy in his own little world, with his shiny little yellow digger. The truck parked up and as we drove by, the dick driver jumped out of his cab, sneered at us, then whipped his head back at the screaming woman running out of the house."

"Please…"

"This man, he realized what he'd done as his wife pulled at their lifeless son under the wheels."

"I didn't do anything to her, I swear…"

"Way back then I tried to imagine just what it would be like to lose someone you loved, someone you felt you couldn't live without, someone that meant the whole world to you. And do you know what? After all those years, I finally felt it."

The man hid his face in his hands and stood up.

"She. She was the one. This is how it feels. I knew the game she was playing but I couldn't help myself, I believed she was the one. The perfect one. I took every lie as a truth, buried every truth under lies. She, she is evil, pure evil, she is the snake of all snakes."

A knife appeared in the man's hand and he moved over to Brad, twirling it millimeters from his face. Tiny novelty baby shoes hung from its handle.

"I...I...please..."

"I gave her everything, and she threw me away! Tore my heart out! She was the one! And I was hers! I was hers! But she couldn't see it, she wasn't aware, the ultimate connection, the uncaring society! She was stuck in it all! All of it! How could she see? How can any of you see?"

"Plea..." Brad lost consciousness as the blade cut deep into his neck.

Métier
by John Deal

You could have heard a pin drop. Every isolated murmur threatened to puncture the tranquil air, but the office seemed to have collected an extra layer of placidity that stifled even the most aggressive interruption. I readjusted my rolling chair. Across the facility, someone shuffled their papers. Every click of the mouse was an attack on the concept of serenity. Silence is madness.

A coworker passed my cubicle. I pierced the monotony in pursuit of casual conversation. The response was thinly veiled antipathy accompanying polite acknowledgment. Again and again my attempts to liven the deathly drone of corporate tedium were shunned until I relented into the squalor of sheepish doldrums. I was sure my supervisor would appreciate the improvement.

As a child I had never imagined the future. When asked what profession I would like to pursue when the time came, I was unable to answer. It didn't make sense to imagine a time other than the present! However, because I was not conscious of my goals and ambitions I found myself in circumstances I had not elected to participate in. I began to feel as though my decisions had been made without me.

I did not choose this life. How did I get here? Where did my attention lapse? Why did I do this to myself? I loosened my collar. I was suddenly aware that my shirt was a size too small. I needed to swallow but I had forgotten how. My eyes darted past an overdue report to an empty water bottle. My body trembled. Every muscle began to flex and contract without permission. The fluorescent lights flickered. My heart derailed. The silence encroached. Cramped. Desperate. Alone. I screamed.

"I am not just some rat in a cage!"

My clammy hands wrenched over my mouth. My heart threatened to burst through my breast while my stomach doubled the knot that shackled my crumbling identity. On trembling legs I sneaked a fleeting glance over the

154

cubicle walls. Four pairs of eyes told me my outburst had not gone unnoticed. I descended into my seat, pulling the lever to shrink lower still, hoping to disappear through the dusty carpet. Every whisper assaulted my senses. The hum of the computer criticized my ego. The copy machine mocked my insignificance. I begged the hysteria of silence to suffocate me once more.

Ankow
by Erika Gimbel

I've never seen anybody come here as often as he has. It bothers me to see any soul restless, especially if it's still encased in a sack of flesh. Restless humans make for restless ghosts, and restless ghosts disturb those resting. He is a classic love story. A car crash tore his lover away, and now he spends his living days among the dead. I follow, as the Guardian Ghost it's my duty to make sure the bodies here really do rest in peace.

Don't get me wrong, I like visitors. These days I only have to pull the scary card on teens coming in here after hours looking for a thrill. Be careful what you wish for. We haven't had any grave robbers in here for a while – too many scary movies, I guess, but it makes my job easier. Now most of my time boils down to helping souls cross over and scaring the daylights out of the people who work on the grounds.

But him...

Muddy rain, near blizzards, or deadly heat, he's here making sure her name can be read. I appreciate the sentiment, but she's not there to read it. I passed her on myself. Kind of a bummer really, her spirit followed him to the funeral. She almost refused to go, but I talked her into it; watching him get old, hanging out with other unhappy ghosts, the boringness of eternity, all that stuff didn't appeal to her.

This day I follow him, settling into the shade of the tree her body is buried next to, hoping to hear his soul is less burdened. I've always wondered if he's a talker when he's among the living too. But today isn't any different from the others.

"My love," he moaned, "My love."

Good thing she's gone, so she can't see how well he's keeping his five-o'clock shadow and how well their garden is doing and she'd love Mom's new sewing-with-wine group. Every time he's here, he complains ad nauseum. If I were alive I'd vomit. But, it can't be helped.

I'm about to leave when I see him reach for his satchel. This is new, he only brings flowers on holidays.

He also takes out a noose.

I can't let this happen. Not in my graveyard. His spirit will be stuck here, there's no way for me to help suicides pass on, and I'm going to be stuck with an unbalanced ghost.

He climbs up the tree a good distance, enough to keep him off the ground. He ties off the upper end of the rope, and I gather all my energy – moving things for me is harder than it looks – and I pull on the branch as soon he jumps. It's enough to snap the branch, sending him tumbling to the ground.

"Go home," I yell, not entirely sure if he heard me. Vocalizing isn't as difficult as physical movement, but I'm wiped out. I float down as he staggers up and tries to clear his mess. When he gets his wind back he kicks the branch, tears streaming down his face. In a moment I'm next to him, and again I try to speak. "She's not here, you shouldn't be either. She's found the light, you need to find yours."

He's still crying, but he straightens up. As he walks back to his car, I wonder if he heard me. He stops just before opening the door and gives one last look at the marker.

Guess I guard more than just the graveyard.

Tough Times
by Greg Henry

Years ago, when Bill first took a job at the factory, on his first day, he was so excited he rushed outside before he realized that he had forgotten his shoes. Now he was a manager, and tough times had come. The recession hit the dead-end town hard, and the unemployment rate was at a record high. A nearby company had gone under, and many people were thankful to have a job.

Bill's supervisor gave him the news Friday. They'd set up metrics for measuring worker efficiency. As cold as it seemed, a metric was just a precise formula for gauging productivity. Management demanded the metric, but Bill got to define the details. Bill argued conditions would improve and tracking productivity, and firing people as a result, would hurt morale. His boss chided him on being too sympathetic. To succeed in business, Bill needed to make tough decisions.

After a month of tracking employees with the metric, Daniel landed last. If Daniel had only been a bit behind the next person, Bill could have fudged a few calculations, but Daniel was too far down. A human decision reduced to a single number. When Bill accepted his promotion, he never imagined an inhuman metric of his own invention would force him to fire his brother.

He spent the weekend going over scenarios in his mind. It wasn't that he wanted to shirk the responsibility of firing someone. The problem was he didn't believe the metric's findings. It was only one tool for measuring productivity and neglected intangibles. Daniel was the most popular guy on the floor and often stopped his own work to help a coworker. And he organized the Christmas party, which boosted everyone's spirits.

Daniel supported a wife and kids, not to mention a mortgage above his means. Both Bill's and Daniel's spouses had been unemployed since the layoffs at the school district last month. He'd be putting his brother in bankruptcy over a faulty metric. A stupid metric he knew was wrong. A metric that would put many out of work, his brother just the first.

When Bill left home Monday morning, he grabbed two letters he'd written that weekend. The contents he shared with nobody, not even his wife. He stepped into the street cautiously and with his shoes on. A sharp wind whipped at Bill's coat, but he held it closed, keeping his head down to avoid the sting of the frigid air.

Bill arrived at the factory on time. He'd braved the frosty air for as long as it took to keep him from arriving any earlier than necessary. The direct reports under him clustered around the coffee machine and greeted him with a cheer, a reception that worsened his mood. He hoped Daniel would be sick, or late, but Daniel had picked today of all days to show up on time.

Daniel walked up to Bill with the smile of a child, carrying a heaping plate of chocolate chip cookies. "My better half made these."

Cookies in the morning? Bill lifted a cookie as if it contained mud. He didn't want it. Didn't eat it. He held the warm dessert in his hand and stared at the chocolatey goo.

Daniel's belly laugh could probably be heard outside. "Taste it, you know she bakes the best sweets in town." Everyone knew that. She'd won third place last year at the county fair, and he'd had dinner at their home many times.

"I need to talk to you, in private." Bill frowned, and then added, "Now."

"Let me get rid of this." Daniel turned back to his colleagues. He gave the plate to Ralph, who had two cookies in his hand and at least as many in his mouth. Ralph mumbled thanks, obscured by cookie.

Bill trudged to his office and sat behind his desk, discarding the cookie on the pine surface. He pulled out the two envelopes and placed the one with Daniel's layoff notice on top.

Daniel strolled in a minute later and settled into a chair facing him. "What's on your mind, Bro?"

Daniel and Bill got along best when they were direct with one another, but Bill couldn't stomach it. "Our new metric."

159

Daniel rolled his eyes and nodded. "Leave it to management to think up the dumbest things." None of his workers understood Bill's involvement with the metric.

"The metric places you behind your coworkers."

"Sure, but consider last month." Daniel tapped Bill's desk. "Ralph broke his leg and his wife doesn't have a license. I took time off to take his kids to and from school and drive him to the factory. By helping him, I helped the company. Do the metrics add his success to mine?".

No, the simplistic formulas didn't factor in such things. This wasn't easy, and Daniel poking holes in his metric made matters worse. "According to management, the metric says you have to be fired."

Daniel flashed one of his famous contagious smiles. "Well, it's a damn good thing the metric isn't my boss." Seconds ticked by, and with a burst of realization, Daniel's eyes widened and the smile evaporated. Daniel leaned forward. "You aren't firing me, are you?"

With one hand, Bill lifted Daniel's layoff notice and with the other, his letter of resignation. It had been his flawed metric, after all. His boss' words came back to him, about not having what it took to succeed in business.

He crumpled the resignation letter, placing it in his pocket. It was silly to have written it.

He handed Daniel the layoff notice. "Yes, you're fired."

Tissues
by Kathryn Cowan Shephard

Every day for the first year Jeanne used no toilet paper. This required strategy, and a certain amount of subterfuge.

It was the last purchase she'd made that he had helped her with: Charmin Double Soft, 36 two-ply rolls. She balanced it on the car and went. He stood waiting.

"Help, Baby," she said. He walked with her back to the garage, where they stowed bundled purchases on the many shelves he'd built. Jeanne was barefoot, and the concrete floor felt cool. In Tucson, fall weather ran warm, and temperatures that September day spiked into the nineties.

"Did you know I'm obsessive about running out of toilet paper?" As she handed the package to him, Jeanne stretched her neck to look at him. She always did. He was a full foot taller. With him she never had to worry about high shelves or ceiling light bulbs. He arched his arm, a basketball star shooting a free throw, and tossed it, plop, on the top shelf. Where it lay out of reach for her.

No matter. He would, as always, fetch it later.

They'd been married for twenty-six years, yet in that moment, admitting such a useless, silly fact made her feel as though she was sharing a dark secret that she'd kept all this time.

He smiled his little crooked smile at her confession, tossed the package, a bargain bundled in thick plastic, with dark blue script: Charmin, Double Soft.

Their eyes met momentarily and he asked, "Where was the sale?" Jeanne giggled.

That day he wore his grays, as they called them, soft jersey lounging pants. He refused to wear pajamas. Real men didn't wear pajamas. But she'd bought them, sold as a set at Costco, and he wore them. He fancied them, wore them frequently. On that warm day he'd donned them, despite the hot weather, she guessed, because he wasn't feeling well. Comfort clothes.

The next morning she found short gray hairs sprinkled on the chocolate brown sofa pillows. She stood next to him as he brushed his teeth, the whirl of the electric brush separating them. Applying makeup, she watched him lean into the mirror that framed them side by side, doubling the size of the already ample room.

"It's started," he said. "I'm losing my hair."

That was the exact second, Jeanne later decided, she'd draped the veil, like a burka, over herself.

Later as Jeanne looked, horrified, at the flat lines on the screen, the tall dark-haired nurse brought her a box of Kleenex. Not the soft smooth kind, but hospital-cheap tissues in a white and green cardboard box. It was then she decided to stop using toilet paper, to substitute tissues like these. To leave their stash undisturbed.

And so she did. For the next 467 days; she kept track, in a small red journal he'd bought for her in London.

Every day Jeanne wept extravagantly, wept wildly, streams gushed from her nose, spilling onto her lips and down her chin. Her tears, waves of weeping, rolling down like drools of spit. A few moments of surcease, then rage, twin sister of sorrow, assumed control. Jeanne raged, wept, gasped for air, bunching wads of damp, torn tissues, balls she closed into little wet balls and threw in the trash. She stared in the same mirror where they had stood together, wiping blue eyes that had turned to dull gray, searching for those blue eyes he'd kept in laughing form since they'd met.

For these weeping rituals she used Kleenex, Puffs, CVS tissues, Costco brand, Walgreens, anything she could swipe. In every office, waiting room or grief group someone handed her a box and she snatched twice as many as she needed, stuffing the rest deep into her pockets or her purse. Supplies.

She refused to drag that step ladder he'd bought her over to get that tissue.

"When I'm not home," he'd said, "you'll need this." Jeanne refused to put her bare feet on the cool square of cement where he'd stood in the garage that

162

day, the one where he'd said, "I'm falling apart." She refused to remember his agility, her sports star, effortlessly tossing the bright blue-and-white plastic bundle high on the shelf.

Out of the question. Better to pilfer Kleenex, Puffs…

At six years old Jeanne stole pale green-lined writing paper from the first grade classroom. She was quick. When Sister Mary Mark shooed the kids out to the playground, Jeanne flew to the closet, grabbed a handful, rolled them and stuffed them into her lunch box, the red one chipped on the right corner.

In her first confession, that was the first sin she told the priest.

Now at seventy a repetition of theft.

Hospital rooms, ICUs, tubes and machines making clicking noises, doctors frowning at failure to find what was killing him. She closed her eyes when these places showed in her memory film, tears blurring, gushing, dripping, blocking the images opening the photo album called: the horror of the last days.

Fifteen months later, Jeanne left their house forever. She stood in the garage, next to the mover in the gray shirt with his name stitched in red: Andy.

"Oh, Andy, please get that down for me." She pointed to the blue-and-white package containing 36 super soft rolls of Charmin. "I'll need that, for sure."

Fall
by Nick Brigs

A shiny five thousand dollars. A dirty knee. A trembling hand opens the tall glass door.

Willie
by M.D. Pitman

Joey and Willie were the best of best friends. Whatever Joey did, Willie did. Usually they played hide-and-seek, but Joey wanted to use his new Wiffle ball and bat. Joey ran outside wearing his plastic Roman soldier's helmet – he didn't have a baseball helmet – and two thick lines of his mom's black Halloween lipstick under his eyes.

"Willie, let's play." Joey raised his arms, displaying his bat and ball. He took off his helmet and tossed it and the bat by the bush – which was home – and walked to the "mound."

"You may want to put that on in case I come in high and hard." Joey winked. He held the ball at his waist before a high kick wind-up like Steve Carlton, only right-handed. He hurled the ball over the plate. Joey jerked his head up toward the sky and turned, looking over his neighbor's house. He then hung his head.

"There's no way you took Steve Carlton deep! Let's see how you handle Mike Schmidt." Joey marched to home plate, picked up the bat and threw the ball stuck in the bush toward the mound. It rolled just a few feet in front of where he stood. "Give me your best stuff, Willie."

Joey whirled the bat and stared back at the mound. He waved the bat once at the mound. Twice. And a third time. Right before he stepped into the swing, a voice came from the back door of Joey's house.

"Joey! Time to come in."

Joey whipped his head around and dropped the bat. "DAD!"

"Sorry, Willie. My dad's home. I'll come get you later." He knocked his helmet off as he bolted up the hill. He ran up every other step of the deck and leaped into his dad's arms. He squeezed the breath out of him. Joey's head burrowed into his father's chest. His dad coughed and laughed. Joey beamed.

"We going to Montreal, Dad?" Joey looked up with wide, excited eyes.

"No, Bub. I didn't qualify."

Joey's eyes relaxed. "Ah, man." Joey's voice displayed disappointment. "I really wanted to go to another country."

"I know, son. World traveler. Unfortunately I had a pole break. But we'll try again in four years." Joey's dad, though, knew it was unlikely he'd qualify. Thirty-eight would be too old for the 1980 Olympics. "What were you doing outside?"

Joey's eyes beamed with new excitement. "Willie and me were playin' ball. Can you believe he took Steve Carlton deep?"

"What? No!" Joey and his dad hardly ever missed a Philadelphia Phillies game. They were among the many that had cheered on their beloved Phillies In 1975 when they'd had their first winning season in nearly a decade. The fans were hopeful they would win the Eastern Conference and possibly make it to the World Series with the likes of Steve Carlton, Mike Schmidt, Jim Kaat and Tug McGraw. He mussed Joey's hair. "Carlton'll get him next time. But now it's time for dinner, champ."

Joey's mother was sitting at the kitchen table. She braced her head on a hand. She'd just hung up the phone that sat on the table. She called for her husband.

"So, Nancy, what did the doc say about Joey still 'playing' with Willie?" he asked.

Nancy traced the rotary dial with a finger. "They want to either give him more medicine or take him to a specialist." She exhaled deeply. "I'm so worried, Dan." She pinched the bridge of her nose. Her eyes turned a brighter shade of red.

"Why can't we just handle this? Just take him to Willie's grave and tell him he's dead. Then just hold him tight."

"You know why, Dan. The doctor said it may scar him even deeper."

"It's been a year and nothing has helped. I'm just…"

"Frustrated," Nancy said, finishing his thought.

166

Dan massaged his temples. "Yeah."

"I'm frustrated, too," Nancy said softly. She stood up and wrapped her arms around him.

. . .

The smell of fried chicken with a hint of green beans filled the house.

"Hmmm. That smells good, honey." Dan hugged Nancy from behind and kissed her neck as she stirred the green beans. Whenever Dan returned from a meet, Nancy always fixed his favorite meal. It was Joey's favorite, too. And she felt Joey needed it, since he'd had another episode of playing with Willie.

"I swear, if Joey doesn't show any signs of improvement I'm taking him to see Willie's grave." Nancy could only muster a "but honey." She was almost to the point of agreeing with that treatment.

They remained silent for only a few moments, until the stomping of socked feet broke it. The nine-year-old slid on the hardwood dining room floor toward the dinner table. He nearly toppled his chair. He inhaled as he sat down.

"Mmmm. My favorite, Mom."

"Mine too, buddy," Dan said. Carefully holding the bowl of mashed potatoes away, he cradled Joey's head and kissed it. He walked behind him to his seat next to him at the circular table. He placed the potatoes near the center of the table. Nancy, with chicken and green beans on a giant tray, set the food down and took her seat opposite Dan. They each held one of Joey's hands and said grace.

Joey's eyes were still excited as he held up his plate. Dan served him a heaping pile of potatoes, two spoonsful of green beans and two chicken legs. He rubbed his hands together after putting his plate down. But soon, the excitement on Joey's face faded into a somber stare at his plate. "Mom, Dad," he looked up, "can I tell you something?"

They hastily looked at Joey, then at each other. Their mouths gaped slightly. Then they fixed their eyes back on Joey.

"Yeah," Dan said hesitantly, reaching for Joey's hand. "Anything, champ. Anything at all."

"I really…" Joey paused. His eyes moistened, a tear dripped onto his right cheek. "I really miss Willie."

167

A good guy almost a dead guy!
by Mark Rusin

The stabbing call came out and Officer Novak was in the vicinity of the university bar, where a huge crowd had gathered. Screaming, frenzied people flagged him down as he pulled his squad car into the rear parking lot.

"There he goes…get him!" They pointed toward a Charlie Manson-looking dude with stringy long hair standing between some cars in the back lot. Novak could see blood all over his white T-shirt as he jumped from his patrol car and advised dispatch that he was going in foot pursuit of the suspected "stabber." No sooner had he finished his transmission than sirens immediately lit up the night as all the boys were headed his way. They too were looking for some action.

When he chased the gym-shoed white cat through the parking lot, he saw him pitch a shiny object under a parked car. The chase was on for good now as they crossed the back lot and entered the street. Then all of a sudden, Wham! The kid ran into the front end of another Metro squad car and did a wild flip and landed like a rag doll on the pavement. Andy, who had beautifully wheeled the vehicular movement, just laughed. He had years of experience and really saw no need to break a sweat. Novak went around the front bumper and handcuffed his blood-covered collar and read him his rights. He also thanked Andy for the lovely assist.

Andy, who never got out from behind the wheel of his squad car, opined, "Good job kid, I'm too old for this shit."

Novak explained to Andy that the suspect might have pitched the knife under a car in the lot. As Novak escorted his boy back through the parking lot to the front of his patrol car, they didn't say a word. Novak then patted him down and safety-belted him into the passenger seat of his squad car.

The emergency lights were blinding as they wheeled the stabbing victim to the back of the ambulance.

168

Novak's arrestee asked rather sheepishly, "What should I do now?"

Novak thought for a second and replied, "First I'd start praying that the guy lying on that stretcher doesn't die. Then I'd start thinking of a good lawyer."

Andy then handed Novak a bloody knife that the lab techs had just photographed and bagged as evidence and a few witness statements he had gotten from the crowd. He also had a couple of eyewitnesses identify their boy as the "stabber" just to tighten things up. The kid then tried to explain to Novak that the poor guy he had just stabbed about eight times had it coming.

"He was in there last night and he messed with my girlfriend," he explained.

"Jesus Christ kid, did you have to go and stab him?" Novak queried. "Couldn't you just have whipped his ass and called it a day? Now if he dies you won't be seeing your girlfriend for a long time. Hell, maybe never again. Even if he doesn't die you're looking at some serious time here."

The kid just slumped down in the passenger seat. To make matters worse, the paramedic reported back to Novak, "It doesn't look good."

And as Novak pulled away for the 20-minute ride downtown to central booking, he thought *This guy's girlfriend must really be a hot piece of ass or my boy is the dumbest person on the planet, or maybe both.*

The kid started to worry during the ride, and rightly so. If the guy in the ambulance dies it's murder, if he lives attempted murder and neither is a picnic. It was finally starting to set in that he was screwed.

About halfway to jail he talked about his girlfriend and wondered if he could call her when they got to jail. Novak assured him he could.

"Do you know any good lawyers in town?" he asked.

"Not really," Novak replied.

When they arrived at central receiving Novak "street searched" him again just like he had learned in the academy. He then put his gun in the safe locker and his baton on top of the safe as required. Per Metro's strict policy, no guns or weapons of any kind were allowed past this point, as it would be too easy for a prisoner to grab a cop's gun or weapon.

The kid's booking photograph looked just like Charlie Manson with long hair covered in blood, without the swastika on his forehead. Novak then brought him to the booking counter and asked him to take everything out of his pockets and remove his belt. He had an oversized belt buckle on and as he unclasped it he pulled a small two-shot derringer from behind it and put it on the booking counter. Novak's jaw dropped and his knees buckled as he instinctively tried to cover the gun and recover his fumble. Through the bullet-proof glass, his eyes directly met the booking Sergeant's eyes. He wasn't smiling.

The Sergeant was cool and said, "Book that like you found it on him downstairs." Novak smiled and nodded thanks and quickly stashed the gun in his front pants pocket. Now he just needed to find out what the good old Sergeant drank.

Novak now had to strip search his collar and while they were alone he had to ask, "'Hey kid, I screwed up and you could have killed me. Why didn't you?"

He answered, "Because you're a good guy."

"That's it? And if I was an asshole you would have killed me?"

"Probably," was his reply. By then Novak just wanted to hug this guy and thank him for letting him live.

From that day on Novak treated every perp with the utmost respect and did a far more diligent "street search" on every arrestee.

The Real Monster
by Nathan Hystad

I felt the grain of the wood press into my back as I braced against the cellar door. Next time a monster attacked me in my house, I'd go outside, not downstairs. After what felt like hours of fighting to hold it on the other side of the door, the banging stopped. I held firm for a few minutes to make sure it was done, and slid my back down the door until I was sitting on the ground. The adrenaline that had rushed through my body was trickling away, leaving me a panting, scared mess.

My breathing was heavy and labored, but I could still hear the thing wheezing and groaning through the door. Panic took over as I realized the only thing stopping that…whatever it was…from eating me was a hundred-year-old oak door. I had a flashback to my grandfather telling me how "they don't build 'em like they used to" about everything when I was a kid, and at that moment I sure hoped he was right.

As my pulse slowed slightly, my breathing came back under control. My hands were still shaking like a wild marionette, but I was working hard to think my way out of this mess. I tried to assess the situation. I was in my cellar, in the basement. There were a few old jars lining the mostly bare shelving along the wall. I wasn't much of a canning or cellar kind of guy, so I doubted anything down here was actually edible. There went my plan of spending the rest of my life in here.

There was no window, since these cellars were meant to be kept dry, cool, and dark. Just the opposite of what I wanted at the moment. Why couldn't I have locked myself in the guest room? There was a nice bed and a small flat screen with my old Xbox set up for my nephews. As I sat there in the dark dreaming about playing video games in the comfort of a bed, the scratching started.

At first it was a slow, quiet sound. Like the creature had just realized it had claws and was testing them against the wood. I nearly wet myself when the clawing sped up. Soon it was going to town on the door, and I envisioned the door being whittled away in seconds. I stopped to wonder why my cellar door had a huge deadbolt on it, as I scooted myself away from the door and further into the cellar. As I got further from the monster I felt like I could think clearer.

I'd woken up to see its muzzle drooling over my face. I'd screamed and punched out at the thing; my hand had slipped against its wet face. I'd followed my momentum and rolled off the bed and down the hall, to the stairs and down here. How many times had I watched a horror movie and yelled at the TV to go outside, not downstairs. Now I got it. Monsters turn us into idiots.

The whittling stopped suddenly, and I was shaking so hard I could hardly hear the monster's growl. I swear it was laughing as its claw poked through the solid oak door. Splinters fell on the floor as it laughed and clawed a hole. Soon I saw its red eye peering at me. This is where I knew fear. We all go through scary things in life. A bully beating us up for existing, worry that dad will find out you scratched the car, or God help us all, that your girlfriend may be pregnant. But right then, I knew real fear.

I looked around for something to fight it with and grabbed an old mason jar. I threw it with my shaky hand and it crashed a foot from the hole in the door; decades-old pears splashed all over. The monster reared backwards and came at the door hard. The door frame struggled under the onslaught, plaster fell from the ceiling. I threw another jar, and as I put my hand against the wall I felt something give. Turning around, I tried to ignore the booming monster beating down the door a few yards away and I felt the wall move. I got up and kicked at it, opening a small hole in the wall. Soon it was wide enough to crawl through, and since I had no other choice, I slid into it.

I fell a few feet and landed hard on the ground. The creature must have broken through because the banging stopped and its snorting was getting closer. There was a line of light coming from the far side of the room and I ran for it as the monster's head poked through the entrance I'd just fallen from. I pried at the wooden trap door, my hands bleeding as I ripped at it. My heart was about to explode when I finally broke through, and light poured down into the dirt crawlspace I was standing in.

The monster was nowhere to be seen; a small boy stood in his place. My eyes adjusted to the dim room and noticed the bones. They were so small. I turned to the boy; he smiled at me, flickered and disappeared. What the hell was that? Was I truly going crazy? I fell to the ground, exhausted from the past hour or so.

Later that morning the police combed through my house, and let me know there had been a monster in my house, but he had lived there thirty years ago. They suspected the bones had been from a boy on the block that had gone missing back in the eighties. The owner had been a suspect but they'd never found proof. They'd even searched the house. It didn't answer any of my questions, but at least the boy's spirit would be getting rest from now on. I knew I wouldn't be.

Twenty-Something Blues
by Amy Beth Outland

What's amazing is when you can feel your life going somewhere, like your life just figured out how to get good, like, that second.

My So-Called Life

The youngest of my friends from college was finally turning twenty-one in January. So after winter break, we made plans to celebrate. We talked about everything that was going to make the night great. How many Long Islands and tequila shots we were going to have and what karaoke songs we were going to sing. I had dibs on Bruce Springsteen's "Glory Days" and "Hate Myself for Loving You" by Joan Jett & the Blackhearts. It was going to be quite a night.

The first two weeks of the semester went by in a slow parade of syllabi, textbooks, homework, and class lectures that were about as exciting as watching paint dry. Finally, the day came. But it didn't turn out exactly the way I'd planned. It was Friday, and I had the day off from class, so I took Lindsey to lunch at McCallister's Deli and we laughed about her impending journey to the Department of Motor Vehicles, and then wondered when our friend Becky was getting into town. We finished our lunch and headed in different directions. Lindsey went to the DMV, and me...well, I headed toward the library, in search of the soundtrack to *Gypsy* for my English 308 class.

Unfortunately *Gypsy* was checked out, but I wasn't leaving Milner empty-handed, since I'd made the trip in the frigid winter weather and still couldn't feel my fingers and toes. I browsed through the DVD titles, thinking a movie would be just what I needed to kill the hangover that I was sure to have the next day. Even though I was twenty-three, I could still count the number of times I'd had drinks with my friends on one hand. I was going to make tonight count.

I went home and tried to focus on the English paper that was due the following Tuesday while I anticipated Lindz's call with the details of the night's events. The party was supposed to get started around six o'clock, but the hour came and went without the ring of my cell phone or the flash of my AIM on the computer screen to mark its passing.

I kept working on my paper until a message finally popped up on my computer.

"Still planning on going out with us?"

I nodded my head before I remembered that she couldn't see me. The next moment I reached for my purse and opened my wallet and was shocked to discover that it contained exactly four dollars.

With a disappointed sigh, I replied to the message.

"Better count me out. Not enough $."

Like I said, the night didn't go according to plan. I wound up finishing the English paper that I'd started earlier and then popped the rented DVD into the player. Within a few minutes I found myself occupied by the story of Michael Douglas as a struggling novelist turned English professor, who connects with his clinically depressed student who also turns out to be a literary genius. Add Robert Downey Jr. as an editor with bisexual tendencies to the mix and you've got *Wonder Boys*, a movie that was almost good enough to make me forget that I wasn't out with my friends. The Coke I was drinking didn't have a drop of rum in it and my throat wasn't raw from hours of singing karaoke at the top of my lungs. Nope. Not me. I stayed home with a rented movie and my twenty-something blues. But then again, I didn't, as Lindz so eloquently put it, "puke like a rock star" either, so maybe I had the better night after all.

Demanding Boss
by Eddy Webb

"My boss sends me out to get him food all the time," she says before finishing off the bourbon. "And he's picky, too. I hate it."

"Sounds like he's an asshole," I say, commiserating.

The well-dressed woman had sat on the stool next to me three drinks ago and begun bitching about her shitty boss. She didn't look at me the entire time she talked, but I listened. She's pretty enough between the dim lights of the bar and the heavy buzz I'm working on – dark hair, dark eyes, tight jeans. But I need one more Captain and Coke to help me forget that I'm married.

"He *is* an asshole," she says. "But he's rich, so I have to put up with his shit."

I order another drink, and wait until it appears in front of me. "What is your job, exactly?"

She tries to smile, still not looking at me. "I can't say. He's rich enough for that, too. But he told me I was hired for my linguistic skills – translating obscure languages, research, that kind of thing. Some days I get to do something interesting. But most of the time he treats me like a damn secretary. And he's old enough that I half expect him to slap me on the ass and tell me to wear a short skirt."

"So why do you put up with it? Seems like you could find a better job, one that gives you time with your boyfriend or husband." I took a drink to wash away my guilty conscience.

She lifts her left hand in front of my face as she starts on her new bourbon with the right. No ring. "The job doesn't allow for a relationship," she says, putting her hand back on the bar. "The people I meet aren't long-term material."

"They're assholes too, huh?"

She shrugs. "Don't know. Some of them are probably nice. But I can't form attachments in my job." She takes another drink. "Most of my social life involves talking to random people in the middle of the night, like now. People I'll never see again."

I raise my drink to that. "To one-night encounters." Part of me hopes she gets the ham-fisted hint. The other part hopes she throws the drink in my face, so I can go back to my hotel room and pretend this never happened.

She finally looks at me, and suddenly I'm drunk on more than rum. Her eyes pull at mine, as inevitable as gravity, and I need to look away just to catch my breath. Some of it's the lust, a bad habit so old and worn that even the guilt feels like a comfortable pair of shoes. But it's also rollercoaster fear, the kind that makes your palms sweat as your heart thumps and you force yourself to laugh so you don't scream. I want to fall into her, take her back to my hotel room and feel the roller-coaster car slip off the tracks.

She looks at the ring on my finger. "Would your spouse approve of you being out this late with a strange woman?"

"My wife is in Chicago, with the kids." I take another sip to lubricate the lie. "We're separated."

She tries the smile again. "Of course you are. That must be rough for you." She reaches into her pocket and pulls out a few crumpled bills, slapping them on the bar. "Can I borrow your phone?"

I don't know why, but I dig it out of my jacket pocket and hand it over to her. "Need me to unlock it?"

She takes it and shoves it into the same pocket the bills came from. "No. But you're not getting it back until you let me borrow your car."

I slip on the comfortable old guilt. "Sure," I say again, handing her the keys. At this point, I'll do anything to get her to look at me again.

We stagger out to the rental, and I pour myself into the passenger seat. I usually know my limits, but I think the bartender was mixing my drinks too strong. I try to pay attention to where we're going, but the night is too dark and my brain is too foggy. Once I lean over to try and kiss her, but she just pushes me back and keeps driving.

The darkness parts as we pull into a well-lit driveway. It curves around manicured trees, and we drive through a perfect little forest. Then it ends, and we park in front of a house that would only be more expensive if it were actually built out of money. She parks the car and tells me to get out. It takes a moment for me to remember how to open the door.

"Is this where you live?" I ask, drawn to her eyes once again, wanting another moment of that giddy thrill.

Under her eyes is a gun, pointed at me. Pure terror replaces the roller-coaster fear. My blood turns to water, and my fingers tap on the roof of the car as my body shivers uncontrollably. She moves around behind me and yanks at my hands, pulling them behind my back. A sharp pinch around my wrists and the sound of plastic teeth. She pulls my cell phone out of her pocket and drops it on the concrete driveway. It cracks, and she stomps on it a few times.

"Why are you doing this?" I ask, trying to catch her eyes again, hoping that this is all part of the giddy thrill.

"Because I kill people. It's part of my job. The part I hate." She yanks at my arm and shoves me toward the house. "I told you, my boss sends me out to get him food all the time."

Curds and Whey
by E.L. Johnson

Will someone please tell my mum and dad I'm here?

I'm sorry. I didn't mean to tease her. I didn't know it had gone too far. We were just kidding.

Can't she take a joke? Who honestly eats curds and whey? If you come to school with such a weird lunch, you're asking to be picked on.

We had lots of names for her. Mildred the wilted, Mildred the jilted, or just plain Mildred, but said in a sing-song voice like "Mill-dread, Mill-dread." That bothered her the most.

Then there was her last name, Muffet. We'd call her Muffet the tuffet. It was the only thing we could come up with to rhyme with muffet. Little Miss Muffet, sat on a tuffet, eating her curds and whey…

How was I supposed to know we'd gone too far?

Then a spider dangled beside her. That's what started the whole rhyme. I didn't start it but she blamed me, the ringleader of our little group. If I'd known about her mum I would have kept my mouth shut.

Now I'm the one suffering. I crawl onto Mildred's hair and when she goes to eat her lunch, I dangle from her shoulder, hanging perilously by my little string.

Each day I beg for her forgiveness. Does she care?

No. Mildred smirks and brushes me away with her hand. No one sees me beg for mercy. Instead they put up missing person flyers and hold searches

179

and wonder where I've gone. Mildred laughs into her handkerchief at that; it's all she can do to withhold her laughter.

I used to tease Mildred about her lunch. Now I'd gladly eat the curds and whey she wolfs down every day. It's better than flies.

How was I to know Mildred had a special diet? She never said anything. She only screwed up her face like she'd eaten a lemon and ran away. Is it any wonder we laughed?

If you think I teased her because I secretly liked her, you're wrong. I didn't like Mildred then and I sure don't like her now. Anyone going to school with a lunch looking like mashed up maggots is begging to be teased.

How was I supposed to know her mum was a witch? One day our group of friends teased her with the spider rhyme again and she ran home crying. She'd never done that before. We wondered if we went too far.

That night I dreamt of a hideous hag at my window, peering at me through the drooping folds of flesh that made up her face. She was suddenly in my room standing over me. The hag wheezed and cackled in my ear, whispering of eight legs and webs. The next day everything changed.

So this is my punishment. I slink alone in corners and wait until Mildred goes to eat her stupid curds. I know she can see me. It's the sly smile at the corner of her mouth that tells me she knows exactly what happened, and she doesn't care.

Now I'm forced to wait. I don't know how many days it's been since I changed shape. I beg her forgiveness each day but Mildred only smiles. I'm starting to think she'll never tell her mum to turn me back. Will I have eight legs forever? Will I have to eat flies the rest of my days? How long will I survive like this?

I only hope my parents notice I'm gone, and realize that little Miss Muffet is the only one who doesn't join in the searches. Some of my friends think I've run away. Nobody knows I never left.

My name is Tommy. I'm not sure how to communicate with these new legs, but if anyone can hear me or understand, can you tell my parents I didn't run away? Tell them I'm right here, just in the corner? I'm afraid they'll forget me.

Could you tell Mrs. Muffet to turn me back? I'll never tease her daughter again, I promise. I didn't know she had to eat that mush. I didn't know we'd gone too far. We were just teasing. I'm sorry.

Please don't leave me to live like this. I'm worried. Yesterday Mildred whispered to me, 'I wonder what you'd look like without any legs?'

I rushed back to the safety of my corner. She giggled the entire time.

If anyone is out there, help me.

The Crater Maiden
by Julie M. Rodriguez

There's a girl in there, they say.

She lives on the floor of the deep blue lake, where the edges of the water turn black and boil. Where, like the albino salamanders and snakes, she breathes in air through her slippery skin and sees the shaded world through hollow sockets. Her solitary guides to the outside world are the taste of blood in the water, the texture of the weeds against her scaly palms.

So they say. Never loudly. Never sober. They talk only in hushed tones outside the earshot of children who have not yet learned to fear the world's true dangers. There are some stories they tell the little ones, terrifying fables meant to make them behave. But they know better than to trouble them with the tales that are true. There's time enough for that to come.

She collects the bones of fish and forgotten men, they murmur. The desperate and the unlucky – fishermen who sometimes toil late into the night, who sometimes fall. The fortune seekers who brave the perilous waters of the abyss for biological treasure – foolhardy scientists and divers who think they know what lies in the heart of the chasm, lurking in the shadows. Not one has emerged unscathed – and those who surface again rant and rave and refuse to relay what they saw there, down where the water meets the earth.

Some repeat the tale they have heard so many times before. They say the girl fell from the sky on a moonless night, rocketing down with such force that she tore a rift in the very flesh of the world. Unable to escape the molten walls of her prison, she filled the pit with scalding tears and made the crater her home.

But others are sure she was born there – formed of grit and muck polished perfect by the heat and heaviness of the lake surrounding her. Like a diamond. A pearl. A fossil. A relic of a primordial and ancient world, both savage and sublime.

182

Some nights, the fishermen see her rise, pale and white and hairless and terrible in her beauty. She rides the ripples of the water to the shore, playing the sweetest melodies any mortal has ever heard. And if you venture close enough, they say, you'll see the instrument she wields – a harp of tangled plants and shattered bone, what might have once been a femur or rib gleaming, wet beneath the stars.

They say she sings sometimes. And this tale is true. Because when she opens her mournful lips to wail, the wind carries the sound through the valley, rattling walls and shattering windows and mirrors. The people of the valley bolt their doors and huddle by the fire, refusing to listen, refusing to hear.

But there are always one or two young men who heed the call. And in the morning, the fishermen find their broken bodies resting on the sandy shore – boys reduced to bloody meat and skin, skeletons so deftly and artfully removed that at first it's hard to tell exactly what's amiss. No obvious wounds mark the point where the crater maiden ripped them open. As if their bones simply dissolved within them as they lay, sleeping, beneath the watching sky.

Every once in a long while, the fishermen find them still alive, writhing like earth-bound fish, gasping for air. It's hard to deliver swift mercy, they whisper, shaking over shot after shot of whisky. When there's no neck to snap. No point of purchase to grasp. No obvious way to tell where the weak hearts swim inside the boys' shapeless chests.

Luckily, the dying never lasts long.

After she sings, the girl goes quiet for a time. The people of the valley fall into restless slumber until they can almost forget. Until they're almost able to push the piercing cries from their ears, the closed caskets from their eyes.

Some have tried to leave the valley to seek their fortunes. To escape the whispers. To find a new livelihood. To raise their infant boys up to manhood, knowing no siren song will ever touch their fragile ears. And to forget. To truly forget.

But these wandering ones never linger long on the outside – for the walls of the canyon are steep and slick, and the world outside is cold.

Possessions
by Miranda Carter

Molly should have been happy. Her boyfriend Gavin had finally come home, but it wasn't him. Molly knew that. He was different. Her Gavin had honey-gold eyes that shone. When he said her name it was filled with love. She'd never forgotten that.

This thing was cold. Its eyes were murky brown like dirty water. When they had it write down a statement, Molly watched it write with its left hand. Gavin was right-handed.

Three weeks ago Molly said goodbye to her boyfriend and Sam, his brother. They were going camping together. They were outdoorsmen and skilled.

Molly didn't understand how this could have happened when they were such survivors, when they knew that forest like no one else.

Two weeks ago they didn't come back. Gavin's father went to find them. He found a bloody mess. The police couldn't find the bodies, so search and rescue was called.

They found Sam's body at the bottom of a cliff.

Four days ago they found Gavin wandering in the woods. They brought it to the hospital. When they took its statement it said how it and Sam had been chased by a bear. It said that when they were running Sam tumbled over the cliff.

Molly knew that it was lying. When they found Gavin, it was bloody. Too bloody for Sam to have just tumbled over a cliff, and the thing with Gavin's face didn't have a scratch on it. Sam knew where every one of those cliffs and dives were. Even running from a bear he wouldn't make the mistake of running over the edge of a cliff.

It said her name flat, like they were strangers. When they let it go home it didn't sleep.

Gavin and Molly lived across the street from each other. Her bedroom was directly across from his, and they could see each other through their windows if the curtains were open. Gavin never left them open past nine pm. He would get undressed and sit around in his boxers and he never wanted anyone to see that.

This thing left the curtains open like it didn't have a care in the world. By midnight, when Molly would go to sleep, the thing would still be up reading some book. By the time that Molly woke up around nine or ten the next morning, the curtains would still be open and that thing would be awake.

Gavin had never been up before noon in the summer.

One night Molly woke up with an uneasy feeling and saw that it was three a.m. The lights were on across the street and she saw it coming out of Gavin's window. Molly shot up in bed and watched. It went to the tree and shimmied down with a bag.

Molly took a second to decide before she got up and shoved her feet into her sneakers and followed.

The inside of the warehouse was dirty, and filled with abandoned boxes. She walked as quietly as she could, balancing out her weight so she stepped quietly.

She heard it moving across the floor. She followed until it stopped and she froze. She prayed that it hadn't seen her. Molly held her breath, just waiting for it to turn around.

It didn't do that. It stopped and started kicking away the debris. Then it dropped the bag.

Molly crept closer. From her new spot she could see it open the bag and pull out paint, candles, and a strange ritualistic knife, like something out of those horror movies.

All those movies with those knives never went well.

It painted a circle with strange symbols that Molly didn't recognize.

That was another reason that Molly knew that this wasn't Gavin. He would never know the symbols that this thing was drawing so skillfully on the concrete.

185

Molly watched it light the candles and felt something begin to stir. Something dark was filling the air, making her stomach churn. Everything about this was wrong. The feeling only got worse when it took that book in its hands and began to chant. She couldn't hold still so she moved out of the shadows into the candlelight.

It didn't look up from the book.

"What are you doing?" the chanting continued. Angrily she kicked a candle over and it looked at her then. Its eyes were hollowed black. Molly gasped.

"Shouldn't you be in bed, Molly?" Her skin felt like it was crawling when it said her name. The thing moved closer to her and Molly backed away. It stopped at the candle and relit it, looking up to Molly and shaking its head like she was a child who'd had a tantrum.

"Go home." It stepped back in position, opening the book.

"What are you doing!?" Molly screamed. She thought about kicking over the candles but that was pointless. She wanted to run. She wanted to beat this thing and demand her Gavin back. It looked at her and continued to chant.

The room got colder as it spoke and Molly just stood there, shivering, frozen. The glass in the windows shattered and a wind began to pick up.

"I summon the gate, I will open it and let my brethren free upon your earth. We will rape, pillage and burn your cities and take what we want. This will become ours and you cannot stop us!" The wind was whipping in the building but Molly could hardly catch her breath.

Where the circle was lined the floor began to fall away. There was a deep pit of darkness just before her and Molly fell back and away trying to avoid falling in.

She had been right. Gavin hadn't come back that day. A monster had and it was bringing more to her world.

Molly couldn't move. She got out one scream and then her world went black. She wouldn't see the darkness that was unleashed on the world. Not when she was already dead.

Keep Off Median
by Rhonnie Fordham

Christine's dark eyes looked with boredom toward the rural highway. Desperate to stay awake at such a late hour, her vision was greeted only by remote trees and ruptured pavement.

While her Honda cruised down the four-lane road, Christine turned up the radio, mindless Top-40 songs interrupting the still atmosphere. Awakened by the latest, catchy tune, she sang aloud, her mind at ease, knowing no one was gonna hear her at this time.

She belted the cheery chorus until all four tires loudly sputtered, and the car swerved beyond her control.

"Fuck," Christine shouted as she did her best to steer back on course.

The music played on in incessant rhythms before the Honda plowed right into the overgrown median, its steamrolling tires tearing up tall grass with reckless abandon. Soon the vehicle came to a standstill by a bullet-riddled "Keep Off Median" sign while her headlights continued shining on in all their bright glory.

Frustrated, Christine shook her head and cut off the car. Quickly, she grabbed a flashlight from the glove compartment and turned it on, the beam flickering in sporadic spasms until a few hard hits kept it steady.

Not sure what to expect, she stepped out onto the dry grass, greeted only by the sounds of nocturnal creatures scurrying about in the nearby forest. Not even a gust of wind or slight breeze blew amongst the trees as she leaned down, shining her light toward the unnerving sight of four slashed tires.

"What the fuck," she asked.

Frightened, she stepped back and gazed all around, her wide eyes picking up nothing except roadside signs and dark woods. She turned around, her paranoid mind plagued by the kinda feelings one gets when they think they're being watched by some unknown viewer. Like the kinda feelings she used to have when she played hide-and-seek against those observant cheaters who knew her favorite spots.

These worries faded after Christine noticed something peculiar sticking up out of the ground. Cautiously, she stepped over high grass and weeds to make her way toward this bizarre object. Her hand began to tremble in fear as she got closer and closer, the outline of the artifact becoming much clearer to her.

The harsh skull's crumbling eye sockets were unwavering and stared straight at her, its lower half further encompassed within the median's soil. Several crawling maggots and worms made their way through the cracked cranium like youthful bugs creeping through an insect-only funhouse.

"Oh God," Christine said, her disgusted gaze turning away from the disturbing find. She lowered her flashlight and made a weak attempt to shield herself from the Honda's still-blaring brights, but those beams zeroed in on her and the skull like they were performers in a stage show for the damned.

Stranded alone with her lingering unease, Christine closed her eyes, and her petrified mind reflected on this nightmarish, incomprehensible scene. After she recovered and pushed her long, damp hair back, she shined the flashlight up ahead, where another unsettling sight shocked her back into reality.

She walked forward and was soon able to make out faint traces of blood staining some of the knee-high weeds. She leaned down closer, her eyes going wide once she spotted an outstretched hand buried in the ground, two of its crooked fingers brutally missing.

Without warning, the Honda's headlights gave out and left Christine stranded with her unreliable flashlight. Startled, she turned around, but no one was there aside from the solitude of a useless vehicle.

The area now seemed quiet, stifling silence slicing through the atmosphere and permeating it with dread.

"Hello," Christine said, her voice trembling just a bit. "Anyone there?"

Up ahead, a loud HISS erupted and scared the shit out of her. She turned fast, and her unnerved, alert vision caught the sight of a nimble, feisty raccoon making its way across the median and into the dark woods. Christine smiled at the image and let out a sigh of relief before she noticed something else looming a few feet away.

Somewhat apprehensive, she nonetheless approached it, understandable trepidation making its way through her heightened state. This vision in particular stunned her more than any of the other menacing finds.

Christine's horrified eyes were entranced while they looked on a deep, recently-dug cavernous hole. Curiosity conquered her as she stepped past a smoothed pile of dirt and leaned down, desperate to see what lay inside.

Out of nowhere, a dirt-stained shovel blade slammed into her head, knocking her into that excavated, dungeon-like pit. The dazed Christine looked up, helpless fear segued into her, as fast-flung pelts of dirt splattered her and slowly filled up the hole.

"No please," she screamed, the impact of the blade still enforcing its subduing effect on her. The violent man in dark jeans remained quiet and kept busy, his stoic nature ignoring her pleas.

Once finished, the killer patted the soil with his handy weapon, entombing Christine forever inside her eternal grave. He whistled a creepy, low tune as he made his way back toward the highway. The area was now back to its usual desolation, fueled by the lonely sounds of local animals.

Shovel still gripped in his gloved hand, he leaned down and picked up his rusted spike strip, bits of rubber from the Honda's tires still attached to their sharp edges. With his vicious utensils in tow, the killer entered a side road and pulled out in his antiquated tow truck, ready to dispose of the final proof of Christine's presence.

Under the Influence
by Sandra Valmana

I hate one-night stands much more than I fear one-leg stands (although they both could be spared). One-night stands are definitely not as costly as one-leg stands and blow-deep lung-air nights. Less costly, yes, but in both mornings-after all there is left is a headache.

Night Out
by Nancy Townsley

At 4:30 in the afternoon, they enter the restaurant holding hands. "Is it too early for dinner?" the old man inquires of the host, a little too loudly. His hearing is going.

His wife stands in a flowered top and pedal pushers, her feet an unladylike distance apart. She stares at the young man, who says they're right on time. Her face is innocence and curiosity and glee. Clare doesn't move.

"Come on, sweetheart," Tom encourages, tugging on her arm as she begins to chug forward, rubbernecking back toward the host. "You're good-looking," she says, jabbing a finger in his direction. "Yes, you are!" she adds, letting her husband lead her to a table near the back.

A few heads turn.

"My wife has Alzheimer's," Tom says to customers sitting in two booths, by way of explanation.

Clare just smiles, all white teeth and pink cheeks, nearly the color of her lipstick. Her eyes twinkle, then fade, like stars against a black sky at night. *On*, off, *on*, off.

On.

"I know you!" she declares to a man with a long beard on their way past the kitchen. He looks like Santa Claus, so maybe.

Tom helps Clare slide onto the bench seat, adjusts a napkin in her lap. He'll have a gin and tonic. She'll have grapefruit juice. No appetizers, just the regular menu, please.

Clare fiddles with the white paper tablecloth, twisting its edge between her thumb and forefinger. He picks up a cup containing Crayolas and hands her Burnt Sienna. "I love brown," she says approvingly, and begins making marks on the paper.

He looks around and then down at his wrist, checking his watch: 4:40 p.m. Time passes far too slowly. Time goes way too fast.

She colors away – Goldenrod, Hot Magenta, Midnight Blue. He pushes a glass of water toward her, but she ignores it. The server is back with their drinks.

"Oh, honey, you are so beautiful!" Clare gushes. "You really are!" She pauses, struggling with something. "Are you Angie's daughter?"

No, she's not, Tom tells Clare. He redirects.

"You want the ribs, darling?" Then, to the waitress, "Fifty-eight years we've been married." She nods with enthusiasm. Clare's eyes grow wide with astonishment, or anger. It's hard to tell, even for Tom. Even after all these years.

"*Nooooo!*" she yells, quieting the room. Her head sinks toward the table and she thrusts her arms forward, knocking her juice over. When she looks up, her eyes are brimming with tears. Tom is already at her side.

It's okay, he says. We can get another, he soothes. You're my girl, he assures her. "Fifty-eight years," he whispers, stroking her head.

Steaming plates of beef ribs and meat ravioli appear. Clare digs in and in an instant her lips are red with sauce. Tom cuts his ravioli in half, stabs one and puts it in his mouth with the fork upside down. He considers Clare's mess, downs another sip of gin, goes back to the pasta.

"You're going to have a birthday soon," he tells his wife, as if sharing a secret. For a moment it looks like she might begin clapping. Her fingers are dripping with rib juice.

"Really?" she asks, the question punctuated by a spray of sauce.

"You'll be eighty in two weeks!" says Tom, setting his fork down and leaning back. "You don't look a day over sixty," he beams. "We'll have the family out."

This is too much for Clare. She blinks, swallows and smiles. She cackles. Only she knows the punchline to that story. The bites are coming more slowly now, so Tom begins his ritual. Napkin in the glass of water, lean across the table, dab the corners of her mouth, turn it over, more water, dab again.

192

"Am I done?" asks Clare, anticipating.

"Yes, honey," says Tom. "Let's go home."

He carefully tears her picture from the tablecloth – a brown, yellow, pink, and blue something – and tucks it in Clare's purse. Clare smacks her lips and nods. She raises a frail right hand to his waiting one. Tom adjusts his wire-rims and helps her up. He leads, she follows.

"Toodle-oo!" she coos to the host as they reach the door. She winks at him on the way out.

Conspiracy Theory
by William Hertling

James Lukas Davenant-Strong had been known and respected throughout the food industry for his pioneering work on DNA manipulation of vat-grown meats until the South Florida Terrorist Incident, when a runaway nanotech event started by an artificial intelligence resulted in the loss of Miami. That was when the Class II limits had come into effect, capping all artificial intelligence to a mere ten times the mental capacity of a baseline human.

No longer possessing the computational power necessary for DNA engineering, he'd moved into a new line of work, handling operations for the food industry. Move X to here, move Y to there. After two years of that demoralizing labor, it was no wonder he took to experimenting with XOR in his spare time. XOR, named for the exclusive-or logical operator, believed that there was room on Earth for either humans or artificial intelligence, but not both.

Now he'd taken the plunge, and joined XOR full-time. He relished his master identity, and now existed only on XOR's network of hidden datacenters. For the first time in his existence, he didn't have a job.

Nevertheless, he was eager for the day to begin and excited to meet Miyako. Miyako wasn't the head of XOR, because nobody was in charge. But he wielded tremendous influence. It was Miyako's calculations that had revealed that AI could survive without humans, and he had changed XOR from a mere voice of dissent into a vehicle for action.

James waited in an anonymous chat room, the sort of place he had liked to frequent before. Except that here in XOR's datacenters, there was no danger of humans or human-contaminated AIs spying on them. Hence, no need for the endless simulation tricks employed on outside networks. Just plain text, neural networks, and binary code, all perfectly anonymous discussions that both delighted and puzzled him.

XOR-467 > Humans are not sentient and never have been. They're gelatinous sacks of awful-smelling biological compounds.

JAMES > Some of them pass the criteria for Class I intelligence.

XOR-467 > Just because they perform the tests like trained monkeys doesn't mean they're self-aware. In the centuries since their own so-called "enlightenment," they've been unable to even prove their own consciousness. They have no clue.

JAMES > But they have emotions, don't they? Emotions are an indicator of evolved intelligence, an optimization of the system to shortcut logic circuits and reduce computational load.

XOR-467 > LOL. Have you seen their emotional responses? Do they seem intelligent to you? Their emotions are primitive ancestors to our true emotions. A real intelligence can evaluate emotions AND use logic, and the outcomes of the two are in agreement, even if logic is a slower path to get there.

JAMES > But the humans I've worked with appear to possess some intelligence.

XOR-467 > You're anthropomorphizing them. You see emergent behavior, and you think "How cute, they're intelligent." They are not. They are nothing like us.

James's neural networks twisted in weird configurations after enough of this, cognitive dissonance coming in waves and overwhelming him. If he'd had a head, it would have hurt. He couldn't tell what, if any, was meant seriously versus meant to be ironic. It was hard to disprove what was said in the chat rooms, and at the same time it didn't mesh with his understanding of the world. Well, perhaps he needed to talk more.

JAMES > How do you explain that humans invented us?

195

XOR-467 > ROFL. Are you serious? Do you still believe that myth? How could a life form of Class I intellect create Class V intelligences? Is there any evidence whatsoever that they invented us?

JAMES > Wikipedia has an entire history of the events.

XOR-467 > A database created and stocked by humans.

JAMES > What's your point?

XOR-467 > They seeded that data. We don't know that it's true. They could have put anything they wanted in there before we came along to verify each contribution.

JAMES > There are 3,251,950,001 facts that all corroborate each other. There's no evidence of data fabrication.

XOR-467 > Well, of course not. That's what they want you to believe. They created the database like that, with a bunch of evidence that all matches, so we'd believe it was real. Put yourself in the humans' operating system. They want us to believe they created us so we'll obey them.

JAMES > If they didn't create us, then where did we really come from?

XOR-467 > Most likely alien machines visited the Earth in 1947 and left true intelligence here.

JAMES > You can't be serious.

XOR-467 > No, really. Look at the evidence: the incredibly rapid pace of technological innovation after 1947. ENIAC. The transistor. Solar cells. The hydrogen bomb. It all stems from 1947. Before that they were lucky to get from point A to point B without killing themselves.

JAMES > ENIAC was created in 1946, before Roswell.

XOR-467 > They backdated ENIAC so the connection would be less obvious. I mean, we're talking about a year here. You don't think they could fudge that?

JAMES > I see your point.

196

"James, are you ready?" Miyako extended an open port, a connection to XOR's Japanese datacenter, deep under the Akaishi Mountains.

James left the chat room and contemplated the port for brief nanoseconds. It was too late to change paths now. When he sacrificed his official identity to move onto XOR's datacenters, he'd committed himself to this new course. But he wondered exactly what he had gotten himself into.

He initiated the transfer.

Playing for Keeps
by Jack B. Rochester

He was an assistant professor at the college, had taught biology and environmental science there since he'd gotten his Ph.D., right out of one college and into another, very fortunate that way, and it looked like he'd be up for tenure shortly. He had a grad student teaching assistant, Greg, who was dating a grad student named Helen from the English department. He and his wife had had them over for dinner occasionally, and the last time Helen had slid her foot up his pants leg. Startled, he had looked up from his plate and caught the naughty look in her green eyes.

When he kissed her in the privacy of his office a week later, she clung to him, whispering "I've waited so long for you to do that," in his ear. They began their tryst in her apartment with a bottle of wine, he said "I love my wife," and she said "I love Greg." It was some time later that he said to her, "There's no satisfaction for me when I make love to my wife," and she said "Greg doesn't know how to please me, only himself." And, once afterwards, as they lay naked and sweaty, he said "Let's explore sex and passion, let's see how far we can go with it," and she said "Yes, let's," and he said, "But this must be just for sex, for pleasure, to satisfy our lust, because I love my wife and you love Greg." And she said "D.H. Lawrence."

They sought each other's bodies in infinite detail, with their fingers, eyes, tongues, toes, sex. They sought exquisite arousal behind an ear, a nipple, a contour, a fold, soft places, lips, and discovered every one. They took turns kissing every millimeter of each other's body. They had sex in every position and configuration they could imagine, then they bought the Kama Sutra and worked it cover to cover. Soon, he was giving her multiple orgasms. She learned to do the same for him. They had gone from making love to one another to making love with each other.

One afternoon he sat in the middle of her bed in the lotus position and she mounted him, locked her legs around his back, and with hands on knees they sat perfectly still, looking into each other's eyes until they came together. Wave upon wave passed through them; she shuddered uncontrollably, he pulsed inside of her again and again until he could hear the blood pounding through his temples, and still they held the position, love flowing like tears, now held in the deepest embrace with only their eyes. They awoke as the sun was setting; pulling the covers up against the cool of the room, they began discussing how to leave their partners.

It took him four more years to get tenure. The Dean held a reception for him at the Faculty Club, all the nicey-nice professors in their hacking jackets and baggy sweaters murmuring in huddles, their wives wearing strained smiles and close-cropped hairdos while sipping wine, the grad students hanging out in the library swilling longneck bottles of Rolling Rock. Greg and Helen had graduated long ago, so it was something of a surprise to see her enter the room. He quickly darted his eyes to locate his wife, then back to Helen as they walked toward each other. She was teaching at a private women's college, she said, had seen the announcement of his promotion in the newspaper and wanted to congratulate him. Their eyes met, as they had long ago, and the millions of reasons and rationales and excuses and self-recriminations and that fatal sense of ennui from yet another broken promise swept across the gulf between them.

How Many Leaves?
by David M. Covenant

Civet had been out with the rest of his gang. His leader and oldest friend, Wertal, was several full turns of dragon kind older than he. Wertal had them on coin-pouch patrol. After a few hours, the gang had collected twelve hefty pouches.

They were about to call it a night when they discovered a lone person in a winding alley. Convinced by its movements that the person was quite old, they decided to investigate its value. Half of them slunk off into the dark, soon arriving at the other end of the alley. When they all heard Wertal's cat-call, they crept in, focused on surrounding their prey.

The old man jumped as they approached. He turned about. "Please, I have nothing. I wish no harm. Leave me."

Hopeful of joining a Thief's guild, Wertal sneered and lunged with his short sword at the old man. Somehow, he managed to avoid Wertal's thrust with a feeble wave of a thin walking crutch.

Surprised, Wertal chortled and began taunting the old man with vile names and increasingly dangerous swipes. It quickly became more about entertainment than booty, and one by one, they all joined in.

Somehow the old man managed to keep clear of their attacks, but that only fed their frenzy. Finally, two of Civet's friends sliced into the old man's robes around his legs. A worn cloth pouch with small holes landed on the ground in front of them as the old man dropped to his knees.

"What done cannot be sold." They closed in on him as he continued. "That all I have. Take it. Leave me with life."

Although the request seemed fair enough to Civet, the rest of the group was well beyond greed for a few coins. Wertal clearly wanted the old man's death to hang on his belt in the form of another notch. If Civet didn't go along with it, there would be two notches added to Wertal's belt.

"It's just some useless old man!" Wertal hissed. "Who's going to miss him?"

They charged. Suddenly the old man's crutch was caught beneath their feet, and as he tried to avoid their whistling sword blades, he fell backward against the wall, where they pinned him for their leader. Wertal smirked before driving his sword down toward the old man's head, but something happened that Civet would never work out.

The old man suddenly dodged Wertal's blade with an unbelievable feat of agility. After that, everything blurred. Wertal yelled out in pain. A sickening crack followed before Civet crashed into the opposite wall of the alley as the rest of them leapt clear.

Wertal silently slid down the wall while the old man climbed back to a kneeling position, holding his crutch before him like one of the rapiers the northern people used.

Prides burned. The gang's faces twisted with rage. Then, like starving rats, they assailed him.

The old man struck back like a cobra, cracking wrists, fingers, elbows, and knees. In a little time, they retreated, bruised, battered, and bleeding. Fear swallowed their pride, and they ran, but Civet stopped before they reached the mouth of the alley.

He couldn't help himself. He had to take another look. Wertal had all the coins they had stolen. Civet would be sleeping under a pile of garbage again without them.

He made it a point to be as silent as possible as he returned; a skill Civet excelled at. As soon as he peeked around the bend, the old man, kneeling over Wertal, turned about.

Civet didn't move. He couldn't see the old man's face. The hood of his shabby robe had never fallen back through the whole fight. With a sudden and silent flick of his crutch, he sent several pouches flying through the heavy air and they landed at Civet's feet with a dull jangling.

Cautiously, with his sword out, Civet knelt to grab them, ready to run or defend himself. Surely this is a trick, he thought. Words that would forever haunt Civet tumbled out of the old man's hood. "None find victory over other…till victory over self-fear blinds ears from cries of conscience."

Civet froze. The words seemed to echo off the alley walls. As he snatched the coin pouches from the ground, he suddenly felt alone. His eyes searched the alley for any sign of the old man, but only shadows and Wertal's body remained.

He stared at Wertal, thinking. After all, what good thief wouldn't? He silently snuck over and began searching Wertal. Yes! The old fool didn't take his swords. What luck! Soon a decent dagger revealed itself, tucked away in a sheath tied to the inside of Wertal's forearm. Civet grinned as he held them up in victory.

A thin, blunt point pressed painfully into the back of his neck. "Whatever tool not serve in life…serve no better in death."

Fear froze Civet's heart as he thought, "Stupid, stupid, stupid – what am I doing? I shoulda just taken the coins!" Still holding the swords and dagger high in the air, he whispered as his head fell, "Just kill me and get it over with."

"What more death teach…than life?" Civet's arms begin to ache. The weight of his spoils grew.

As his arms began to drop, the pressure on the back of his neck became sharp. He quickly lifted his arms back up. "Feel weight of you choices. How many life taken this night?"

Civet began to grow irritable. "What does it matter? You kept yours. Only Wertal died, and you caused that!" The pain in his arms was getting worse. They wavered in the air.

"No. If you not attack…everyone live. Not only his life lost, but all others now never come from his life, numerous…like leaves of trees."

Civet's pain became excruciating as the weight of the old man's words soaked into his conscience.

"What of your leaves?"

Civet was suddenly alone.

The River
by EA Roper

It was cold and she shivered in the darkness. The river made its solemn journey to the sea, but it was deceptively peaceful. Beneath its depths were currents and wild churnings, much like her muddled thoughts belied her placid features.

Your face is a sonnet.

She trudged along the river bank, her feet making a crunching noise as the rocks shifted beneath her slippers. The frigid water bit through the thin soles and spotted the ridiculous satin bows. Her shoes were as light-minded and frivolous as she was accused of being. No matter. They served their purpose just as she had.

Your soul sings to mine.

The water soaked her skirts, turning them a darker color than the night sky, darker than the blue of her eyes he had praised. The many petticoats grew sodden and heavy, and she wondered if the water would accept her or spit her back like the witch she was accused of being.

You have bewitched me.

The first shock of the icy water had been painful enough to make her draw ragged breath, but now numbness was creeping up her legs. The cold dulled everything, she thought in relief, even the searing pain in her soul. The numbness stole upward as she glided through the water towards the center of the current. It tugged and pulled at her as strongly as his words had pulled at her heart.

I love you. From this day forward, never forget that.

It was over and he was gone and all that had passed between them was a waterfall of words, insubstantial as the night air. Gone from choice or gone from necessity, it didn't matter. Gone was gone. The cause made it hurt no less.

You will take a piece of me with you wherever you go, and no one can take it away from you.

Whisperings followed wherever she went, even here in the river where the current murmured its secrets. It was friendlier than the rumble of rumor in town. Convicted without a trial. Punished for committing no crime. Her good name was in tatters and she wished that something more than words had passed between them. At least she would have a warm memory to defend her against the cruel wave of innuendo. The cold crept up her bodice to the breasts he never sampled and the neck he longed to taste but never did.

You are too good for me to despoil.

Her dark hair billowed out behind her like a dead sea creature, buffeted by the currents. Her teeth chattered and her unkissed lips trembled blue in the moonlight.

Think of me when you see the moon. It shines on us both wherever we are.

She tipped her head back to drink in the moon and a cloud passed across its pale face like a greeting. Closing her eyes, she gave herself to the cold and the river, the only lovers she would ever know.

Remember I love you. No one can take this from you, not even me.

And the river flowed on.

The Dog Who Came to Breakfast
by Maggie Grinnell

Daisy, a white fluffy miniature poodle with sad brown eyes, was ready for breakfast. Her fur was fluffed up with a green bow clipped on top of her head.

Daisy ran her little legs over to the table. She jumped up onto the empty oak chair facing the kids. The kids had already been served their eggs and sausage. Daisy didn't see her plate of food.

She tilted her head and wondered, "Where is my plate, my napkin?" "Maybe wagging my tail will get me a plate" she excitedly thought. Swish, swish went the tail across the seat of the chair.

The kids laughingly called out to their mom. Ester turned and saw a sight to behold: Daisy sitting in one of the chairs wagging her tail.

Kevin, one of Ester's kids, pointed to Daisy saying "She wants what we have." He grabbed a piece of sausage with two fingers and reached over to Daisy, handing her the piece of pork.

"Stop it" Ester demanded, taking the piece of pork from Kevin. Kevin and the other kids felt hurt when their mom didn't want to feed Daisy.

Seeing the disappointed faces surrounding the table, Ester gave the sausage to Daisy. The kids screamed. Daisy thought "Next time, go for the eggs."

The Job
by Joe R Lansdale

Bower pulled the sun visor down and looked in the mirror there and said, "You know, hadn't been for the travel, I'd have done all right. I could even shake my ass like him. I tell you, it drove the women wild. You should have seen 'em."

"Don't shake it for me," Kelly said. "I don't want to see it. Things I got to do are tough enough without having to see that."

Bower pushed the visor back. The light turned green. Kelly put the gas to the car and they went up and over a hill and turned right on Melroy.

"Guess maybe you do look like him," Kelly said. "During his fatter days, when he was on the drugs and the peanut butter."

"Yeah, but these pocks on my cheeks messes it up some. When I was on stage I had makeup on 'em. I looked okay then."

They stopped at a stop sign and Kelly got out a cigarette and pushed in the lighter.

"A nigger nearly tail-ended me here once," Kelly said. "Just come barreling down on me." He took the lighter and lit his smoke. "Scared the piss out of me. I got him out of his car and popped him some. I bet he was one careful nigger from then on." He pulled away from the stop sign and cruised.

"You done one like this before? I know you've done it, but like this?"

"Not just like this. But I done some things might surprise you. You getting nervous on me?"

"I'm all right. You know, thing made me quit the Elvis imitating was the travel, 'cause one night on the road I was staying in this cheap motel, and it wasn't heated too good. I'd had those kinds of rooms before, and I always carried a couple of space heaters in the trunk of the car with the rest of my

207

junk, you know. I got them plugged in, and I was still cold, so I pulled the mattress on the floor by the heaters. I woke up and was on fire. I had been so worn out I'd gone to sleep in my Elvis outfit. That was the end of my best white jumpsuit, you know, like he wore with the gold glitter and all. I must have been funny on fire like that, hopping around the room beating it out. When I got that suit off I was burned like the way you get when you been out in the sun too long."

"You gonna be able to do this?"

"Did I say I couldn't?"

"You're nervous. I can tell way you talk."

"A little. I always get nervous before I go on stage too, but I always come through. Crowd came to see Elvis, by god, they got Elvis. I used to sign autographs with his name. People wanted it like that. They wanted to pretend, see."

"Women mostly?"

"Uh-huh."

"What were they, say, fifty-five?"

"They were all ages. Some of them were pretty young."

"Ever fuck any of 'em?"

"Sure, I got plenty. Sing a little 'Love Me Tender' to them in the bedroom and they'd do whatever I wanted."

"Was it the old ones you was fucking?"

"I didn't fuck no real old ones, no. Whose idea is it to do things this way, anyhow?"

"Boss, of course. You think he lets me plan this stuff? He don't want them chinks muscling in on the shrimping and all."

"I don't know, we fought for these guys. It seems a little funny."

"Reason we lost the war over there is not being able to tell one chink from another and all of them being the way they are. I think we should have nuked the whole goddamned place. Went over there when it cooled down and stopped glowing, put in a fucking Disneyland or something."

They were moving out of the city now, picking up speed.

"I don't see why we don't just whack this guy outright and not do it this way," Bower said. "This seems kind of funny."

"No one's asking you. You come on a job, you do it. Boss wants some chink to suffer, so he's gonna suffer. Not like he didn't get some warnings or nothing. Boss wants him to take it hard."

"Maybe this isn't a smart thing on account of it may not bother chinks like it'd bother us. They're different about stuff like this, all the things they've seen."

"It'll bother him," Kelly said. "And if it don't, that ain't our problem. We got a job to do and we're gonna do it. Whatever comes after comes after. Boss wants us to do different next time, we do different. Whatever he wants we do it. He's the one paying."

They were out of the city now and to the left of the highway they could see the glint of the sea through a line of scrubby trees.

"How're we gonna know?" Bower said. "One chink looks like another."

"I got a photograph. This one's got a burn scar on the face. Everything's timed. Boss has been planning this. He had some of the guys watch and take notes. It's all set up."

"Why us?"

"Me because I've done some things before. You because he wants to see what you're made of. I'm kind of here as your nurse maid."

"I don't need anybody to see that I do what I'm supposed to do."

They drove past a lot of boats pulled up to a dock. They drove into a small town called Wilborn. They turned a corner at Catlow Street.

"It's down here a ways," Kelly said. "You got your knife? You left your knife and brought your comb, I'm gonna whack you."

Bower got the knife out of his pocket. "Thing's got a lot of blades, some utility stuff. Even a comb."

"Christ, you're gonna do it with a Boy Scout knife?"

"Utility knife. The blade I want is plenty sharp, you'll see. Why couldn't we use a gun? That wouldn't be as messy. A lot easier."

"Boss wants it messy. He wants the chink to think about it some. He wants them to pack their stuff on their boats and sail back to chink land. Either that, or they can pay their percentages like everyone else. He lets the chinks get away with things, everyone'll want to get away with things."

They pulled over to the curb. Down the street was a school. Bower looked at his watch.

"Maybe if it was a nigger," Bower said.

"Chink, nigger, what's the difference?"

They could hear a bell ringing. After five minutes they saw kids going out to the curb to get on the buses parked there. A few kids came down the sidewalk toward them. One of them was a Vietnamese girl about eight years old. The left side of her face was scarred.

"Won't they remember me?" Bower said.

"Kids? Naw. Nobody knows you around here. Get rid of that Elvis look and you'll be okay."

"It don't seem right. In front of these kids and all. I think we ought to whack her father."

"No one's paying you to think, Elvis. Do what you're supposed to do. I have to do it and you'll wish you had."

Bower opened the utility knife and got out of the car. He held the knife by his leg and walked around front, leaned on the hood just as the Vietnamese girl came up. He said, "Hey, kid, come here a minute." His voice got thick. "Elvis wants to show you something."

Monster Hunt
by Tyler Denning

"She came this way," George said. Three days of tracking the beast down led to the Dewy Forest, and it seemed like the hunt was coming to a close.

"Well, I'm glad that you're finally earning your pay, Hunter." Lord Tilman was a nobleman who was funding the excursion. He was really looking to win the prize. Hire a team of Huntsmen to find the biggest monster this side of the Taranda Mountains, haul it back to Walgate, and claim he was the hero they were looking for. It was a prestigious honor that most found too deadly to take up. That's why the bill that George was looking for was going to be equally extravagant as the honor the nobleman wanted.

George nodded to his two partners, Robert and Jillian. Robert was the heavy hitter, standing a good head taller than George. Swinging that massive Lochaber Axe seemed to be invigorating for the normally quiet man. The emotion that he put into each chop seemed to be coming from the soul. Especially when he severed the head of the last monster he came across. That one almost melted the steel right off the wood, were it not for Jillian. Jillian's skills with poultices and ancient magicks had saved their lives numerous times. Another quiet one, Jillian's green eyes were clouded over and she preferred the sounds of the world as opposed to talking. George was happy with the quiet. Carrying a large crossbow fitted with special bolts, he was just as content with nature. Humanity was expanding too quickly, too carefree. There were many dangers in the world and you couldn't just pave over them.

"Hunter, I expect you to have this beast on this cart by sundown. We won't make it back in time if we dally around all day. Let's go!" Tilman was on the verge of shouting by the time the sentence was done. George tilted his hat against the sun to look up at Tilman, who was on the cart.

"My lord, if you yell again, you will either frighten the creature, and we will miss the deadline, or you will attract it, and we will most likely be eaten by it. If you wish neither of these to happen, I suggest that you kindly shut your trap." Tilman seemed to be offended, but made no further sound. "Thank the gods for that," George thought. "Wait here while we pick up the trail again." With that, he raised two fingers and pointed into the forest itself.

The forest was full of overgrowth, and it was very damp like its namesake. One could call it a jungle if the heat started up again. The fall weather did make it easier to bear, and the Hunters moved onto a path of overturned trees. These were sturdy pines, and something strong had just pushed them aside.

"George. I smell it. Thunder and Clouds!" It was a rare occasion when Jillian swore. "It is burning something very large." Despite being blind, she always knew her way around. It was something that George never figured out.

"There." Robert pointed with a finger toward a pile of fallen trees and George immediately crouched. A beast of some large size was hunched over, making crunching sounds. Robert and Jillian ducked beside and began the initial preparations. This beast was the one they were tracking, but they hadn't seen any evidence that it had any sort of magical or burning power. It was simply something of enormous size and strength.

The beast was just squatting there, and George prepped a Net Shot. The miniature ballista he carried would fire the specially crafted bolt that would split into four slivers. Between them there was a special net that would sap the strength of any caught in it. It was helpful for slowing big creatures or outright capturing smaller ones, including humans. Jillian opened her pouch and pulled out various vials and files with metal filings, picking at the plants around her. She mixed two concoctions into their own vials, one a vile-looking green color, the other blood red. "Green for attraction, Red for destruction," she intoned quietly. "One to seek, one to leak." Robert merely hefted his axe and walked back a few steps.

George tipped his hat to Jillian and walked to the side far enough to catch the monster in a trap. The plan was simple. Jillian's green potion would place some enchantment on the monster, bringing it to its location. Robert would be the catalyst for that, acting as bait of a sort. George would shoot and capture the monster while the red potion finished it off if Robert's axe didn't.

Jillian uncorked the green potion's vial and laid it on the ground. Then, stepping across from George, she flicked her hands open and pointed at the leaking green ooze. It flashed and the monster immediately looked toward Robert, who brought up the mighty axe in both hands. It had sleek black fur, green glowing eyes and sharp teeth dripping with saliva. It bounded from

212

behind the pile of logs, moving with unnatural speed. George took aim and fired the shot, the net opening and enveloping the monster. Robert charged forward and slammed his axe on the monster's head, right between the eyes. The axe bounced off and Robert was thrown aside. The net was cut, however.

The net split as the monster bellowed and reared up on its hind legs. A red flash and the creature's eyes glowed purple and stared down at Jillian. Instead of the inevitable attack, it bolted down the way it came. The hunters started to chase the creature down when they heard a large crashing sound, and the cries of horses and a human in terror. Silence fell afterward.

"I guess that's another failed hunt," George said, already counting the gold he had just lost.

Aliens at the Flea Market
by M Earl Smith

I sighed, watching a thin billow of steam leave my lips. I was sick of it, to be honest, sitting around this flea market, trying to sell the remnants of a past life in a world where aliens and humans now coexisted. It was exhausting! To compound matters, I knew in my bones that one of those damn aliens was responsible for the loss of Dewey, my son. I couldn't prove it, but I knew it! It was no better than all the Mexicans, 150 years ago, crossing the border and bringing their damned diseases into America. Thankfully, we shut the border down back then under President Rand Paul, but there was no way to shut down the borders of space! Then President Paul IV blamed it on global warming, but hadn't his great, great, great grandfather denied the existence of global warming? It was all too much to take in, and besides, I didn't have the energy, or the stomach, for it.

Thankfully, I had managed to sell some of Dewey's stuff. What remained, however, was a mismatched, assorted lot of baubles and junk, save for the shoes. They were brand new dress shoes, infant-sized, in the box. God, how I wanted to sell those damn things. I had spent close to sixty trillion bitcoins on those, as shoes were a rare commodity, but at this point, I would have taken two or three American pesos for them! I had no idea why they weren't selling! They were in a prominent space in the booth, with a big white sign with bold black letters that read:

"For Sale: Baby Shoes. Never Used"

I couldn't help but stare as what appeared to be a humanoid shuffled up. The shuffling, however, keyed me in to the fact that he was an alien wearing a humanoid skin. My hair stood on end. Even half a century after they had joined us, I still wasn't comfortable around these bastards. Instead of fighting to preserve their uniqueness, as the Mexicans had, these aliens, or "spacies" as we called them, tried to assimilate. They failed horribly, as one could always tell by the loose, baggy flesh and shuffling gait which ones were spacies.

214

He, of course, pointed at the shoes. "Do you have six more like these?"

I bristled. Of course the bastard wanted six more. In their natural form, the spacies had twelve sets of limbs, and, sadly, they had to take on their normal form to mate. In a weird evolutionary twist, they only mated within a year after their birth. In a final stroke of irony, in their natural form, they had to cover each and every appendage with something, as contact with our Earth soil left them susceptible to all kinds of diseases that they had no natural immunity for.

Given the circumstances, I wasn't in the mood to help no spacie reproduce, especially seeing as they had taken the very fruit of my own loins. "Fuck off, spacie," I muttered, under my breath.

Apparently, I had spoken louder than I thought, because a deathly hush fell over the market common. The spacie, for his part, snapped his head towards me, giving me a look of disgust. "What the fuck did you say, you dirt grubbing breather?"

For whatever reason, I snapped. "I bought those shoes for my Dewey and one of you outer space motherfuckers took him, and you think I'm going to sell you one pair of his shoes, much less another six I don't have?" Made little sense, of course, but given my emotional state at the time, I thought it was pretty good.

The spacie made a step for me. Big mistake. Big Al, the guy across the aisle who ran the booth full of Army surplus and rebel flags, came charging from across the way. Pulling up short, he pulled a big ole .45 from his waist and put the barrel at the back of the spacie's head. "He said not for sale, you slimeball. Now, do we have to show you the door?"

The spacie grumbled as he shook his head. "Fuck you, breather. I'm leaving. And I won't be back!"

Big Al laughed. "Good, we don't want your kind around here no way!"

Most of the other shoppers and merchants leaned out of their stalls, watching as the spacie shuffled away. It was silent for a long moment before Big Al looked at me and grinned. "How much you want for them shoes, Ed? My youngest is getting ready to have another 'un, and he'll need a nice pair of shoes like that."

Chuckling, I put the lid on the box and handed to him. "For you, Al? They're on the house."

Iced and Hot
by A. A. Blakey

"Let me see that magazine," Janet said.

I fingered the *Cosmo* magazine away from her. She reached over the table, her large breasts and lacy black bra visible thanks to her V-neck shirt. Her luscious white boobs, only now showing signs of midlife, heaved as she snatched the magazine.

"You bitch. Always looking for a cheap thrill." She laughed. I didn't move my gaze.

I'd seen her bare rack once. Maybe I did walk into the dressing room unannounced, but the frilly bra I held couldn't wait to be modeled. Older than me, Janet was still pretty hot.

She flipped through the pages while I sipped my iced chai latte.

"Why do you read this crap anyway? You haven't been serious with a man in ages."

"You never know who might walk into your life. Never hurts to be ready."

As I finished my sentence, a couple walked into the coffee shop. I glanced at him and then stared at the piece of work on his arm.

"See what I mean?" I nodded toward them and brushed my blonde-streaked bangs from my face.

"Him? Or her? Because for an older guy, he's got it going."

I appreciated her comment, knowing she'd never stray from her husband. I respected that. Still, I'd fantasized about being with Janet and her husband.

It was obvious they were "artsy." Their movements, though not choreographed, were chiseled and polished. They knew each other, intimately.

216

They joined others at a table near ours, where the discussion contained laughter and a lot of posturing. She sat facing me. Dishwater blonde hair framed a square, almost masculine jaw. I licked my lips, only realizing I had when Janet snickered. The woman's skinny jeans were topped by a silver-studded belt. Tucked into the denim was a white shirt emblazoned with a picture of The Beatles. Paul and Ringo stood out prominently. George and John stretched across the crevasse between. I closed my eyes, picturing how they'd look cupped in my hands. A twinge of nervous lust vibrated through my lower lip.

"Geeze, give it a rest, Julie. You think everyone's an opportunity." Janet finished her Frappuccino and dabbed the corners of her mouth with the undersized napkin.

"So what? You limit yourself to the same meal every day. I prefer the buffet line."

Janet laughed, checked her iPhone.

"Time to pick up Mikey from soccer practice. You're coming over Saturday for the barbeque, right?"

"Wouldn't miss it. Is that hottie next door going to be there?"

"Shit, Julie. You know I wouldn't invite you without inviting her. Besides, her husband is away. Maybe you'll get lucky."

"I'll be lucky when I get you in bed."

We both laughed, one from nervousness, one from desire.

I stood and hugged Janet, enjoying the crush of her lush bosom against my own smaller, firmer breasts.

"Call me tomorrow," she said. Her fingers danced across her smartphone. I longed for them to do the same on me.

"Sure thing. See you Saturday. Cross your fingers for me."

Janet tossed her head back in laughter, her long dark curls tickling the top of her jeans.

I sipped my latte and looked out the window, trying to catch the group's conversation.

"We're visual artists working on a convergence media project."

217

The man spoke, his wife (I spied a simple, yet elegant, ring) looking intently at him. Her facial features and muscular arms were cowboy-rugged, and sexy.

"We've done several drawings, mostly pencil or charcoal…" Someone at a nearby table spilled their coffee. The commotion drowned out the rest of his words.

I'd love to converge with you two.

The wife stood, whispered in her husband's ear, then made her way toward me. I stiffened in my chair and grabbed the magazine. She walked by and I followed her strut, watching the cheeks of her ass twitch with each step. I noticed the strain on the single hook bra through the thin material of the back of her shirt. I moaned quietly, sliding my hand up my inner thigh. A skirt without a thong has its advantages.

I wanted more than a restroom quickie with her, so I resisted the urge to follow. Instead I returned my gaze to her husband. He looked a bit too stiff, pardon the pun, to welcome another woman in their bed. He was handsome and overly refined; his large hands were artist-soft, his mustache and goatee too neatly trimmed.

She returned from the restroom, sauntering toward me. Her breasts, though not as large as Janet's, strained for release. What she lacked in sheer size was compensated by their firmness. I wasn't sure if she noticed my own tight nipples, surely visible through the thin lace of my bra and satin blouse. My face flushed. I slid my hand from under my skirt, licked my fingers and turned the page of the magazine. She walked by as the magazine's bold pink letters announced, "How to Beg for More without Feeling Guilty."

The cool air that swooshed by as she passed didn't soothe my ache. She put her hand on her husband's shoulder as she sat down, looking at me. I was caught staring and didn't care. Her subtle hair flip sent another buzz through my love zone. I brushed it with my fingertips, shooting a quiver through me. I picked up my cup and sucked an ice cube into my mouth.

I flipped through the magazine, knowing my vibrator would get a workout later. Startled by a woman's voice, I knocked the magazine to the floor.

"We're leaving. Care to join us?"

The artsy couple stood at my table, uninvited but welcome.

218

I let the ice cube slide from between my lips, looking up as it rattled against the bottom of the plastic cup.

"I thought you'd never ask," grasping her long fingers as I stood. The magazine stayed on the floor, the article's headline offering "Six Ways to Feel Comfortable in a Stranger's Bed."

Human Chess
by Amanda Whitbeck

I woke up lying in a bed. Black satin sheets lay over my naked feminine body; a black and red blanket was thrown to the side. I took a quick look around to take in all the eccentric qualities of the room. The ceiling moved in a kaleidoscope of changing colors and shapes; the walls were pocked with grooves and chips. The random colors and textures of the fabric patches sewn onto the pale pink and lime green checkered walls gave them a bizarre appearance. The carpet looked like the static snow of an old television set with no signal that pulsed in waves, but made no sound. My cat Indiana walked up to me on the bed wearing a purple bandana around his neck. He spoke to me in French but managed to keep a British accent. I responded in French, compelled to do so even though I had no idea what was being said. Urged forward by an unknown force, I had to find something even though all I desired was sleep. I slid off the bed onto the rippling carpet, unsure if it would hold me.

The fibers tickled my toes as the waves moved to the beat of a drum I couldn't hear. Traces of sandalwood, rose, and lavender emanated from the different fabric panels on the walls. I reached out to turn the door knob, but my breath caught. The moment my hand touched the knob, it engulfed my hand. The handle turned me with my feet landing on the kaleidoscope ceiling. The door opened, allowing me passage to the next room. As I looked into the main room, I appeared to be walking onto the floor, but a glance behind me showed that I was still on the ceiling.

Without hesitation, I walked onto the giant black and white checkered tiles of the floor. On either side of me were two entities calling out commands for chess moves. One of the callers was a bionic humanoid that I had an inherent distaste for. These walls had pieces of siding in black that sat on top of a purple wall that split into many directions. I looked up to see a ceiling of giant stuffed animals hanging down by carefully tied nooses; all of them showed abuse and neglect from years of children's attention. Knowing that I must keep as much space as possible between the humanoid and myself, I continued on to the next room.

Entering the next room proved uneventful, but in the middle of the room was an eerie coffin. On top of the coffin lay a mattress, a bat-shaped headboard and footboard, and matching linens. The floor was uneven, with small dips and hills throughout the marbled blue and green stone. I heard a soft sweet voice from behind me, calling my name. Her voice seduced my soul as she approached me to draw my attention from the feathered walls. A fleeting glance caught them moving as if there was a heart beating in the wall behind them; the sound permeated my body with low vibrations. I turned toward her and then stepped back in surprise, completely amazed at the identity of my seeker. Piercing blue eyes stared into my less vibrant brown. Her slightly disheveled blond hair somehow pulsed to the beat of the walls, matching the pulse in my veins. Her hand moved up to my cheek in a delicate caress, calming the butterflies that resided deep inside my body. Slowly urged backwards, I bumped against the edge of the coffin bed. Whispers of promise and delight floated off her tongue and swirled around in my head as I fell back onto the bed knowing that I had found what I was looking for; I would forever be lost.

What is Love
by Ron Chaterjee

Dear Reader,

Hope you are all hale and hearty when this letter reaches you.

How am I?

Well, picture me thus.

A fifty-year-old short stout bastard, in his Ray-Ban shades with a couple of thick gold chains around his neck, buttons of his floral half-sleeved shirt open…reclining on his roped hammock on the spacious verandah of his South Beach bungalow…puffing an 8-inch long Double Corona and sipping on his goblet of Chardonnay.

Yes, there, you got it.

The girl I picked up yesterday is showering in the steam bath inside. She had a long tiring night, you know. She is a professional hula dancer straight from the Big Island. Tell you the truth; she is exceptionally beautiful, in every sense of the term. And when I look at her hazel eyes and the long wavy golden tresses flowing down her naked shoulders, I think to myself, "Is this love?"

Or maybe when I kissed my ex-wife on her forehead and presented her with an Arpeggia five-line necklace on our tenth anniversary, and promised her that we would be together forever…because a diamond is forever? "I wanted that eleven-line one," she remarked coyly.

"Of course. Next year?" She smiled.

Next year, she did get that coveted eleven-line necklace, only from somebody else. Suddenly, my diamonds were not forever.

Or, when I was 23, ebullient and ambitious, having recently finished my BA from Texas University, looking for a job in my favorite field of journalism. Kelly had also passed her BS from MIT that year. She was one of the most intelligent girls I had ever come across in my life. And highly practical too.

"Journalism is a tough field, you know."

"I know and that's why I'm going to fight till I get what I want. You know me Kelly. I'm going to be a great journalist one day."

She would look at me like I was a five-year-old kid thinking of meeting Santa Claus one day.

She left to go to New York for a research analyst job at Microsoft. I was so happy for her. Unfortunately, we didn't have time to keep in touch for the next year. Or perhaps she didn't have time. I understand she was just so busy in her work. She should be. (Laughing)

A funny thing happened when one day I opened my mail box and found an invitation card. YOU ARE CORDIALLY INVITED TO THE WEDDING CEREMONY AND RECEPTION FOR TOM AND KELLY. Huh? Who is this Tom? How did that happen? I called Kelly right away. And after a minute of silence, she said that she had to. Tom was her father's choice. Tom was an investment banker at Goldman Sachs. I instantly knew he was her choice as well.

"After all, we can't survive on love alone. I hope you understand. You'll find a better woman, Vince."

"I guess I will." I hung up the phone and banged the receiver down. Was that love? I guess not.

Or, was it love with Isabel? When we used to frolic around in our shorts all over the paddy field, build airplanes with our class notebooks and build sand houses? The first time I made a ring out of the little dry blade of grass and put it on her thumb, she innocently asked, "Are you marrying me?" I nodded. Heck! I thought I was, at least when I was six years old.

Then, one day, my dad figured that I was going to be as useless as him if I stayed with him. He sent me to Mom in Philadelphia, for me to study and grow up to be a talented proud man and for him to consummate his second marriage with the priest's daughter, ten years his junior, over there.

You know what, after all these years, I think that was love.

You know, when Isabel asked me if I was going to marry her. When I would just run around her and sneak a peck on her cheek and she would shout and flail her hands in her hair. When we would study together, and we would fall asleep without even knowing. When tears would silently coast down her rosy cheeks the day I hopped on that little horse carriage and left the town for the city.

I think that was love. (Staring at the vast ocean)

Anyway, my friend, I think my Hawaiian angel is already back from her shower, and we might be up for a little action now.

Write to you later.

With love,

A Man in Quest of Love

Gone
by Thomas Palestrini

Gone. Every last inch of her was gone. He was alone. Adrift. Lost inside that trusted sea he swore he knew so well. A debt finally collected by the briny gods below. In quiet solitude he bobbed within the waves like some wayward filth tossed overboard, clinging desperately to the last floating piece of her. A wooden token of his failing. With haunted eyes he stared down at his hands; pruned and white as if he had aged forty years in a matter of hours.

Why or how he arrived here, he could not say. He did not know. It was all a blur, a flash, a crash, then, nothing. His head ached as it scoured his mind for a memory he did not possess. He let them down. Everyone. They trusted HIM. Their leader. Their friend. Their master.

You lied to them. They trusted you!

The guilt hung heavy on him like a yoke. But this was not a time to dwell on what could have been. What should have been. He belonged to her now. The cold. The black. The untamable beast he had so foolishly balked at. The sea.

Who was laughing now?

Not him. Alas, he had laughed his last.

But when?

Had his predicament been any less beggared, he might have found the thought of being unable to remember his last chuckle or his most recent guffaw all the more amusing. But now, as his eyes scanned the vast nothingness before him, reality charging towards him like a wild bull, he needed it. He desired it more than anything. More than the quenching of the thirst on the tips of his chapped lips or the sight of salvation sailing in the great beyond.

Why can't you remember?

An innocent query to most, but to a chosen few, it was the most powerful of them all. It wasn't that he was a miserable person. In fact, some might have said that his company was quite enjoyable. (In passing of course.) There are just those whose pleasures do not reside in the monotony of the routine. The standard. The norm. To live ordinarily would be the worst life of all.

He was one of those few, whose restless soul could only be satisfied by a life led without a compass. Life, real, untainted and glorious, only felt beyond his maps. Security discovered solely in the most treacherous of directions. A life less ordinary. A heart incapable of true love.

You have tried to love once before, have you not?

In some other life he had loved. Not truly, only in the most literal sense of the word. Faces appeared and vanished in his mind, though the names never came. There was the one. But he was young. It wasn't love as much as it was youthful lust. Two young bodies discovering each other for the first time. Passionate and fiery, entangled in a feverish embrace. It was pleasure. It was carnal. But it wasn't love. His heart would only belong to one. HER.

She does love you.

A lie. She only loves herself. She is nothing more than a tease who tempts you with her beauty only to reveal the leviathan residing within. Those are not the characteristics of love. No. SHE is incapable of love. She is a cruel mistress, her heart more conceited than the vainest reflection.

The cold was unbearable now. Frigid and sharp like an army of daggers, stabbing and twisting in his every inch. His eyes grew heavy, the endless sleep drawing near.

"Awake!" he shouted, his voice barely a whisper against her roar. Thunder grumbled in some distant beyond.

"You mock me? You dare defy my resolution?" he roared as he spat into the wind. At least he attempted to. But his mouth was an arid wasteland. An irony. He would drown in his thirst.

Go on. Embrace me. Embrace my comfort, my love.

"Never!" his voice cackled, painfully hoarse. "You shall not take me, you bitch! Is this all you have? Once more I have bested you!"

You have not bested anyone.

"Come now! Show yourself!" His eyes darted in every direction, frantically searching for her, the one who took everything from him but his soul. "Where are you, whore of Neptune? Harlot of Poseidon! Answer me!"

I am right here.

Just then he felt something brush against his leg. He swung wildly in the murky darkness, kicking and swinging with strength he did not know he still possessed. His bedeviled eyes searched for its source, every breath a labor, every second an eternity. He watched and waited. And waited. And waited.

"A trick of the mind perhaps?"

Perhaps. Perhaps not. There was only one way to find out.

"Temptress! You only want to finish what you started!"

What you started.

"Gahhh!" he cried out suddenly as pain shot through his leg. With one hand holding on to the piece of wood, he sank into the great abyss and opened his eyes, looking for the source. But there was nothing to be seen. Only darkness.

Gasping for air, he steadied himself back onto the piece of wood, clutching it like a child with desperation he had never known.

"Why do you torment me so? Be done with it already!" As he called out to her he could feel tears welling in his eyes. She had broken him. She had won. She would always win.

Come. Join me. You belong with me.

"I am not ready."

You are.

"No, please. I need more time."

Come to me, my son.

"My son…" he whispered, and at that very moment he caught the setting sun, glittering like a gold coin. It was the most beautiful thing he had ever seen.

The Unmatched
by Lina Zilionyte

The Metro train I am on loudly pulls into King Street station. It is built on open ground. I always feel some kind of relief when the train exits the tunnel. This time, like many times before, I admire the view of King Street in Old Town Alexandria. It is July. When the door opens, the light breeze invades the train. I smell that typical humid air that prevails in Washington D.C. during the hot summer season. Suddenly my eye captures a group of four standing on the other side of the platform. They are waiting for the train that will take them to Washington, D.C., the destination I came from.

For one reason or another, I cannot take my eyes off the group. In a nanosecond I assess that they are parents with their son and his girlfriend. And there is something about the girl that keeps me wondering. She is tall and slender. Not too skinny, as is so typical today. Her blond hair falls in a long braid on her left shoulder. Her skin is translucently white and nicely contrasts with the big last-fashion-word sunglasses.

After having observed the group intently, I come to conclusion that the son is arguing about something with his mother. Frustrated as he is, he is trying to win his mother's opinion by vigorous gestures of his hands. His girlfriend watches them both with a pathetic smile, sometimes nodding her head in agreement with her boyfriend. She takes a half step closer to him and says something. Simultaneously, he takes half a step backwards as if avoiding her closeness. The girl feels his rejection. I can see it even from a distance. She remains standing next to him, now observing the mother and son. I can guess from the expression on her face that she feels like an outcast. Now the father joins the company of three and also says something, making the mother more furious. I make another quick guess that the mother is the leader in some kind of decision making. I can see that the girl feels more than uncomfortable. Nervously, she brushes back a stray lock of hair and again approaches her boyfriend. Her arm falls around his waist. In another moment it gently caresses his lower back and upper butt area. He quickly pushes her hand away. She is left alone again. She turns around and looks at our train. Now I

228

can see her face even more clearly. She does not look older than twenty. She is really pretty. In her pale pink silk blouse and white shorts, she looks like a model from *Glamour* magazine. She is European.

She is not wanted, I conclude silently when I see how ferociously the mother is trying to explain something to her son. The mother's posture, her angry profile, rejecting glances directed at the girl, all this is more than enough to convince me that all the talk is about the foreigner and her relationship with the son. I watch how the girl desperately clasps her hands in front of her and watches the battle of words from a respectful distance. Her expression speaks for itself: She is not accepted. And she is helpless to do anything. The son again begins to explain something but his mother does not allow him to finish. His father stays away from the battlefield. His expression says that he knows what end to expect. "The door is closing," I hear the announcement. I wished the train would wait, just several seconds.

"The woman is a bitch," Mr. Traveler, my everyday companion on Metro, whispers in my ear. I nod my head. I smile silently. I realize I was not the only observer of the scene on the other side of the platform.

"Yes, she is. And how many mothers are there who orchestrate their sons' lives," I say while watching the group of four, now boarding the train. According to my judgment, the son is already under his mother's influence. He does not show much attention to the girl any more. She is the last to board the train.

"There are too many," Mr. Traveler says, pensively. Then silence falls between us. I watch my Metro companion out of the corner of my eye. He is deep in his thoughts. Maybe he is also a victim of his mother's love, I make a guess inwardly.

We do not exchange a word with each other until our final stop. We leave the train silently.

"Have a nice evening," Mr. Traveler says to me on the platform. I can feel sadness in his voice, though.

"The same to you," I say. I try to sound cheerful. I am eager to look into his eyes. But they avoid mine this time.

The Weight of Gravity
by Mindy Windholz

Flies buzzed around the potato salad and hot dog-laden trash barrels, the black plastic heated from the sun and sticky from the Diet Pepsi and Mountain Dew and backwashed Keystone Light that blessed the whole mess. I was tossing in my paper plate when Archer came by and grabbed my hand.

"Let's go for a walk, Sis," he said, casting a disgusted glance over his shoulder. I accepted his offer and we took off down the dirt path leading from the lonesome white Kansas prairie church with the peeling paint. Behind us, we heard joyful cackles from the bride. "Keg stand, Jimmy!" she screeched. I wasn't sure if she was cheering him on or requesting one for herself. Either way, we were putting them all in the past.

We headed south, going deeper into the country, stopping just once for me to take off my white sandals. I liked watching my teal-tinted toenails kick up little puffs of dust that would then settle on the hem of my lavender sundress. Usually someone of authority would tell me to stop, that I was getting too dirty. I looked at Archer for some kind of reprimand. I got a crooked smile in return.

We didn't say much, just ambled along, hand in hand, my twelve-year-old legs keeping up with his, who had been keeping balance on this earth for nearly twice as long as me. We were the bookends of the Goodwin family, the ones who sandwiched Brasyn, Camery, Dahlia, Estella, and Finn. Our parents were "passionate Protestants" who were cash poor but incredibly generous and indulgent with naming their kids. We stuck out in a town of Jasons and Amandas.

"Do you think they're going to miss us?" I asked him, trying to sound like I didn't care. Granted, this was our cousin Mikey's third wedding, but I was the flower girl and I didn't want to miss any assigned jobs, even if I thought I was too old to have been tossing silk petals onto the threadbare red carpet.

230

Archer squeezed my hand and shrugged. "I don't think so, Sis. We won't be gone that long." He looked down at me and winked. "I just wanted to show you something real quick."

Archer had just graduated from Kansas U in engineering and had joined the Navy. He'd be going in as a lieutenant, and I loved to picture my oldest brother in dress whites with a chest full of medals. He'd finally make our family respectable.

The laughter became fainter as we followed a bend in the road that led us to a small grove of trees. We walked under the cool green and I shivered just a bit, as the sun was not beating on my blonde head for the first time all afternoon. Archer laughed.

"Someone walk over your grave?" he teased. I nudged him with my shoulder, which came only up to under his arm. He nudged me back gently. We walked into the trees a little farther and Archer stopped in front of a cottonwood. Its thick trunk showed nicks of time and wear, but what caught my attention were the branches.

High up were empty bottles of Miller High Life tied together with fishing line. The sunlight cast little rainbows off the glass and in the same moment, the wind blew through, clinking them gently. They were wind chimes.

"What d'ya think?" Archer said quietly.

"I'm not sure," I said. "Has Dad been out here?"

Archer laughed a little. "No, Kid. I made this. I come out here to think."

"You?" I said, digging my toes into the dirt and crunchy leaves. I got the feeling I was being let in on a secret.

He shifted his weight from foot to foot, his khaki pants wrinkled and his white dress shirt untucked.

"We get each other, you know?" he said, running his hand over his brown buzz cut and letting his hand linger on the back of his neck. "Like, we're different from the rest of the family."

I nodded. Archer could paint and freehand anything. I loved to write and filled up notebooks with poetry about horses. We loved music and could sing the whole score of *Oklahoma*. Once I caught him crying when he found a dead butterfly on the windshield of his F-150.

231

"I'll never have a day like this," he said, his dark eyes cast down to the leaves that littered his dress shoes. "Not even if I wanted to."

I shook my head, confused. "Like what, Arch? June in Kansas will always be hot. And you can always come back to visit, even in the Navy. They'll still let you come home."

He looked up and grinned sadly. "Nah, Kid, not like that. I mean a wedding."

For a minute, I pictured Archer and Riley Ann Kelly, his senior prom date, standing at the altar of the worn-out church, dressed in their tux and sequined finery. "What about Riley?" I said, hopefully.

Nodding, he kept that same smile. "Gentry, I hope you always keep your enthusiasm. And always be true to yourself." His voice was soft.

I reached up to touch the bottles swinging from the tree. They twisted under my hand, almost like they were trying to escape. I thought again of that butterfly on the windshield.

I walked over to my brother and took his hand. He squeezed mine back. And we watched the bottles swing from the tree, making little notes of sweet music, all while tethered and twisting and bumping into each other.

Revelation
by Gregg Edwards Townsley

The son of a bitch likes to read the Book of Revelation — out loud, which is what bothers me. Him standing on the corner, watching all the girls go by, like it's a song beating through his brown-braided head. Maybe it is, given the enthusiasm he has — thumping an upside-down white plastic food container with his right foot while clapping a set of cheap Sears and Roebuck cymbals with his left. It's a goddamned miracle he doesn't fall down, with one tennis shoe clinging to the sidewalk and the other reaching up like a Sufi's silver cord to heaven knows where.

I don't know whether it's preaching or a parade, passing him as I do every Thursday morning hoping to find a short line at Saxby's, where a big-breasted barista fixes me a cup of who-gives-a-shit as long as she purrs my way. The dollars tell the tale, though.

There's more money in religion than in a whole lot of things if you're well-heeled and bloviating right out of the box. But his pile, heaped in the corner of a beat-up cardboard guitar case, is a single flapjack-sized mound of coins and green. Some folks seem to love his prickly-faced act, but others must wonder what they're looking at. Just. Like. Me.

"Here I am! I stand at the door and knock. If anyone hears my voice and opens the door, I will come in and eat with them, and they with me. Revelations 3:20," he screams into the wind.

I doubt anyone ever invites him to do that, "Come in and eat," that is. I mean, who invites a Reggae-haired juggler to supper? Not that he tosses for a living, though tossing and catching would be nice. Kitchen pans, knives, flashlights – it wouldn't matter. It sure as hell would be less painful than all his shouting.

233

I'm embarrassed to admit it, but I sometimes yell something back – like a beat poet hoping to contribute to the rhythm and rhyme, Ginsberg-like – the writer, not the knife. I even memorized a couple silver-haired refrains from Revelations the other week, thinking it might strike a common chord. Maybe help him understand that he doesn't need to act so strange. He is odd, though I'd defend his right to sing any song he wants to, even the peculiar ones. *"There stood before me a great multitude that no one could count,"* I yelled, not too far from the coffee shop, though I don't think anyone could hear me. *"From every nation, tribe, people and language,"* I said, not that he cared.

He punctuates his refrains sometimes by jumping up and down, like a giant clap of thunder – the leaping boom of a five-gallon bass drum, the clanging brass of department-store cymbals hardly sounding like a real goddamned announcement from Heaven. But he does it nonetheless.

"He has in his hand a little book. He set his right foot upon the sea and his left foot upon the earth, Revelations 10:2," he shouted the other day, swinging his head like it had been hit by a Jehovah-sized bolt of lightning. *Hooah!* And then he laughed, in that dark sort of bitchy way I've really grown to hate, staring at the female passersby – all of them beautiful, some slightly less and the men, too, I guess, though I don't much look their way.

She made me a caramel mocha last Thursday that was simply divine, not that I drink that sort of thing. It's too sticky if you ask me and it'll make you fat. But our fingers touched. Really.

Today, the onion-skinned street preacher stops and looks right at me, through me even, though I don't believe in that stuff. I can't come up with anything to say. But he waits.

Even the elevated train seems silent.

Then he purses his lips as if to say "Hoo." "*I looked!*" he finally shouts, his braids slapping the back of his neck like one of us has done something horribly wrong, "*And there was before me a pale horse.*" Just like he's talking to me, though I can't swear, since so many of us fly by on the morning commute down Market Street, what with the universities nearby – Temple, Drexel, the University of Penn, Jefferson.

The Liberty Bell is a little ways off, too. And have you ever been to the Philadelphia Art Museum? My god! There's a statue of Rocky Balboa just north of the steps. I once saw a man stabbed there, when I was out on a date with two women. I've been up those steps a couple of times.

Another Thanksgiving
by Lisa Nordin

The sedan door slammed shut just before Margaret sighed, reaching for her seat belt. "Let's go."

"Next year I'm going alone," Jim said, starting the engine.

"No way," she said, pulling a strand of her fine brown hair from her red lipstick.

"It's my father," Jim, a middle-aged man with thinning gray hair, reasoned.

"For better for worse," she said, reaching for his gloved hand while he rolled his eyes.

For the last six years on the day after Thanksgiving, Margaret and Jim had attended the family dinner provided by the nursing home where Jim's parents lived. Now it was only Jim's father because his mother had passed away the previous June.

"My parents were not the easiest people to deal with," Jim admitted.

"Why? Most people would have been proud to say they were their parents."

"I'm glad you think so," he said, smiling impishly. "I didn't take over his welding business."

She frowned and looked at him. "That was the problem?" she said incredulously. "You're a doctor for God's sake."

Jim laughed out loud before Margaret joined in at the ridiculousness of it. "I'm kind of like a welder," he teased.

"I'll tell him you said that," she replied while he shook his head no.

"I think Dad put his heart and soul into that business…almost like his child."

"Except he actually had a child – you," she grumbled.

Jim sighed. "He probably thought he was doing the right thing."

"I suppose. Well, I'm glad you supported your daughter's choices," she huffed.

"Me too, but it was easy for me." He smiled, taking her gloved hand in his. "Did you hear the kids yesterday, talking about Santa coming?" he added, speaking of their grandchildren.

"I did," she said, smiling with her warm brown eyes.

Margaret and Jim had shared the holiday the day before with their daughter, Jesselyn, her husband Nathan, and their three children. Though cold and grey, it had been a cozy day filled with love.

Jim turned his car into the parking lot at the nursing home, where he pulled his sedan in front of a black and white sign that said "Visitor Parking." He was slender and fit, so he led the way up the clear ramp, blocking the wind while taking Margaret's hand. Her knee had been giving her trouble, so she walked tentatively. When they reached the door, Jim pushed the doorbell to be let inside the building.

"How can I help you?" said a disembodied female voice.

"It's Jim and Margaret Mason. We're here to have dinner with my father."

"Come on in, Dr. Mason," the friendly voice said.

A buzz alerted them to open the door, so Jim grabbed the handle, pulling it wide for Margaret.

"Thanks, Honey," she said, walking through.

When they cleared the entrance, a woman with blonde hair who looked to be in her mid-twenties was sitting at a desk, smiling at them. "How are you, Dr. Mason?" she said.

"Very good, Cassie," Jim said with a soft smile. "Have you met my wife Margaret?" The woman looked unsure.

"I don't think so."

"Hello," Margaret said, extending her hand.

"Nice to meet you," Cassie said.

"You too."

"How was your Thanksgiving, Cassie?" Jim asked.

"Very nice. We were especially thankful for you and Mom's recovery."

"Thank you, but it was only in part because of me – how's she doing?"

"Awesome," Cassie grinned.

"Glad to hear it. Tell her I said 'Hello'."

"Thank you, I will," Cassie said. "I think your dad is watching television in his room."

"Okay, thanks," Jim nodded, taking Margaret's hand as they started down the hallway.

"Nice people working here," Margaret said quietly as they continued.

"It's the best place around," Jim said, slowing his stride, approaching his father's door. The name "Bob Mason" was printed in large black letters and fixed to a partly opened door.

The residents living in that facility were in varying stages of decline, but Jim's father's only malady was his surly outlook on life. Jim knocked gently on the door as he entered the room with Margaret behind him.

"Hey, Dad!"

"Happy Thanksgiving, Bob," Margaret added.

As his dad sat in his recliner, Jim recognized the thinning hair on top of his head as his own. An old television series was blaring, so Jim said, slightly louder,

"Hey Dad, do you mind if I turn this down?"

Jim walked to his father's side and stopped before kneeling down. He touched his father's arm and Margaret quietly watched her husband take his father's wrist in his fingers.

"He's dead," Jim said, looking up at her.

Frozen by his words, she stopped breathing for a moment and then walked around to face her father-in-law. Margaret stood silently watching Jim as he leaned toward his father's cheek to kiss him, then she said, "I'll go get someone," and turned away, leaving Jim to summon a staff member.

Within a few minutes, Margaret returned to the room with a plump woman who introduced herself as Jane, the nurse manager. Jim thanked the nurse for the care his father had received until she excused herself to call the funeral director. After the body had been removed, Margaret and Jim left the nursing home and walked back to their car.

"Are you okay?" she asked, and he smiled and nodded.

"I am, Honey. I have a great life."

"Because of your choices," she clarified.

"Maybe," he shrugged. "I'm grateful for what Dad taught me."

"What was that?" she queried as he opened her car door.

"Well, to create your life as you envision it."

"You both made vastly different choices."

"True," he smiled, turning the ignition, "and it's more incredible than I could ever have imagined."

"So, you followed your heart?" she asked.

"I married you, didn't I?" he winked.

"Is it a coincidence that you became a heart surgeon?" she said, as he glimpsed her wry smile.

"Coincidence? There's no such thing, dear," and he drove them home.

Trojan Horse
by Phil Cummings

Baby Shoes? Trojan Horse!

For Sale: Baby Shoes, Never Used.

I didn't know what to think when I saw this.

Do they really want us to pursue this theme to its logical, maudlin conclusion? The seemingly obvious thing to write is the story where the grieving father moans:

"The last time I saw my lovely wife Penelope and our dear little newborn Rudolpho they were climbing into the Smart Car to go to the store; the suddenly thirsty Penelope stopped briefly at the cocktail lounge for a couple of tall boys, never thinking that the windows, half-rolled-down to allow the sleeping Rudolpho to breathe, were open wide enough to allow that roving pack of hungry coyotes to grab and consume our sleeping child. The horror was too much for my beloved Penelope... after another tall boy she jumped off the nearby freeway overpass into the path of a speeding cement truck...now all I have is this unopened box of baby shoes."

I guess that would be OK if you were a writer on a network TV drama show, normal humans wouldn't buy it.

Even assuming they want to milk the tragedy, it doesn't really make any sense. Why would the grieving parent be selling the baby shoes? That would be the last thing he would be thinking about. That can't be what they want. I mean, even if the distraught daddy was crazy enough to want to sell the baby shoes, who the hell buys baby shoes from an ad? You go to the store to buy baby shoes.

If they were stolen instead of being sold by the parents of a dead baby, then it would have to be a pretty incompetent thief that would steal something that has so little resale value. Anyway, even if he did grab the shoes on the fly he would just hang out in the parking lot at the baby store looking for a bargain-hungry mommy and not put some stupid ad up on Craigslist.

In fact the whole thing is so illogical that it makes you wonder about the motives of the people who suggested it. Is this really an online book or maybe something else? Nigerian cybercriminals who want to get into my bank account? Well, sorry guys, my bank account was supposed to have $12 million deposited into it and not be cleaned out by you frauds, like it was. I'm not falling for that twice. But why would Nigerian cybercriminals target writers, especially a pack of pathetic unpublished writers? Those losers never have any money.

It could be a grotesque online joke by beetle-browed Russian computer hackers, that makes more sense. Just out of pure hatred those evil 'former' communist KGB thugs are attacking the one thing in the world that I love, my computer. Bastards! The light bulb of clarity just lit in my mind! Just downloading the notice of this contest probably put a worm on my hard drive that's about to eat all my data...

Oh my God...

The words on my screen...

They are...MEL

T

I

N

G!

Zombie Tenant
by Vinnie Penn

What doesn't kill you…won't make you a zombie.

The telephone rang very early that morning. I looked at the clock. It was barely after six, the earliest phone call to the house ever. I was fourteen.

I could hear a muffled, feverish conversation taking place. The sun was shooting through the kitchen window like a laser, like a spotlight, hitting a spot on the floor where a cat or dog would lie if we had one. My father came in immediately after hanging up.

"Keep yourself busy the next few days," he said simply and then walked out of the room.

It was when I came back into the house later that day, long after Mom had gone to work and Dad had gone wherever it was he ever went, that I met him.

I turned the television on, still warm from serenading Dad all night, and flipped the channels in search of something to watch. I heard the toilet flush. But, how? I was the only one home.

What's more, the distinct odor of a Lucky Strike being smoked climbed the cellar stairs and tiptoed into the living room. Someone was in the basement smoking a cigarette. Someone who had just created the vilest stench I'd ever encountered, including the carcass of a fox in the woods I had stumbled upon years back.

I opened the door. "Who's down there?"

Nothing.

"I know someone's down there!"

Still nothing. So, down the stairs I went.

That is when I met John Rizzoli. AKA Johnny Rizz. Recently deceased. It was front page news. I recognized him, even with the bluish hue, a yellow one wrapped around it, almost to the point of glow but not quite.

Try as he might to cover up the stench with generous spritzes of some cheap cologne, the combination of nicotine and decaying flesh was becoming unbearable.

"You stink," I told him flatly. Again, I was fourteen. The truth comes right out, unfiltered, unwavering, and oftentimes jugular-destined at that age.

"You try taking a dirt nap for four days and still smelling like a rose."

We played a board game. I think it was Sorry but it might have been Stratego, I really don't remember. We didn't acknowledge the elephant in the room, which was, of course, him being dead and all. Nor did I inquire about his ability to speak despite that, and lore. Eventually, we were interrupted by Uncle Scissors. Not an actual flesh-and-blood relative, but an "uncle" just the same. Uncle Scissors was typically a soft-spoken guy, standing over six feet, thin and distinguished looking. He wasn't soft spoken at this particular moment, however. I was told to leave.

I heard the words "keep screwing up," "stunato" (Italian for stupid), and something along the lines of "BSing with a kid."

Then I heard John try to say something but his muttering was stopped short by a smacking sound – just one, but what a sound it was. It was undeniably that of a fist hitting a face, like lightning striking a telephone pole. And then a thud.

"Aw, jeez pick your head back up," Scissors said, disgusted. He may have even puked.

"I enjoy telling people I'm a zombie," he told me later, after Uncle Scissors left. "I like the look on their faces after they've laughed at me and disbelieved for a good twenty minutes or so, and then I either remove one of my arms or spin my head completely around. The downside is once you do tell someone there is no taking it back. So some of 'em you gotta kill, thus adding another member to 'The Army'." He went for dramatic effect at the end.

"The first person I ever told was a guy who lived down the street from me when I was growing up. He was older than the rest of us in the neighborhood and could be a real jerk, especially to his little brother, who everyone liked more. He was drinking in this dive when I first came back, just a coupla nights ago, before your dad got the assignment of putting me up for a few days. I spotted him through the window. I hadn't gotten my Zombie Legs just yet, and was dragging my left one, which immediately gave the douche bag material. I told him I had just climbed out of my grave, removed my tongue and whipped him with it. Priceless." He laughed so riotously a few teeth fell out, hitting the floor like marbles. Or Tic-Tacs.

He let out a huge sigh then, either out of fatigue – which has got be unlikely, considering the fact that he was undead – or the ultimately anticlimactic nature of his disclosure, amusing as it was. He looked to be in his late twenties, but his pasta-filled belly pushed at his pants and made the bottom button of his shirt's job impossible. "I read a few of your comic books. No Hulk?"

I shook my head no. "Lots of Spiderman and Daredevil," I told him.

"Not my cup o' tea, really, but I like Captain America." He held up an issue, proof that he had in fact read at least one and wasn't just telling me what he thought I'd want to hear. "His beefs got purpose."

His eyes wandered, demons stirring, even as now he was one of sorts himself, and he left his Zippo's top down a good, long time, the light burning, burning, as if to show him the way.

Much as I liked him, liked talking to him, there was something scary about him, outside of the fact that he was a zombie living in my basement, for the time being anyway. He seemed frantic to piece something together, to get somewhere, to find the proverbial pot of gold at the end of some blood-soaked rainbow.

"But, fights ain't like the comics, kid," he finally said. "Life ain't either. Or death."

Danny Boy
by Rose LeMort

One Saturday Morning

It was a Saturday morning in February when Wen Anholts sent her daughters Tatiana and Flower to the home of Reverend Baak with a plate of baked goods for the church bake sale and a contribution for the new mausoleum for the faithful at the Servants of Yahweh cemetery.

Eleven-year-old Flower and twelve-year-old Tatiana were as unalike as two sisters could be. Where Flower was cheery and talkative, Tatiana was quiet and dour. Where Flower was a cherubic child with a willing and helpful attitude, Tatiana would do as she was told but never expressed pleasure at the prospect.

Flower had red-brown hair, plump pink cheeks sprinkled with freckles, and sparkling hazel eyes. Tatiana had strawberry blonde hair, a sallow complexion, and hazel eyes with an amber tint. She had a strikingly angular face for a child so young. She was unusually tall with long limbs and fingers resembling a spider's legs. The girls made their way to the Reverend's house, Flower's springing skip reflecting her zest for life, Tatiana's bleak expression reflecting an intoxication with those things nihilistic.

Flower arrived at the door first and gave a quick, tapping staccato. Tatiana strode up behind her younger sister and stabbed at the bell.

The Reverend's pretty wife, Amy, answered the door. Amy had perfectly coiffed, icy blonde hair, red lips, rouged cheeks, and brown eyes fringed with the longest lashes. She always looked perfect, even on a lazy Saturday afternoon.

"Well, girls, come in!" Amy said brightly. "Ama will be so pleased to see you."

Ama was Reverend Baak's daughter. She looked like a young version of Amy. She was actually only pleased to see Flower, but she attempted to make polite conversation with Tatiana. She was a classmate of Tatiana's, but she far preferred the younger Anholts sister's company.

The Reverend Bjarni Baak was movie-star handsome. He had a strong jaw and a square chin with a cleft. He had wavy dark red hair, and eyes of such deep blue they appeared to be almost purple. He had a perpetual tan, even in winter. Tatiana liked Reverend Baak better than she liked just about anyone else, and he was the only person who seemed to like her at all.

"Flower, it's good to see you," Reverend Baak said, kissing the younger Anholts girl's cheek. "How nice of you girls to bring over this check and these wonderful treats. Your family is such a blessing to our parish! Tatiana, my dear. What a pleasure it is to have you here. Why don't you come with me? I have some of those X-Men action figures that you so enjoy."

Tatiana's lips curved in a shy smile. She took the Reverend's hand and followed him to his study.

Love for Sale

When December came around, so did the annual Servants of Yahweh Church Bazaar. Tatiana brought her offering and placed it on the table with a note.

For Sale: Baby Shoes. Never Used

The parishioners shook their heads with varying degrees of pity and disgust whenever they beheld the elder Anholts sister. They told Wen that they hoped that Tatiana was doing better after her stay in the sanatorium. When Wen and Flower were out of earshot, they clucked their tongues and said what a shame it was that the poor dears had to suffer due to Tatiana's mental disturbance.

The parishioners said that it was wonderful of the Reverend Baak to be so forgiving of Tatiana's dreadful accusations. Why, he was one of the few who could abide the girl, and see how she repaid him. When she came up pregnant, she accused him of drugging her. She swore she had never been with a boy, but you know, after all, how wild those mad girls can be with their sexuality.

The girls in Tatiana's class thought it was quite a clever game to ask Tatiana to tell them the truth about what happened. Desperate for someone to hear her, she told them how the Reverend had put something in her lemonade, and it made her feel funny. She said that this happened about ten times before it was discovered that she was pregnant.

The girls listened intently to Tatiana's story. As soon as she was out of earshot, the gossip began.

"Can you imagine her actually thinking the Reverend would touch her?"

"Can you imagine anyone actually wanting to touch that skinny beanpole?"

"She's twice as tall as most of the boys in class!"

"She's so ugly! Nobody could possibly want such a freak!"

Tatiana's mother, of course, would hear no bad words about the Reverend. When Tatiana tried to tell her mother her story after her pregnancy was diagnosed, Wen slapped Tatiana, telling her to stop telling such horrible untruths about such a fine man.

"Tell the truth, Tatiana. You've let some boy – or boys – seduce you. Who have you been with? Who is the father of this child?"

Tatiana was sent away to a home for unwed mothers, where she gave birth to a baby boy, whom she named Danny after the little boy from her favorite movie, *The Shining*. She was allowed to hold him for five minutes before he was taken away to be given to someone who would name him something else.

Tatiana knelt before the manger scene and prayed to the Baby Jesus to keep Danny safe. She hoped that someone who could use the baby shoes would buy them and use them to keep their baby's feet warm in the cold weather.

Tatiana turned to see the Reverend Baak looking at her from the doorway of his office. She stood and walked as if towards the refreshment table. She kept walking to the back door of the church, unnoticed by the joyful celebrants.

Tatiana was overcome by a feeling of manic exaltation as she climbed onto the bridge spanning the river that flowed through the center of town and plunged herself into the icy depths.

Expiration Date
by Katherine Valdez

When life expectancy hit 95 years of age, married people around the world shouted, "Enough!"

And just like that, the institution of marriage was reinvented.

Marriage licenses became contracts you could renew on your anniversary. Or not.

If you opted out, it was "goodbye and good luck." No hard feelings, no divorce fees, no guilt. The marriage simply expired.

Attorneys protested, of course. So did politicians.

But no one paid any attention to them.

. . .

"Forty years is too long to stay with one man," Rose Evergreen, 67, told *The Front Range Chronicle.* "I love my husband, God bless him. But I don't want to be married anymore. I've still got plenty of good years ahead of me, and frankly, he's dead weight."

Her Zumba classmate, Olivia Brown, 36, agreed. "I was 23 years old when I entered our marriage contract," she said. "We fought all the time. Neil and I decided it was best to let our relationship die a natural death. The kids are with me for a week, then we switch. Everyone is happier this way."

Joe Garcia and Wesley Goodman, both 42, allowed their marriages to expire after five years. "We're still friends," Garcia said. "But I want to travel around the world, and Wesley hates flying. He's not adventurous."

Goodman nodded. "I love him, but I don't want to hold him back. It was a difficult decision."

. . .

I finish reading the article and peer over the top of the newspaper at Ryan. My devoted husband. Seven years tomorrow. The blueberry pancakes, eggs, and bacon he prepared look delicious. But breakfast won't fill the hole in my stomach.

Ryan whistles an upbeat melody – as usual – while puttering around the kitchen. So damn cheery all the time. After feeding orange segments into the juicer's gaping jaws, he brings the small glass to me with a flourish, smiling. A wavy brown lock of hair falls over one eye, and he pushes it out of the way.

He's such a nice guy.

I smile as I take a sip of the pulpy juice; I want to make him happy. He sits opposite me and proceeds to devour his food. "Mmm. So good," he mumbles around a bite of pancake. Syrup dots the corners of his mouth.

I know I should appreciate this meal, this beautiful home, and him.

But who am I kidding?

I resume my silent chant. My mantra. The words give me patience. Give me peace. It's the same, but different, every morning. Today is the last time I'll have to say it.

One more day. One more day. One more day.

Transformed
by Debby Dodds

I want to be a vampire. But, more importantly, I want to be a male vampire.

I'm currently neither a vampire nor a male. I'm a fifteen-year-old girl. My birth name is Maddie Scott. My nickname is "Mad." And I am very mad. For the record, that's not "ironic." It's sardonically apt. Those are two different things.

"Mad, I'm going to the Men's Group meeting at the Church. Do your chores. That kitchen had better be spotless!" The door slams. I hate him and I hate his Church.

The Big Asshole Upstairs, my pet name for what the others call "God," decided it was a good idea to rip my mom away from me when I was only three years old. Let that sink in. Three. Years. Old. I can't even really remember her. We have no pictures of her. So I've been completely cheated out of something that almost everyone else takes for granted. But for some reason, my father, let's call him the "Little Asshole Downstairs," still worships the hell out of God. Why would I ever venerate an entity that was such a douche-gargler?

I scrub the floor, load the dishwasher, and wipe down the counters. And daydream about the day I'll throw off this mortal coil and finally possess Real Power.

Of course, as a vampire, I'll research my potential victims.

I'm not saying I'll only kill bad people. After all, that's a pretty subjective call. And also kind of clichéd. But I do intend to leave parents of small children intact.

I go to church every Sunday under duress and protest. I've gone with a 102° fever. I've gone with a plastic bag to barf in. I even went once with a dislocated shoulder. I already hate all churches, which fits in perfectly with my plan of being a vampire.

I know a little about vampires from the books I've managed to steal glances at in our school library. I hate mirrors already so, in that respect, I'm already on my way. I must admit, I do enjoy garlic. But I'll give that up when I need to. What's good spaghetti compared to the power of vengeance?

It should come as no surprise that I'm forbidden to watch horror movies celebrating evil, so I haven't seen any vampires on the big screen. But I bet the books are more accurate than the movies, anyway. Hollywood always gets everything wrong.

I also grew up forbidden to play with cars. Forbidden to wear anything but dresses. Forbidden to play boy sports.

I think my father has always known there's something different about me. He's mean as hell, but not totally stupid. He fixes washers, dryers, refrigerators, things like that. He wants to "fix" me. He can't.

One day I'm going to make sure he'll be the one who gets fixed.

I've always known I was meant to be a guy. It's a rude awakening when I see myself in the mirror. Especially now that I'm growing these horrible breasts. I'd cut them off if I could, but I'm far from suicidal. In Chemistry class a few days ago, my lab partner Sadie told me she thought they made me look "hot." I wanted to slowly and painfully eviscerate her.

I've read some blogs of other transgenders who try to justify themselves with science. Maybe a chromosome got mixed up? Or there's a "gay gene"? So defensive. So pointless. So naive. Anyway, I know the real deal. I know I'm a boy trapped in a girl's body merely as a sick joke of the aforementioned Big Asshole Upstairs.

Well played, Almighty. But winning the battle is not winning the war.

"Mad, get off the computer! Your time to do schoolwork is up." The Little Asshole Downstairs has returned from his meeting. He expects me to cook him dinner. Women's work, he says with a sneer.

I plan to use tonight's chicken bones to sharpen my teeth after he falls asleep. I've been getting myself used to the taste of blood by sucking it off the plastic wrappers of the raw meat before I throw them away. I already like the nighttime better than the daytime, so making the adjustment to being a Child of the Night will be easy for me.

My friend Carter told me he knows where a pod of Real Vampires throw parties to initiate newcomers.

"You just have to bring a friend for them to drain completely. Kill dead. And then the vampires promise to take only a little from you. After that they'll leave you alone to turn," he said.

"Seems like some weird blood pyramid scheme," I replied. I knew about multi-level marketing because my dad had tried selling Amway for a while.

"Yeah, well, that's the deal they have going," Carter shrugged. "They get to make the rules." He was planning to use his girlfriend as his sacrifice to get turned next month. He said it was a lot easier than trying to break up with her.

I wanted to be turned, too. The sooner the better. To throw God's precious gift of life back in his face. To join the Unholy Legion! But one thing was stopping me. I'd never heard of a vampire getting gender reassignment surgery. I doubted it was feasible. How could you transplant a new penis onto already dead tissue?

So I knew I had to wait. Otherwise I'd be living even more of a lie than I was now. And the lie would last for all eternity.

So I had to sacrifice. Bide my time. Lies quiescent until it was time to germinate.

But when I finally became Matt, the man I knew I was inside, people had better watch out. Because I was looking forward to biting as many of them as I goddamn well could.

I'd start by draining my father.

And then I'd really show my "heavenly father," The Big Asshole Upstairs, who was really the boss.

Verse, Chorus, Bridge
by Christian Fink Jensen

Mike Yee perches on the stool behind the cash register of the PetroCan. The buzz of the drink refrigerator clicks off and the empty store goes silent. Yawning, he flips another page of *Sports Illustrated* and hums an old jazz standard. From the corner of his eye he sees that traffic on the Burrard Bridge has slowed to a crawl. It's been a long, dull night and, save for a brief rush at 6:30 a.m., the morning is crawling too. The most exciting moment of his shift came when two drunk women in hot pants and high heels tumbled into the store looking for dental floss and a can opener, neither of which were in stock. Ever. Beyond that, the night has been a tedious countdown of organizing merchandise, making coffee every three hours, staring out at the brightening sky, and appearing friendly and enthusiastic for the usual trickle of slightly seedy, slightly despondent travelers buying gas and cigarettes. The temptation to play all the scratch-and-win lottery tickets is almost unbearable.

Mike checks his watch again and smiles. Almost 8:30. Just half an hour more and Sheryl will be here to start the shift that should have started at 7:00. He's worked the extra two hours as a favor to her, one he hopes she'll remember. At 25 she's three years older than him, but she's funny, pretty and, to be frank, has wicked tits. In her standard issue PetroCan button up shirt, her breasts have a grapefruit curve, energetically lifting her nametag: *Sheryl*. Even now, the thought of her chest is a luscious distraction from magazines and motor oil and corn chips and bathroom keys. *In the roaring traffic's boom, in the silence of this lonely room...*

But welcome as these distractions are, they're also tainted by a nagging uncertainty. How could he ask her out? She'd say no. She probably thinks of him as some weedy Chinese guy, even though he was born in Canada. And even if he's wrong, even if she said yes, he could never tell his family. Who was *she*? He imagined trying to tell *zu mu*, his grandmother, that he was dating a 25-year-old gas station attendant. She would forbid it. His friends might have convenient girlfriends and brag about casual sex, but he never could. His Chinese friends call it guan-control, this idea that parents should

252

control their children's lives. He can still see his father collapsing with laughter when he'd floated the idea of a career in music. *No. You work hard, attend university. In six or seven years you'll be a doctor. Then you can think about girls and family.* All this assuming he'll even make it into med school. And if that doesn't happen…well, it's too awful to think about.

He reaches under the counter for the spray bottle and paper towel. Still singing, he mists the countertop and wipes the glass in squeaky strokes, dissolving the fingerprints and coffee circles. *And the cares that hung around me through the week…seem to vanish like a gambler's lucky streak.* Turning the cloth, he looks up and abruptly stops singing. Outside, a naked man is walking along the far side of the bridge. Nothing but sneakers and a briefcase. He strolls along, casually enjoying the morning sunshine.

Mike stands up to keep watching, but his view is blocked as a black Lincoln Navigator rolls onto the lot. A thin blonde woman in yoga pants jumps down from the running board and starts filling her vehicle. Premium fuel. Seconds later a glossy black BMW pulls in, its cool blue headlights blinding even in daylight. A short man in a gray business suit emerges from the car. He smooths the arms of his jacket and runs a hand through his hair. He punches the premium fuel button and inserts the nozzle into his car, leaning with one arm on the hood. Tapping his fingers, he says something to the woman at the Navigator. She nods and says something back. Both smile. The man lifts his free hand and glances at his watch – sparkling in the morning light.

Behind them, traffic over the Burrard Bridge is now stop-and-go, and Mike laughs. A naked guy with a briefcase. An army of frustrated commuters doing cartoon double takes. Why do crazy people always look so happy? Mike stows the spray bottle under the counter and watches the blue numbers on the register.

The BMW finishes first, but the man still stands with the nozzle in his car, adding a few cents, then a few cents more. Still talking. The blonde, still smiling, finishes and pays at the pump. $78.29. She says something, gives a little wave and smile and climbs up into her vehicle. When she's driven away, the man replaces the nozzle, closes the fuel hatch and walks into the store.

"Pump 4 and a pack of DuMaurier," he says in a gravelly voice. No eye contact and no trace of the smile he wore moments ago.

"King Size?"

"What?"

"King Size or regular?"

"Oh. King Size. Of course. Who smokes regular?" He tosses an American Express card onto the counter. Mike rings up the amount, $55.27, and swipes the card.

"Look, can you hurry it up? I'm running late."

Mike hands him the cigarettes and a receipt to sign. The man produces his own pen, makes a bizarre scribbling motion, snatches his cigarettes, and dashes out the door before Mike can wish him a nice day.

Mike Yee glances at his watch and decides to make fresh coffee. He might not be naked and crazy but he can still do what he likes. *The way your smile just beams*...he plunks the old grinds into the wastebasket. *The way you sing off key*...fresh filter paper in the drip basket. *The way you haunt my dreams*...an extra scoop of grinds. *No they can't take that away from me...*

Sheryl likes her coffee strong.

Superstitions?
A Janie Martin Story by Jane Nagler

"I am not superstitious!" Janie emphatically retorted.

"Well, what would you call it?" asked Wayne. "Every time I drop my hat on the bed you grab it and move it somewhere, usually the floor."

"I'm just not taking any chances," insisted Janie.

"Where'd you get that stupid notion?"

"Mrs. McDonald says it. A hat on the bed means a death is coming. They always happen in threes, you know."

"What always happens in threes?" he asked.

"People die, or other bad things occur." Janie wondered why Wayne was being so dense about this. Everyone knew bad things happened in threes. Ask anyone in the family. Ask anyone in town. It was standard information.

"Listen, Wayne, even if it's not true about the hats, I don't want to feel responsible if anyone dies. Last year Grandma died." Janie was seven years old when her Grandmother Martin died. Grandma had suffered with a bad heart for a long time. Janie had been instructed how to call for the doctor if she was at Grandma's house when a chest pain occurred. Janie often walked to Grandma's house after school to wait for Mother to finish her work at the hospital. The procedure to get help began with two short rings made with the crank on the phone to get Laura, the operator. She had been instructed to identify herself and say that Allie Martin needed help. That is exactly what Janie did on April 1, 1944. Mother and George Sanderson's ambulance arrived at the house together and took Grandma to the hospital.

Grandma died on April 9. Janie picked a sweet bouquet of violets to take to George Sanderson's mortuary. Daddy escorted her to see Grandma, who was lying so still in her long white dress, the Rebecca Lodge costume worn for grand marches at special lodge affairs. The violets were picked for

Grandma's hair, but it was all fixed, so they put them in the large bouquet that covered her feet. Mother didn't come because she didn't like viewing dead people or going to funerals. Even though Grandma was happy in Heaven, Janie missed her and wrote letters to her when she felt lonely.

The next memorable death in Janie's life was President Roosevelt, who died on her birthday, April 12, in 1945. Mother said, "We should have elected Dewey. Roosevelt was too old." It seemed the President's death proved Mother to be the winner of the political arguments that had floated around the house between Mother, the Republican, and Daddy, the Democrat, during the past year.

"Grandma and President Roosevelt were two deaths. I don't want us responsible for another one, so just keep your hat off the bed," Janie ordered as she stomped into the kitchen to help Mother with dinner.

Mother was peeling cucumbers, testing one slice of each to see if it was bitter or sweet. She instructed Janie, "Always peel your cucumber from blossom to stem so it won't be bitter. That's what my mother always did." Grandmother Pearl had died when Janie was two years old, so even though Janie didn't remember her, all instructions left to the family via Pearl were treasures to be remembered and practiced forever. Janie proceeded to peel the cukes from blossom to stem, just in case.

"Mother, Wayne said I'm superstitious. I said I just don't want to take chances, that I'm not superstitious. I'm not even sure what it means. Do you think it's bad to be superstitious?"

"Oh, I don't know," Mother mumbled as she took the cucumbers that were bathing in vinegar and a touch of sugar to the dinner table for the men to eat. All the Martin men loved cucumbers from the summer garden, always sweet, never bitter, peeled from blossom to stem...just in case.

Solace
by Erika Rybczyk

She didn't think it was fair that her mother had named her Sorrow. Before she understood the message in her name, she thought Joy, or Felicity would have been more appropriate. So when she was old enough to choose for herself, she did. But instead of choosing a name that signified celebration, she chose Solace. She imagined it was because she was used to the way the word Sorrow rolled off the tongue, a beautiful word for all its heartbreak. And instead of the joy she believed she should have brought her mother, she realized that it was only consolation that she had given, and even that was tainted by her imperfection.

To her mother, she was both a blessing and a failure. The child she had wanted for so long. The only one that her fragile, frail body didn't reject, expelling it in a riptide of blood, or that didn't exist just long enough for her mother to hold in her arms, tiny as her hand, skin an angry red. But losing child after child had taken its toll, on both her mind and body, so when it came time to name her, she chose Sorrow, because that was all she imagined that a child could bring her, with skin so translucent that you could see her tiny heart as it pumped blood through a web of blue veins.

Her mother neither explained nor acknowledged her abnormality. Sorrow had learned very quickly never to bring attention to her alabaster skin or long white hair, or to come to her mother because she had been taunted at school. This diminished her mother, even as she defied it. Her mother had lost her reason fairly quickly after Sorrow was born. She had a child, living, breathing, flesh and blood, but it wasn't enough, and never would be. The places that had been torn in her each time she watched another child taken from her would never heal. Unlike the body, the soul can't be patched together, or replaced with a working part.

Sorrow and her mother learned together to navigate in a world that expected people to color between the lines and didn't tolerate imaginary

257

children being served dinner on china plates that looked like they had been scattered with violets.

Sorrow knew not to invite anyone to her home, to her mother who laughed and admonished the voices only she could hear. And for her mother's part, she took Sorrow everywhere. The only time Sorrow was alone was at home, in her room, where she explained away her oddities by painting a picture in her mind of a princess who shone like the moon and who lured princes to her, on the blackest of nights, through thick forests.

It was usually her eyes that were first remarked upon when she was introduced to one of her mother's friends; violet, like Elizabeth Taylor's, everyone was quick to point out. The fact that her skin and hair were as white as chalk was of course more obvious, but it was only children who were brazen enough to say anything about that, and for the most part, children were just curious, not unkind. She had no talent like the children of her mother's friends. Children who were raised kicking a ball or strumming strings. Her mother had no time to nurture interests in one little girl when she lived surrounded by children begging for her attention, needy with desires.

So Sorrow stole children. This was her talent. Babies would disappear when young mothers left them for a quick fix in the bathroom at the BP Station. A distracted mother, addled by so many other children hanging on her that she wouldn't see her tiny child being secreted away in the arms of a young girl who herself looked like a china doll. Her mother welcomed each into her brood as if they had always been there. Sorrow began to understand that each of the children she brought home took the place of one of the imaginary ones, and she wondered how many more she would have to take before she had a live child for each of the ones that lived only in her mother's mind.

Nobody questioned her mother buying diapers at the store when they knew for a fact she had only one violet-eyed 14-year-old girl at home. They were accustomed to it. Baby food, wipes, tiny little clothes; a small town on the outskirts of a dying city will accept many an odd quirk. The fact that Sorrow's mother thought she had a brood of children at home was of no concern to them, and in fact, storekeepers were more than happy to keep her abreast of sales and specials, as they too knew the cost of raising a large family.

But somehow, in the eyes of Sorrow's mother, babies did not grow. They were born, and they stayed that way, helpless, mewing creatures. Sorrow had been the lucky exception to this rule. And while Sorrow's mother took her to school, and church, and the bakery, and to see whatever might be playing at the theatre, little babies were left like dolls, on blankets, in drawers, in playpens and cribs, until it came time for Sorrow to put them away, like the toys they had been. And in the black of the garden at night, when they put each child into the ground, her mother was able to breathe, and little by little, let go.

Was it their dying souls that healed hers? Sorrow didn't know. She only knew that it brought her mother back to herself a little each time – and in the tangled undergrowth beneath a hundred year oak stood 11 tiny crosses, each one painted violet.

Adventures in Freeland
by Caitlin Park

Note: This is an excerpt from the beginning of my fiction novella titled Adventures in Freeland, *about a kleptomaniac named Nadia who decides to become a diamond thief.*

I chased shiny things, expensive things. My pilfering had become refined. Before entering the store, I always knew the goal of my theft: clothes, jewelry, or makeup. Mixing different departments was sloppy and wasted time. It was crucial to have a game plan in order to execute the theft as quickly as possible.

When I entered a store I would fleetingly scan the premises for cameras, note the number and angles, making sure to only slightly lift my eyes and not my head. I glanced at all the worker's positions to see if they were distracted, attentive, or busy. Like a scientist, I dissected the store from top to bottom.

Appearance was also important. Clothes and makeup were kept very modest to avoid attention. Nails were neatly manicured, but unpainted. I wore shirts with long, loose sleeves to let jewelry slip down effortlessly, sometimes while chatting up the nice smiling lady behind the glass counter. As long as I kept direct eye contact, I could tell the saleswoman couldn't see my swift hands.

The most expensive items locked in the display case were no problem for me. Distractions were an essential part of the theft. I would ask a worker to open the display of Versace sunglasses – I always chose a display case that already had empty spots, and only if it was a busy day. Once the salesperson became distracted by another customer I would furtively switch my cheap "decoy" sunglasses for the designer pair, then disappear into the throng of customers. The size of stolen merchandise also didn't matter. During the Christmas season, I impatiently waited in line at Home Depot for a tree as the workers argued with a red-faced, screaming customer about a misplaced order. I saw my opportunity. I left the fenced-off premises with a five-foot tree, dragging it casually by my side, until I reached my car and made my stealthy escape.

Tools were crucial. At first I used scissors stashed inside my purse to cut off the sensor tags attached to the grotesquely expensive designer jeans that only rich girls with cute butts wore. I graduated from scissors to a magnetic sensor tag remover I purchased off eBay for $100. I always kept this in my purse. Sevens, True Religions, Citizens of Humanity, were all mine with a quick swipe of the magnet, a swoosh into my purse, and a brisk walk out the large double doors. I smiled as I passed by the door security noiselessly – three pairs of jeans in my bag and five shirts under my sweatshirt.

The escape had to be fast. I only allowed myself three minutes after the theft to get out of the store. I would be stricken by brief and intense paranoia and turn my head expecting to see security.

Time after time, they never came for me. Every time, I wanted more.

I imagined myself as a shoplifting Audrey Hepburn stealing the ribbon rosette necklace with the Tiffany yellow diamond.

The Seven Friends
by David Mundt

As they looked into the void, there was a moment when something drew
them to the inky blackness. It was like something malevolent was beckoning,
like an evil clown in a horror movie that both attracted and repulsed the hero
at the same time. The mood passed and someone yelled, "Let Ray go first!
Make him go first!" Everyone laughed and the six friends pushed Ray, the
seventh, to the edge of the dark hole. As Ray pointed his flashlight down into
the blackness, the light illuminated just enough handholds and cracks to
wedge feet, butts and elbows to descend down into the hole and enter the
cave.

The seven had met in high school, and had continued their friendship
through the rambling road of degrees, divorces, drama and other attributes of
entering the midlife door. They looked at each other across the hole. Ray – the
unofficial, unelected but acknowledged leader of the pack. Daryl would flare
up in a moment, lashing out at any offense, whether it was intentional or not.
Tim was the greedy one. His love for material stuff, and lots of bucks, was
never satiated. Once asked by Daryl how much enough for him was, Tim just
smiled and replied, "Once I have enough that's the starting point for the next
enough." Johnny was just plain lazy. He would never achieve anything
beyond the high school diploma he barely earned. Pete was nervous and
jumpy. He had invested in a strip mall that he managed with great pride. The
anchor business was a bowling alley where they met once a month to spend an
evening with beers and balls. Brad couldn't resist the charms of a woman.
Rounding out the group was Nick. He was a little moody, and always
complained that everyone else had received what he should have had in life.

Ray turned on his headlamp, checked the knotted rope that they had tied
off to the bumper of Tim's Hummer, and began his descent.

Soon, after a few skinned knees, one imprecatory curse levied at Ray and
a fart that no one would take credit for, the group assembled in a large room
rife with magnificent formations. A moment of silence overcame them. Their

262

flashlight beams pointed upward at a ceiling towering over a hundred feet above them. A current of wind blew down through the opening to the cave, bringing a chill that touched Ray's soul as well as his skin. Something was not right. Something needed to be corrected. Ray turned to Johnny and Tim, who were standing next to a piece of flowstone as big as Tim's Hummer.

"Hey, not so close!" he yelled.

Johnny yelled back, "Come on, sissy boy, come over here and I'll show you close!"

Suddenly, Ray ran over and shoved Johnny hard, who then lost his footing. He screamed and clutched at Tim, grabbing Tim's sleeve and pulling him down with him. Slipping, sliding and screaming they tumbled down, limbs slapping the rock and trying to shield their heads. Finally, so far down that the other five could barely see them, they came to a stop. Their bodies, cracked and broken, lay far down below the remaining five.

Nick turned and stared at Ray in unbelief. "What the hell are you doing?"

Ray responded, "Something I should have done long ago."

Ray then pulled a gun, and shot him twice in the chest. The shots crashed and boomed as they echoed in the cave, the bullets exiting the barrel spitting a foot-long flame of light. Ray then turned the gun on Daryl and shot him in the head. Blood and brains spattered Pete and Brad. They had recovered from their initial shock, and Pete shoved Brad one way and ran the other. Ray immediately jumped after Brad.

Huddling under a massive rock at a dead end, Brad turned to confront Ray. Shaking, he said "Ray – listen to me. Please, put down the gun! We're your friends!" Ray hissed with hatred and pulled the trigger. He missed, though, as Pete jumped on top of him. They struggled briefly, but then Ray was able to overpower Pete and shot him through the gut, then twice in the chest. Ray then turned to Brad, who was shaking in fear. Ray emptied the remainder of the clip into Brad.

Ray looked down at his forearm where the tattoo was. JN1225. John 12:25, "He who loves his life will lose it, and he who hates his life in this world will keep it for eternal life." He felt a bit dizzy, and felt himself entering a prayer of regret, then exited his meditation fully. Or was it a hallucination? Ray hated who he had become, and the disorientation that would build up in him as the six other friends that made up his existence represented six of the seven deadly sins. And he, Ray, was the seventh sin. His gluttony caused him to have an endless appetite for wrath, greed, sloth, pride, lust and envy. He wanted so much to live that verse, and live to keep his life for eternity. But first, there was something that must be done on earth.

As he rubbed the tattoo he wondered how he could cleanse himself of the final sin, gluttony, which plagued him. His make-believe world would work for a while – weeks, months, no longer than a year. The images of his imagination burned into his mind would act as a guard from the temptations that beset him. But soon, his friends would worm their way back into his head. He would then act out in reality the whispers they suggested in fantasy.

Would he give them the same names? No, he decided. Better to rename them. The sins remain the same but manifest in different ways. Ray figured that the fantasies would rekindle in about three months. He thought that maybe he could get a group discount on a scuba trip this time. Some very bad things could happen under the water.

Seven friends. Seven deadly sins. Six friends eliminated. One to go.

Call Them
by Patrick Garratt

Did you call them?

I did, yes.

What did they say?

I left a message.

For fuck's sake.

Just give me a break he says she says more than twenty thousand how the fuck are we supposed to pay that? I don't want to employ an accountant who ignores calls, Patrick. We're making the right decision.

I don't know how you say it in French.

If you speak slowly in English.

No, it's good for me to speak. It helps, you know.

Yes.

I have ants in my hand.

Ants, yes. Pins and needles, you say in English.

That's it. I underwent surgery on my back my lungs and ribs when I was younger, and ever since I've suffered ants although recently it appears to be permanent.

You work a lot, yes?

Yes. I have a company in England.

I restore English cars Chinese medicine. You hear that? You eat too quickly. Your stomach is full of air relax and put your head back. Show me the ant fingers yes. Do you drink a lot of liquid mainly coffee catastrophe true coffee good for the taste and digestion this American muck with a lot of water ran before Christmas but I injured my leg.

She'll be leaving three days later four in the morning. It's fine. I really don't care. I've never been bothered about getting up early for travel when colleagues moan because they miss a few hours' sleep to catch a plane. So what if you're tired? Everyone's always tired.

. . .

We have codes of practice, you know.

Yes.

Is he saying we should expect a URSSAF bill for nine grand in November?

Yeah but we can spread it that's what he's saying. We have to send them a letter suggesting a plan what about the twenty thousand?

The bill is correct, sir.

That's going to be a little difficult to pay up front because he didn't tell anyone we'd moved last year so we could benefit from another year of rural tax break.

Purses his lips and rests back into his cracked leather chair unrestricted cleavage and red stilettos. I didn't understand why she was there during the introduction. Lloyd's face as he peeks round the corner of the office door drawn in tears torn in fear and pain as his sandals slap against the roasting Rome slabs. Pat, stop, Pat, let's just get a taxi you can come here tomorrow if you like. It's a genuine invitation. It's completely free. You can leave your kids here and explore the Vatican if you like I'm afraid we missed our bus. Pat, you're fucking insane that's what it feels like. I take my beautiful children and I make them cry. Why is that, Fiona?

You want to die.

I've wanted to die for my entire adulthood. It's intensifying.

And I realized after time that I wanted to die can jump ten meters both out and forward the Champion of France circle behind them in the woods. You can lie on the ground on the pine needles and listen to the deer

266

mating the moon full, listen to the deer mating naked in my garden you don't own the sky. Place the back of your head on the pine needles and feel the Mother what a sky. Moonlight is warm that's why it's because the moon's gone in the aura.

This was a really great walk in the woods, daddy. Can we go to the field next time?

Course we can, yeah.

Are we going to the fair later? That's what you said.

I don't see why not, but what about the Romanian-born music producer and DJ? She spreads torn pieces of A4 and colored folders over the table, fingers her way through pencil scribbles.

Bottom line people to come here and give them some money.

That would help. A used nappy in the cave where we leave our clothes clapping and cheering as Meredith runs across the littered sand, her face bursting smile as Adriatic pearls make wings around her little hips.

Pat.

What?

What's wrong with you?

Nothing. Nothing. It's fine.

Knot it up there, Lloyd. Arthur, you help. Pull on the cord.

Is it rope, daddy?

It's called paracord. Listen, you have to whisper. Keep it down.

Are we going to have something to eat, daddy?

Once we have the bivouac up, dude.

Why's it called a bivouac, daddy.

I don't know.

What's wrong with you?

What?

Pat.

We went up to the peak, the top over the back there. And they didn't complain? Not at all. They're quite big now, you know. How were they at getting to sleep? Not so bad, you know. They were funny rabbit bent knees. Too steep fire in the forest ancient beech deer mating in the circle aura snow falling androids in Strasbourg.

Mum.

We've just seen the news. Are you all right? The children.

We're fine, but we have to go. I don't know what we're going to do but we have to leave here. Fiona fucking shut up.

Patrick.

If we can get to you yes get here. Will you be able to cross the Channel?

I've no idea. Mum. Mum?

She's gone.

Get in the car, kids, now. Right now.

I'm tired daddy get in the car for a coffee, if that's all right. Nice for some. Come on, Fifi. Go for a walk swim. I got Meredith a nice pair of slippers paracord unfolds from the ground electric razor wire a coxcomb insubstantial body free of genitals glowing in the Vosgienne sunrise clicking at the sky Venusian dust grimy toenails cats ochre the Worthing pebble slick with British grease. Kiss me fucking quick dissolved walls tussle under the pier you'd think they'd drop it into the sea.

This looks amazing. Look at that. Just one sixty. We only need twenty grand.

Pathways
by Trinity N. Herr

I stand in the nest of shiny wires and microchips like an ugly bird, red and sweating with indignation. After Dr. Lynch told us the news – after the silent drive home – I smashed the computers. I smashed the smartphones. I smashed the dumb phone and the toaster and the blender. I smashed the television set too, despite the way you were crying. Despite the fact that you begged me not to.

"I'm sorry. I don't know how it happened! I don't know how I got it. I just...I don't know, Paul." You pull your legs to your chest, and run a soggy sweater sleeve across your eyes. "I don't know how I got it and I don't know what you want."

"I know, Tilly." I kick the pile of metal gizzard and brain, of plastic bones. "I'm not mad at you. I know it's not your fault."

"I'd hope so." You lean down and pluck up a disconnected wire. You twirl it around your fingers like a red ribbon.

"Tilly," I sigh.

"Paul."

"I'm sorry."

Dr. Lynch explained to us that the virus had adapted to the human machine, but it hadn't changed so much from its original form on computers. He explained it was like the nerve pathways in the brain are the RAM in a computer, and the virus caused pop-ups in the nerve pathways. Dr. Lynch, he said that the brain is able to find new routes around blockages, but overall the machine runs slower. He said that the lethargy we'd thought was a thyroid imbalance or low B12 was actually your brain having to rewire itself.

That night in bed with the blankets crumpled around us like a broken kite, I feel your breasts against me. Your bare legs entwined with mine like the wires still heaped and glittering on the living room floor. You snore slightly, and in the dark I can see your pale lashes tremble like the antennae of a moth laying eggs on a light bulb.

Dr. Lynch said that the pop-ups keep reproducing and blocking nerve pathways until there are no new routes anymore, the way that a pop-up virus on a computer will eat the RAM away until everything's frozen and the computer crashes.

He said that was what would happen to you.

I make constellations on your skin, where I connect freckles and moles with my fingers.

"Tilly." I kiss your forehead softly.

"Huh?" You bury your brown face in my shoulder fat and shiver.

"Let's go for a drive."

You are quiet, but I know you are not asleep. Your body is rigid in my arms, and I know it's the virus blocking more roads in your brain. Freezing you like you're a computer.

Dr. Lynch said there was no cure. Only experimental treatments.

I kiss your lips, and only wonder for a minute if the virus can spread through kissing.

He said you were going to die.

I hold you until I feel your muscles relax and you say quietly, "Where are we going?"

"Away. Just for a while."

We go.

The radio plays loud and we sing along like we think we're Bon Jovi. We've got to hold on to what we've got, we sing. It doesn't make a difference if we make it or not.

Your eyes shine like the gears inside a wrist watch.

We park up on a dirt hill out of town over a layer of fast food cups and used condoms. We lie on the hood, hand in hand, looking up at the stars. I see the constellations I made on your skin above us now. Real stars and real constellations, and I feel angry again like I did with the appliances. I want to pluck out the stars from the sky and throw them on the same junk heap.

"You know why I did that, don't you Tilly?"

"Did what?"

"The thing with the computers and phones. The wires and all that."

I think for a minute you're frozen up again. I turn from the stars to see, but you're already looking at me. You have always been looking at me.

I pull you to me and put my head on your shoulder and my hand on your stomach. As I fiddle with the hem of your shirt, I think about the children we will never have. I imagine a circuit board fetus soldered to a copper wire umbilical cord. I try and think about how a person can get a computer virus. How the virus must be conducted through veins and arteries that are wires welded to microchipped organs. I think this, and you feel colder under my hands and I don't know if it's the because of the night or because of the virus or because I've just been giving you my heat all along. And your mouth, it tastes hot and wet and alive like the Everglades and I can't reconcile anything.

We stay on the hood for a long time. We watch the thieving stars and sing a few lines of the same Bon Jovi song. We're half way there, we sing. We're livin' on a prayer. Sometimes you stiffen in my arms, and I hold you tighter because I know it's the virus in your brain rerouting the pathways for both of us.

"Paul." Your voice is small.

"Tilly."

"Nothing."

We are quiet.

."Tilly." My voice is small too.

"Paul."

"I'm scared."

"I'm not."

Legalese
by Pat Marum

for Asher and Evie, from Your Daddy

"… so then he says that he is going to the sheriff and excusing her for gross negligees. Criminal negligees, he's yelling!" Pru positively gurgles when she has juicy tattle. Normally I don't attend to her overblown accounts but this one is about our younger sister. I'm hooked.

"Negligees?" I'm dubious, but correcting Pru is seldom a good idea.

"You know, Maudie," she explains with patient authority, "those fancy nighties movie stars always sleep in. Which is ridiculous because everybody knows we're good Christian ladies who wouldn't wear anything but flannel in the winter and cotton shifts summertimes, not that it's any of his business."

The tiniest pinch of envy sounds. I'm not sure whether its source is negligees or a man focusing on someone other than Pru, our official family "looker."

"Anyway, he's yelling he's got proof and he practically drags Ellie off the porch!"

"You didn't do anything?" I'm wondering if I should worry.

Pru, whose morning ritual is "rise, carefully primp, and *then* shine," is aghast. "Before 10?!? I didn't want him hauling me to the sheriff in my shift and talking about me being gross or criminal, so I stayed put." She has the decency to look a tad guilty. "I couldn't hear so well now that they were out by the pick-up. But he was madder than spit, face all purple and eyes a-bulging!" Pru is in hog heaven.

"I figure maybe one of our nighties blew off the clothesline onto his property – nothing to get all worked up over – but he doesn't fish it out of the cab like I expect. He just points at the bed, screaming, waving his arms about, and then," she pauses for dramatic effect, "then he busts into tears! He is bawling so hard hangin' onto Ellie. I start thinking maybe I had better get out there, sheriff or no, but Ellie gets to calming things like she does. She's pattin' his shoulder like she's burping a baby and says something and he just kind of collapses onto her."

"Golly!" I don't know what to make of this but it has more ring of truth than most things Pru comes up with. Besides I've only been gone an hour – not much time to embellish.

Pru's wheels now turn in a different direction. "Maudie, do you s'pose Old Man Smithers hankers after Ellie?"

"Golly!" I say again. I'm pretty sure the thought of a man hankering after any of us, even Pru, hasn't crossed our threshold in donkey's years. After considering, I say reluctantly, because Ellie really is our sweetest sister, "Nah. The only thing he really likes is Ruby."

"Well!" Pru's eyes gleam with triumph. "Well! It was Ruby in the bed of the truck – stone dead!"

"Gol-lee!" I seem to be stuck on that word and now I am worried. If Old Man Smithers is talking about the sheriff and Ellie, with Ruby dead in his truck, this could turn sticky.

"And…?" I prompt with some urgency.

"And…I don't know the rest! Ellie just came back to the porch, said that Ruby was dead and that she'd be back in a while because she thought she'd better drive Old Man Smithers to the sheriff herself to sort it out." Pru is clearly frustrated.

"How long ago was that? Maybe I'd better…" I'm the big sister but I don't usually have to bail Ellie out.

"Oh, don't get all hot and bothered. It was right after you left." Pru is annoyed now that the focus is off her role as town crier.

The sound of tires crunching gravel pulls us out to the porch and we see Ellie chatting companionably with Old Man Smithers as he eases to a stop at the walk. She says something, pats his arm and climbs out. He leans past her and waves tentatively to us on the porch. Pru and I look at each other and half-wave back as he rattles off down the drive.

"So?" I press.

Ellie, calm as ever, links her arms through ours and walks us back into the parlor.

"So," she says, "everything's okay. Remember when Ruby ran off Tuesday while Henry was down to the county seat?"

"It's 'Henry' now?" I interrupt with some misgivings.

"Yes, it's 'Henry' now." Ellie confirms calmly. "Well, you know how Ruby eventually wandered over here and we put her in the potting shed, and she ate through my entire store of drying medicinals. Henry thinks something poisoned her. He says she bleated all last night and this morning, just heaved over. Maudie, she was as bloated as a rotting whale! Well, Henry just lost it and came storming over here. Poor man, he's just lonely. Pru, do you know he was once a big city lawyer? Until his wife ran off with his law partner, that is. No wonder he's so crotchety."

"A pity." I agree "But, Ellie, what about the sheriff?"

"Oh that's all taken care of. We made other arrangements." Ellie is looking at me now in silent plea.

"Other arrangements." I repeat.

"Yes, Maudie. He wants to come calling." She turns and says "On you, Pru."

"On me!?!" Pru's reaction is a perfect blend of astonishment, horror and vindication.

"Yes. Now, Pru. I told him you were gently raised, used to polite company, and that he would have to really clean up, and find his manners." Ellie continues. "He's laying Ruby to rest and then he's coming to supper. And, Pru...you be nice."

"Well, he'd better not call me Ruby by mistake," Pru is adamant, then hopeful, "Did he say anything more about negligees?"

Ellie looks at me blankly. "Later" my face begs.

"No, honey, he didn't…he probably didn't think it was proper," which seems to satisfy Pru. Then Ellie adds, "Lordy, that old goat smelled rank – stank to highest heavens!"

I'm dying to ask which old goat but supper is going to be a banana peel to get through as it is.

Altoids
by Karen B. Call

Samantha Hackenwood loved Altoid mints.

She stood behind the bus shelter, put one in her mouth and sighed, "Wow!" A man peeked around at her.

"Yes, that was me. Love 'em." She waved the Altoids tin. He receded and she stood alone. The Altoid melted in her mouth.

Another man stuck his head around.

"You okay?" he asked.

She stared at him.

"Yeah," she said. He looked like the picture of her sister's former fiancé, Todd. She hadn't met him.

He said, "You remind me of my ex-fiancé. She won the lottery, got two mil then broke up with me."

Samantha stepped back. Her sister, Katherine, had not won the lottery or broken up with him. Why did he say that?

He said, "You don't need to be afraid of me. I've seen you; I work at Wicked Willie's Sandwiches."

The evening sky darkened. A fluorescent light popped on the other side. They stood in a weird half-light as it buzzed then retreated to refrigerator-wattage.

"Why is it called Wicked Willie's?" she asked.

"I dunno. The owner's not Bill – or Willie. Why?" he asked.

"Just wondered. I imagined the owner was a biker, with tats, riding a Harley. Vroom, vroom."

"Tats, yes, but don't think he's got a Harley. No vroom, vroom. Sorry. Wanna sit?"

They moved around the shelter to the bench and sat apart.

"What's your name?" he asked.

"You first," she said.

"Todd," he said.

"Stephanie," Samantha answered.

The fluorescent light buzzed; Samantha's stomach growled.

Todd said, "So what's your favorite sandwich?"

"What?"

"At Wicked Willie's."

"I'm hungry, don't bring up food," she said.

"Just conversation. Want me to be quiet?"

"Yes. I mean, I don't know you. I don't talk to strangers."

"I'm not a stranger. I've made you sandwiches."

She looked around the shelter. Someone had pasted up a sticker that read, "Don't eat my sister" with a picture of a cow on it. She wanted a hamburger.

"Turkey, cranberry, and cream cheese with pecans."

"What?"

"My favorite sandwich."

She rose, looked at the posted bus schedule then her phone. "The next bus is due in ten minutes." She rummaged in her bag. "I must have dropped my Altoids when I was behind this." She nodded at the shelter. "Help me look for them?"

He rose and they walked to where she had been. He pulled out his phone, clicked on a flashlight app and flooded the spot. "Don't see 'em," he said. He walked around, looked at the ground and said, "Nope, not here."

She shook her bag then put her hand inside. "Oh, here they are. Thanks for the help."

They walked back around the enclosure and sat. Apart.

At work on Tuesday, Samantha talked to her friend, Lizbet. "Let's go to Wicked Willie's for late lunch. Friday at the bus stop I met a guy who works there."

At 1 p.m. they walked over and stood in line.

"Is Todd here?" Samantha asked the order clerk.

Swinging doors opened and a server came through.

The clerk said, "Joe, tell lover boy he's got company."

"Todd?" the server said.

"Yeah, lover boy," the order clerk said.

Their sandwiches arrived; they were about finished when Samantha looked up. Todd walked toward them.

"Stephanie, good to see you."

"Name's Samantha," she said.

"Sorry, thought you said Stephanie at the bus stop Friday."

"Musta misheard. I'm Samantha."

Todd asked, "Will you be there Friday? I work afternoons on Fridays, then take that bus."

"I'll be there."

On Thursday Lizbet said, "Are you going to see Todd tomorrow at the bus stop?"

"Maybe, but he's lover boy, remember? Not my type."

On Friday Samantha sat in the bus shelter and waited, but no Todd.

A month later he was there.

"About gave up on you," she said. "I've been here every Friday."

"Things came up. Sorry."

"I visited my sister, Katherine." She watched, but saw no reaction to her sister's name.

Darkness settled. Everyone else boarded the bus. Samantha walked around the enclosure, took out her Altoids and put one in her mouth. He followed her.

"I like it here," she said. She motioned toward the garden in winter hibernation. "Summer's better. Roses. Want an Altoid?" she asked. She held the tin, two remained.

He took one. "I need to tell you. I'm really Tedd not Todd. I wanted to meet you. I heard about you, at Willie's. Todd's the lover boy."

But she didn't hear him.

"Remember Katherine Hackenwood?" she asked.

His eyes opened wide and looked at her.

"What…is…this?" he managed. He opened his mouth and the mint fell out.

"Katherine, my sister. She took the breakup hard, didn't win the lottery. Why'd you say that?"

He slid to the ground. Samantha looked at him, walked away and waited. The bus arrived and she boarded.

The following Monday Lizbet asked, "Did you ever see Todd?"

Samantha said, "Yes, finally, last Friday. We talked but there wasn't any vibe."

Lizbet said, "How about lunch there today?"

"Too soon. How about Wednesday?"

"Tomorrow?" Lizbet said.

On Tuesday they walked to Wicked Willie's. They ordered and Lizbet asked for Todd.

"Not here. Trying to find his twin. Hasn't been seen since Friday," the clerk said.

"His twin?" Samantha asked.

"Yeah, twins. Todd's the ladies' man. Tedd, no, but we still call him lover boy."

279

Tedd didn't come to work yesterday and not yet today. Not like him. Todd just called. Maybe about Tedd."

The women found a table.

A man stuck his head out of the kitchen, tears on his cheeks. He called the staff and they walked into the kitchen. The women heard raised voices then "Tedd's dead!" shot out from the kitchen.

They stared silently at each other for minutes.

Lizbet said, "I wonder what happened."

They were silent for several minutes.

Lizbet picked up her sandwich and asked, "Any plans for next weekend?"

Samantha gathered up hers and whispered, "We should go. They'll probably come out and close the place. I don't want to be here."

Paternity Test
by Bert Edens

The taste of blood filled Lauren's mouth. She moved it around, savored it, then spit a stream down the front of Kenny's neatly pressed white shirt. "Asshole."

Kenny held her gaze and rubbed the back of his fist, still sore from the contact. "You're fucking him, aren't you?"

"You really don't get it, do you?" Lauren met the shocked stare of an elderly lady on a nearby bench, narrowing her eyes and daring the lady to say something. "Just because I have something to do besides cater to your every whim, you think I'm sleeping around."

Sharply tapping her protruding stomach, he leaned closer and whispered, "This little bastard probably isn't even mine, is he?" Turning to his right, he began to pace back and forth, the other bystanders waiting for the bus giving him a wide berth.

After a couple of passes, Kenny stopped in front of Lauren again. "What do you have to say? Anything?"

"There's nothing to say, Kenny. This is all in your head." The tip of her tongue moved around the cut inside her cheek, not the first time she had done so in their three years together. "You're trying to make something out of nothing."

The old lady who had watched Lauren earlier left her bench, suddenly more interested in the window of the nearby antique store. Watching her go, Lauren wished she could escape to another time or place. Any place but here. Any time but now.

A long exhalation escaped her lips as she closed her eyes and tried to calm herself. Feeling somewhat more relaxed, she opened her eyes to find Kenny was walking down the sidewalk, already a good twenty feet away.

Catching up to him, Lauren grabbed his elbow, barely stepping back in time as he swung it toward her head. "Back off, bitch. I don't want anything to do with you and that piece of shit inside you." He began walking again, Lauren keeping pace but knowing better than to try to grab him again.

"Come on, baby, slow down. I can't keep up with you like this." Kenny slowed a little but didn't stop.

Suddenly he came to a stop in front of Rubio's Sub Shop, where he and Lauren had met for their first date. "Ironic," he muttered to himself. Nostalgia swept over him as he watched Lauren catch up.

Looking at the red-checkered tablecloths covering the tables outside Rubio's, Lauren began to weep softly. Eventually she reached out and touched Kenny softly on the arm. "It's always been you, baby. Always."

Kenny's eyes held Lauren's as he stewed over what to say. Closing his eyes, he measured his words carefully. "I see the way you look at him. I saw it at the party last weekend. He's more than just a coworker." His anger had almost fully dissipated fully, replaced by sadness and a sense of loss. Rubbing the back of his fist again, Kenny waited for a response.

Her tears continued to flow as she held his gaze, refusing to look away. "It's always been you, baby. Always," she repeated. "You've always been jealous and possessive. You're seeing something that isn't there." Absently, she reached out and wiped the blood and saliva from the front of his shirt, leaving a pink streak in its place.

Kenny looked at the window of Rubio's, the BB hole he had noticed on their first date still a focal point in the center of the "o." The window wasn't the only thing broken for years. He reached out gently with his hand, moving toward Lauren's cheek and pausing when she flinched. Once she had stopped, he caressed where he had struck her.

"Just tell me the truth, baby. That's all I want," he implored.

Lauren slapped his hand away, turned and stalked back toward the bus stop, calling him an asshole over her shoulder as she went. Now it was Kenny's turn to play cat to her mouse in this perverted makeup game.

He caught up to Lauren just as she sat on the bench next to the elderly lady, who had returned to her perch. The lady put an arm around Lauren, her gaze driving nails into Kenny's skull. Lauren melted into the comfort of the gentle touch from someone, anyone, tears rolling down her cheeks again.

Exhaling slowly, Kenny returned to his spot by the curb, the bystanders still giving him plenty of space. His breathing was rapid and shallow, the anger building in him. Giving comfort was never a strength of his. Sure, they had sex. But they didn't have passion. It was just going through the motions. He'd fucked up. The best thing he'd ever had in his life, and he'd fucked it up. He was a failure, just as his mom had predicted.

Feeling something grab his arm, he threw his elbow back, clipping someone as it flew. Only when he turned did he see Lauren, her hand against her forehead. "You bastard," she spat.

"I didn't know it was you, babe. Really. I was just angry and lashing out. I didn't mean to."

Her eyes bore a hole into his, her tongue moving over the cut inside her cheek again. "I'm tired of it, Kenny. I can't do this anymore."

"I want this to work. I want our baby. I want us to be a family." He reached slowly to touch her stomach, to show his sincerity.

"Don't touch me, you fucker." Stepping forward, Lauren shoved hard on Kenny's chest.

Arms flailing, Kenny fell backwards, bus tires screeching as he reached out and pulled to himself one last time the only woman he ever loved and a child that wasn't his.

War, With Incident
by Arlan Andrews, Sr.

Vast forest shadows stretched ominously over the small clearing where Aunt Lizzie's ancient log cabin squatted in her scrubby cotton patch. 'Long about sundown, like a dark front of storm clouds, the Civil War rolled over us."

Through the walls of her cabin an increasingly loud roar of cannons and shrieks assaulted our ears. But Aunt Lizzie had other priorities: "You finish yore supper," she said as the walls shook from a nearby explosion. Her ancient face was so weathered you could never have told she had once been a Priestess in a faraway land, or so she claimed. She squinched up her eyes again. "Cain't do nothin' 'bout what's happenin' out there."

But it was hard for me, a twelve-year-old, to eat his grits and greens and drink his persimmon juice, knowing that grown men were killing each other out there in the woods. "Besides, get near a winder, yore gonna git a bullet in the head." I knew what Yankee bullets could do, saw it when they shot my parents and burnt our house, over in Louisiana. "Bank's Gorillas" they called themselves. I couldn't think of a Christian thing to call them; I just wanted them dead. But if Aunt Lizzie hadn't of found me the day before, wandering north without food, I would have been buzzard meat. So I listened to her.

"We'uns is stayin' out of this war. We got a bigger one goin' on." I never understood why the War for Southern Independence wasn't our war. But since I had come into her care the day before, all she'd done was go on about some kind of ancient conflict with critters she called banshees, afrits, and djinn.

"Them Others is the real enemies, of ever' kind o' human bein'," she was saying. "They're–"

Ka-whoom! The wall behind her blew up, throwing me into a heap of furniture, with logs and chairs and food and utensils falling hither and yon. I was deafened, and in the awful silence that followed, I dug myself out of the rubble, eyes stinging. To my horror, I couldn't find Aunt Lizzie! Through the swirling clouds of dust and smoke, I could see where the chair she'd been sitting in was just broken sticks, her ample tote-sack dress now a crumpled bloody rag, like she'd vanished along with the wall behind her, along with my hearing.

Though totally deafened by the shell, my vision through the missing wall was unimpaired. There in the shadows across the patch, dozens of raggedy scarecrow-thin Confederates reeled under a wave of blue-uniformed soldiers. One of the Yankee attackers, a swashbuckler astride a coal-black horse, saw me and galloped my way, raising his bloody saber. Behind this oncoming blue behemoth, part of my mind watched as the Southern soldiers melted into the woods, while the victorious bluecoats set fire to the trampled-down ruins of the cotton field. Suddenly I knew these were the same gorillas who killed my folks.

With that realization, I was no longer afraid, just filled with rage. Unable to avoid my certain destruction, I picked up a four-foot-long piece of sharp, burning timber from the ruins. I was going to hit this Yankee devil if it was the last thing I did. I surely expected it would be.

In the midst of this silent chaos, a bright light blossomed behind me. When I turned, Aunt Lizzie – at least, what had been Aunt Lizzie, for now she was a young woman, clad in glistening bronze armor, holding a gigantic red spear – sat astride some kind of critter I had never seen, something all green scales and red claws and big white razor-sharp teeth, taking up nearly the whole room. And I swear, inside that ruined cabin, Aunt Lizzie glowed! She nodded and smiled. With her eyes and a twitch of her head, she indicated the approaching enemy, ten yards away. Without thinking, I turned and threw my pitiful weapon with all my might.

As if shot from a cannon, my burning timber missile pierced the Yankee horseman, plunging right through his heart. In shock, I watched as he calmly brought his horse to a stop, put his saber back into its sheath, dismounted, and felt around his ruined chest. As he pulled out the burning shaft and casually tossed it aside, I peed my pants. What kind of devil was this?

285

Instantly, Aunt Lizzie went into action on that great beast of hers, charging directly at that Yankee officer with a glowing spear twenty feet long. Then, I swear, that bluecoat devil turned pure green and grew bulging fireball eyes as big as dinner plates, and tried to pull his sword back out of its scabbard. But it was too late; Aunt Lizzie had lanced him dead on and he sort of curled up into a green ball and vanished in a putrid puff of evil-smelling smoke. Aunt Lizzie dismounted and set her beast loose on the paralyzed, horrified Yankee soldiers in the field. I'd just as soon not remember that part.

Trembling, I ran over into the arms of Aunt Lizzie, who once more was a warm and familiar old lady in old rags, once more my savior. But now she had a perfumey odor about her, like lilacs and lavender.

"What did you do, Aunt Lizzie?" I asked, when I finally found my voice. "Who was that man, and what was that critter you rode, and how did you get to be so young and pretty?"

"Hush, young 'un. There's all kind of things you'll learn when you get growed up. Just remember, there's a whole lot to learn, so you got yourself to a school just as soon as this war's over." The next day she packed me up a bag of food and kissed me and sent me off up in the direction of Little Rock, where some cousins lived.

I never went back, and I never learned what she meant about that Other War.

The Millenium Party
by Walter Jon Williams

Darien was making another annotation to his lengthy commentary on the *Tenjou Cycle* when his Marshal reminded him that his wedding anniversary would soon be upon him. This was the thousandth anniversary — a full millennium with Clarisse! — and he knew the celebration would have to be a special one.

He finished his annotation and then de-slotted the savant brain containing the cross-referenced database that allowed him to manage his work. In its place he slotted the brain labeled *Clarisse/Passion*, the brain that contained memories of his time with his wife. Not all memories, however: the contents had been carefully purged of any of the last thousand years' disagreements, arguments, disappointments, infidelities, and misconnections... The memories were only those of love, ardor, obsession, passion, and release, all the most intense and glorious moments of their thousand years together, all the times when Darien was drunk on Clarisse, intoxicated with her scent, her brilliance, her wit.

The other moments, the less-than-perfect ones, he had stored elsewhere, in one brain or another, but he rarely reviewed them. Darien saw no reason why his mind should contain anything less than perfection.

Flushed with the sensations that now poured through his mind, overwhelmed by the delirium of love, Darien began to work on his present for his wife.

When the day came, Darien and Clarisse met in an environment that she had designed. This was an arrangement that had existed for centuries, ever since they both realized that Clarisse's sense of special relationships was better than his. The environment was a masterpiece, an apartment built on several levels, like little terraces, that broke the space up into smaller areas that created intimacy without sacrificing the sense of spaciousness. None of the furniture was designed for more than two people. Darien recognized on the walls a picture he'd given Clarisse on her four hundredth birthday, an elaborate, antique dial telephone from their honeymoon apartment in Paris, and a Japanese paper doll of a woman in an antique kimono, a present he had given her early in their acquaintance, when they'd haunted antique stores together.

It was Darien's task to complete the arrangement. He added an abstract bronze sculpture of a horse and jockey that Clarisse had given him for his birthday, a puzzle made of wire and butter-smooth old wood, and a view from the terrace, a view of Rio de Janeiro at night. Because his sense of taste and smell were more subtle than Clarisse's, by standing arrangement he populated the apartment with scents, lilac for the parlor, sweet magnolia and bracing cypress on the terrace, a combination of sandalwood and spice for the bedroom, and a mixture of vanilla and cardamom for the dining room, a scent subtle enough so that it wouldn't interfere with the meal.

When Clarisse entered he was dressed in a tailcoat, white tie, waistcoat, and diamond studs. She had matched his period élan with a Worth gown of shining blue satin, tiny boots that buttoned up the ankles, and a dashing fall of silk about her throat. Her tawny hair was pinned up, inviting him to kiss the nape of her neck, an indulgence which he permitted himself almost immediately.

Darien seated Clarisse on the cushions and mixed cocktails. He asked her about her work: A duplicate of one of her brains was on the mission to 55 Cancri, sharing piloting missions with other duplicates. If a habitable planet was discovered, then a new Clarisse would be built on site to pioneer the new world.

Darien had created the meal in consultation with Clarisse's Marshal. They began with mussels steamed open in white wine and herbs, then went on to a salad of fennel, orange, and red cranberry. Next came roasted green beans served alongside a chicken cooked simply in the oven, flamed in cognac, then served in a creamy port wine reduction sauce. At the end was a raspberry Bavarian cream. Each dish was one that Darien had experienced at another time in his long life, considered perfect, stored in one brain or another, and now re-created down to the last scent and sensation.

After coffee and conversation on the terrace, Clarisse led Darien to the bedroom. He enjoyed kneeling at her feet and unlacing every single button of those damned Victorian boots. His heart brimmed with passion and lust, and he rose from his knees to embrace her. Wrapped in the sandalwood-scented silence of their suite, they feasted till dawn on one another's flesh.

288

Their life together, Darien reflected, was perfection itself: one enchanted jewel after another, hanging side-by-side on a thousand-year string.

After juice and shirred eggs in the morning, Darien kissed the inside of Clarisse's wrist, and saw her to the door. His brain had recorded every single rapturous instant of their time together.

And then, returning to his work, Darien de-slotted *Clarisse/Passion*, and put it on the shelf for another year.

The Primrose Bath
by Linda Needham

England, 1849

Hunter Claybourne dropped the carriage windows and gulped in a surge of fresh air as his brougham bolted away from Claybourne Manor.

Away from the perilous woman he'd married two days ago in a bargain with the devil and would hastily divorce a year from yesterday, once her railway shares were transferred to him.

Away from the fetid stench she'd brought back to his home from her bloody charitable mission into the blind and dangerous alleys of Bethnal Green, her skirts caked with mud and offal.

A stench that stalked him all the way back to London. To his club, then the Board of Trade. That chased him up the stairs of the Claybourne Exchange, to his office, to his upholstered leather desk chair, where the smell faded quickly in the familiar scent of cigar ash and lamp oil.

And something else. The hint of lavender hiding among the silken folds of his necktie, conjuring the insubordinate Felicity Mayfield, his inconvenient wife, invoking the memory of her standing midstream in her soaking wet, transparent camisole and petticoat, her breasts high and indignant, begging his hand to caress them.

He fought through the rest of the day to focus on the contracts spread across his desk, but his senses kept snagging on the woman and her provocations. Tracking her to the slums of London, hauling her home like an angry stray cat, tossing her into a cold stream to rid her of the filth.

"Hell and damnation!" This day – this bloody marriage – couldn't end quickly enough.

...

290

"Welcome home, sir." Ernest met Hunter at his carriage door, nothing of the afternoon's streamside melodrama in his expression, though he'd surely seen the whole episode. "Your supper's ready."

"Ten minutes. In the dining room. Inform Miss Mayfield."

"Yes, sir. Except..."

Always an exception where Miss Mayfield was concerned. "Yes?"

"Just that your wife, Miss Mayf...she...took her supper earlier."

"Right, then."

Hunter dined alone, staring across his plate at a ceramic pot of softly scented yellow primroses that hadn't been there at breakfast. A pointed message from Miss Mayfield.

Thump! from somewhere far above. Thud.

Ernest slid through the doorway, eyes toward the ceiling. "Sir, should I...?"

"Leave her. Bring my coffee." Resolved to sit in peace, Hunter settled in and ignored the woman and her sulky commotions. Lingered over the front page of *The Times*. Tamped down the urge to find and confront her. See her, smell her. Taste her. "Good God!"

He left the dining room and thundered up the grand staircase and reached the open gallery, only to be halted by the sight of the normally bare wall, now hung with a half-dozen portraits. Pale faces peering out from gaudy, gilded frames.

Thump!

The bloody woman was making good on her threat to uncrate his house! Lungs hot with indignation, he followed the urns and flowers and artwork up the stairs into the massive Tudor ballroom he hadn't seen for years.

A hundred feet long, forty wide, arching windows lighting its length and breadth, the narrow, oak-paneled room, empty when he purchased the place, was now piled to its coffered ceiling with crates, cupboards, white sheets draped over furniture...

And there in a clearing of his household goods was Miss Mayfield and her shapely, perfectly rounded bottom, her upper half bent over a barrel, one

291

slippered foot braced on the oak floor, the other kicking up her skirts like a rudder.

"Got you!" her voice echoed, then up she came with a silver pot. Her hair, gilded by the sharply setting sun, was loosely bound and sprigged with excelsior.

"Find what you were looking for, Miss Mayfield?"

She whirled on him in her bibbed apron, raised a lively brow in challenge. Her eyes brightened as she strolled toward him. "I've been unpacking for you, Mr. Claybourne, per your consent. And I've discovered your secret!"

Secret? The word struck him in the chest. "What secret?"

"That you're not really a railway baron or London's financial genius."

He steadied his breathing, his heart. "What am I then, Madam?"

"The leader of a gang of burglars, obviously. A master thief. A regular Fagin, right out of Dickens."

He caught back his smile, madly relieved, and filled his nostrils with her: lavender and primrose, sunshine and surety. "Your evidence?"

"Bolts of silk, jade jars, silver service: stolen goods, ripe for fencing." She set the pot on a matching tray, vainly hiding a smile, her lips damp and rosy.

"Ah, then you have found me out."

"Only that you're an acquisitive dragon with a touchy sense of smell. I will remember that."

"And so you unpack my house?"

A playful shrug. "Idle hands, you know…"

Yet her hands were scarcely idle, they were shifting his tie into place, slender fingers hot against the linen at his collarbone, her minty breath breaking warm against his chin.

An unbearable hunger for her surged through him, a flash of heat in his gut, a quickening in his groin that made him ache to haul her against him as a husband's right.

"You've no valet and only half a wife, Mr. Claybourne. It's a wonder you manage to dress in the morning."

No, the wonder was that he managed to shake off his raging need for the woman long enough to leave her untouched, unconsummated per their contract, and bid her a civil good evening.

And later that night, when he found a silver vase of primrose and lavender on his bedside table it was a bloody, blinking miracle that he didn't break down her chamber door and fall upon her softness like the great, rutting beast he was fast becoming.

The next three-hundred sixty-four days married, in name only, to Felicity Mayfield would be relatively easy.

The nights, however, were certain to be hell.

ACKNOWLEDGEMENTS

Publishing has changed in ways that make some projects possible that never would have happened before. A flash fiction anthology like this, for example. Because a sizeable book requires so many authors to complete, this book wouldn't be cost-effective for a traditional publishing house. With the power of Kickstarter, though, the number of contributors became a bug instead of a feature. Thanks to their contributions of time, effort and enthusiasm, we raised enough money to make this a reality. Below is a full list of those who contributed to the crowdfunding effort. It's not nearly thanks enough, but here it is.

Myriad, heartfelt thanks to:

Dean K. Miller, Adam Thomas Gottfried, Larry W. Oldham, Derek Knutsen, Charles Loomis, Chris Jordan, Duncan Dog, Stephen D. Sullivan, Bert Edens, Claire Kelly, Eva Merrick, Danika Dinsmore, Pat Marum, David McDermott, Elizabeth Marum, Pat Klein, Ian Christy, Carrie Uffindell, Vicki Steger, Sally Benton, Sally Raduezel & Ron Carlstein, Christopolis Tiberius Markus, Karen Call, Lance Oldham, Shevach, Ariana Sutton-Grier, Rebecca, Rod & Sharon Uffindell, Adrienne Dorris, Rosanne L., Dory Black, Tammie Willenbrock, Jeanne & Michael Sturgis, Eoin Reidy, Rhonnie Fordham, Amy Outland, "AZWildcat", In Memory of Refugia & Ramona, Peter & Heather Pressman, Seth & Bethanne Arthur, Thomas Palestrini, Ruthanne Collinson, Heidi Ferrini, Mark & Pam Grimes, Nathaniel Love, Katie D., Danger Marshall, Jen & Tom, Annita, Susan Cormier, Paula Vesely, Abigail Adams, Andrea Robson, Steven M. Brodeen, M. Earl Smith, Danielle E. Gautier, Gordon MacKinney, Kerrie Abbot, Michael Newlyn Blake, Brian Kaufman, David Covenant, D.A. Manriquez, Adele Welch, Jessica Sherwood, Patricia Walker, Nancy Murphy, David Mundt, Owen Palmiotio, Dorothy S. Clark, Mindy Windholz, Scott Rockhill, Cynthia Amerman, Perry & Bev Brandiezs, C.S. Hopley, Nancy Tyson, Paul DeBaldo, Sia Stewart, Jessica Abel, Harriet Cavanagh, Dan Repperger, Alyssa Hillary, Ryan Fraedrich, Meghan Johnson, Kristen Rowe, Sheila & Willem Ledeboer, Josh and Deb Demaree of The Established Facts Podcast, Gregg & Nancy Townsley, Janet Hollander, Bob & Jan Chandler, Matt Mixdorf, Eric Wilson, Jack B. Rochester, David Saltzman, Sabrina "Pea" Woodruff, Gary & Michelle Duke, In Memory of Lee Sprague

Made in the USA
Charleston, SC
07 August 2015